American Policy and the

Division of Germany

THE CLASH WITH RUSSIA
OVER REPARATIONS

American Policy and the
Division of Germany

THE CLASH WITH RUSSIA
OVER REPARATIONS

by BRUCE KUKLICK

Cornell University Press

ITHACA AND LONDON

First published 1972 by Cornell University Press.
Published in the United Kingdom by Cornell University Press Ltd., 2–4 Brook Street, London W1Y 1AA.

International Standard Book Number 0-8014-0710-9
Library of Congress Catalog Card Number 78-38121

PRINTED IN THE UNITED STATES OF AMERICA
BY VAIL-BALLOU PRESS, INC.

Librarians: Library of Congress cataloging information appears on the last page of the book.

For My Father and Mother
Emil Kuklick *and* Emma Roth Kuklick

Acknowledgments

I am obligated to the Group Committee in Political Science at the University of Pennsylvania for awarding me a Penfield Scholarship for 1967–1968, which funded much of the traveling and research necessary in the writing of this study. Yale University also provided a summer research grant.

I have received permission from the *Western Political Quarterly* to use rewritten portions of my article "The Division of Germany and American Policy on Reparations" (June 1970), and from the *American Quarterly* to use rewritten portions of "History as a Way of Learning" (Fall 1970), copyright, 1970, Trustees of the University of Pennsylvania. The staffs of the manuscript divisions of various libraries and archival depositories were without exception efficient and helpful, and I wish to thank the following for permission to quote from their collections: the Historical Office of the Department of State for archival material under State Department control; Yale University Library for material from the Henry L. Stimson Papers; the committee in charge of the John Foster Dulles Papers at the Princeton University Library for material from the Dulles Papers; and Judge Charles Fahy for material from the Fahy Papers at the Franklin D. Roosevelt Library, Hyde Park. I would also like to thank Joy B. Takiff, Richard Doran, and Congressman William Green for expediting my access to a great many published government documents.

Frank Carner, Thomas C. Cochran, Joseph Ellis, Charles Frye, David Horowitz, Robert Alun Jones, Robert Schulzinger, and Russell Stetler were helpful in various stages of my work. Gabriel Kolko, who guided the writing of an earlier version of the manuscript, instilled in me a sense of what others have already called his "passionate scholarship." I have an enormous intellectual debt to William Appleman Williams. Richard Freeland has faithfully followed the tribulations of this essay since the first draft was written and has been an astute and intelligent critic. For four years Leo Ribuffo has stimulated my thinking and tried to make my work readable. No one could want truer or more loyal friends.

W. Averell Harriman, without doubt one of the most distinguished and intelligent American statesmen of this century, was kind enough to spend an afternoon with me discussing some of the problems the book takes up. Although I feel that Mr. Harriman's recollections supported many of my central theses, I am sure he would strongly dissent from my interpretive conclusions. I am, nevertheless, grateful to him for giving me a renewed sense of some of the complexities involved in explaining human motivation.

I am happy to say that my wife has scholarly interests of her own, and I cannot, as is conventionally done, thank her for unpaid secretarial help. But for keeping out of my way at most times and tolerating my incessant conversation about my work at others, she has my lasting affection.

B. K.

New Haven, Connecticut

Contents

American Policy and the
Division of Germany

THE CLASH WITH RUSSIA
OVER REPARATIONS

Introduction

During World War II, Great Britain, the United States, and the Soviet Union formed a grand alliance that vanquished Nazi Germany. But when the victors met in Berlin in 1945, their relationship was already bitter. Two years later Russia and the United States were the leaders of opposing blocs of nations, each accusing the other of malevolent designs for the defeated nation. A divided and prostrate Germany had become the pawn of its conquerors and an instance of their inability to live peaceably together. Ultimately the split between the two Germanys came to symbolize the terrible worldwide tensions associated with the international history of the late forties. But Germany had much more than symbolic significance: the German issue was also a major substantive problem whose resistance to resolution played a major role in the development of the Cold War.

The Americans had had high hopes for the postwar world and had been determined that the mistakes of World War I which had plunged them into a second global conflict would not be repeated after the Nazi defeat. Their positive program for Germany was designed to attack the root causes of war. Germany was the keystone of the central European political economy, and Russo-German relations were crucial

1

to the health of international life and the stability of the
states of eastern Europe. When the Americans failed in their
purpose for Germany, they could not succeed in Europe,
and the ills of Europe were central to the tragic dilemmas of
the postwar years.

If we examine U.S. policy for Germany in 1945 we find a
striking situation. The United States knew that reparations
were a primary concern of the Soviet Union: the German
pillage of Russia left the Soviets with enormous needs for
reconstruction goods and equipment and an intense desire
to punish the Reich. But, defining the German issue almost
entirely in terms of the reparations problem, the Americans
took an intransigent and uncompromising stand: they gave
the USSR nothing from the western zones of Germany,
brushed off all attempts at negotiation, and unrealistically
expected the Russians to accept the American reparation
plan and to moderate their own reparations claims in the
eastern zone. I will contend that a hostile and belligerent
American attitude, on the one hand, and an unrealistic
attitude, on the other, were responsible for the partition of
Germany and perhaps for the rigid division of Europe.

Why did the Americans adopt a position that had such
unfortunate consequences—consequences that were antithetical to their expressed aims and that were obvious to
many people at the time? This is the major question I have
tried to answer in this book. In order to answer it I have had
to explicate the premises from which all American policy
was derived and the historical context in which these premises originated. We can understand U.S. policy for Germany
only within this framework of basic assumptions.

When the war began, many American diplomats were
committed—often explicitly, sometimes implicitly—to creat-

ing a world political and economic system. Similar commitments have had a long history in U.S. diplomacy, from Thomas Jefferson's "Peace, commerce, and honest friendship" to John Hay's "Open Door." But I am referring to a group of temporally bounded beliefs—the set of responses and dispositions to action that governed much American diplomatic behavior during and immediately after the war. In the forties these responses and dispositions had been shaped by a specific set of historical experiences and precedents: Woodrow Wilson's wartime leadership, the Depression, and a renewal of world conflict. These events had confirmed a belief in the need for trade expansion and liberal democracy, but tied the precise meaning of this belief to a particular interpretation of the history of the interwar period: that the failure of Wilson's dream of an international political and economic community was a crucial cause of World War II. I have given the name multilateralism to the belief in global order that was justified by this historical account of the diplomacy of the twenties and thirties.

The Americans would act to establish a worldwide economy ensuring prosperity and rising standards of living to all nations. Governmental obstacles to foreign commerce would be minimal. All nations would lower tariffs, and other barriers to trade would be imposed without discrimination. If a country placed restrictions on imports from another country, the restrictions would apply to every other nation. If these economic arrangements were realized everywhere, American policy makers believed that the United States would be the chief beneficiary. Although every nation would obtain fair and equal treatment, the efficiency and technical superiority of American capitalism would secure for it increased exports and assure its commercial primacy. The markets of all nations would be opened to American goods, and American business interests would be free to establish themselves anywhere. But the diplomats did not think that benefits would accrue to the United States alone. The expansion of trade would raise living standards universally and bring prosperity to all countries. The new commercial order would also eliminate those economic frictions that many believed were the fundamental causes of war. Economic autarchy and discriminatory trade agreements would vanish, and with them, global violence.

A commitment to worldwide political democracy and a new League of Nations complemented this set of economic priorities. In fact, the Americans often argued that a country's economic institutions nearly determined its political structure and the psychology of its citizens. If decision makers could change a nation's economy, its politics would change in predictable ways. In some unexplained way, successful commercial policies would produce pacific democracies, similar to that of the United States, all over the world.

U.S. diplomats perceived no conflict between the demands of morality and the growth of American political and commercial influence. Multilateralism justified U.S. behavior abroad while at the same time served to extend the liberal business interests of American capitalism. Moral and even religious motives permeated actual policy making; diplomats took no step that did not have an ultimate and sincere ethical warrant. The concept of multilateralism simultaneously embraces moral commitment and politico-economic interest.

If the Americans compartmentalized their motives, it was in terms of means and ends. Although the distinction is partially justified as a mode of analysis, diplomats frequently did act in ways that subordinated most factors to economic ones. Commercial measures—demands for multilateral trade and the use of various economic levers—were characteristically seen as means to the ends of diplomacy. But we may construe the ends as principally political in nature, a world federation of peace-loving democracies. Diplomats sought extensive foreign trade because it was thought necessary to the political freedom Americans valued so dearly. By selling abroad, the United States might offset instabilities caused by underconsumption of goods produced at home. Without international commerce, domestic markets would be glutted, unemployment would increase, and depression would ensue. In Germany such a depression led to Nazism. But extensive exports alone were not sufficient to preserve freedom in the United States and around the world; the necessary and sufficient condition of the American order was foreign trade conducted with a minimum of governmental direction. A Nazified Europe in which state trading would predominate threatened just this condition. U.S. diplomats believed that the triumph of German political and economic policies would mean a reduction of U.S. exports and government control of what remained.*

For U.S. diplomats attached to multilateral beliefs, World War II created a uniquely hopeful situation: a set of circumstances in which the Americans could eliminate forever the war-producing conditions of the thirties. The formal diplomatic procedures that had maintained the unsteady peace in that decade imposed severe restraints on American freedom of action. War opened up great opportunities. After the conflict the Americans would begin anew to bring about their world politico-economic order, the conditions for per-

* The Appendix (pp. 237–241) examines the connection between the above interpretive framework and recent historiography.

manent peace. There would be an end to competing blocs
of nations. The states of eastern Europe would no longer be
the pawns of the great powers; certainly there would be no
German satellites, and the Russians would be dissuaded
from creating their own sphere of influence. The eastern
European nations would participate in the new world order
and would, consequently, have economic and political freedom. And the Soviet Union would gradually give up its
totalitarian beliefs as it developed liberal commercial relations with the other nations of the world.

The multilateral view of Germany is our chief concern.
Because fragmentation of Germany would bring economic
disaster and political chaos for all of central Europe, the
State Department planned for a unified state. Germany
would give up autarchy and return to dependence on overseas markets and resources. The Allies would prohibit discriminatory commercial controls, clearing arrangements, and
international cartel agreements. The Germans would export
industrial goods and import foodstuffs and raw materials,
contributing to the expansion of international trade and securing for themselves a decent standard of living. The Allies
would leave the German industrial plant basically intact and
make repairs where necessary to the manufacturing, transportation, and communication systems. But high cost "defense" industries created in the climate of economic nationalism would be dismantled, as would those industries capable of producing only for war.

American policy makers realized that U.S. monetary support would be necessary for the German economy in the
immediate postwar period to make these policies viable, but
although financial help was contemplated to achieve German stability, the Americans would oppose any reparations

program that required them to subsidize the German economy. Nonetheless, a controlled reparations program was part of overall policy and would aid European reconstruction: claimant nations would receive the dismantled German industries and, more importantly, goods from German current production. The program would punish the Germans in the early part of the postwar period—the coal industry, in particular, was to produce for export to western Europe. But the program also meant that Germany would be assured of that measure of industrial strength that was necessary for the manufacture and production of reparations, and would eventually prosper.

These policies would be put into effect beginning with the initial period of occupation and military policy would be subordinate to them. The great powers would strictly coordinate the occupation itself to ensure unified treatment of the defeated country; indeed, if it were possible, the occupation would be joint and, at the very least, there would be a strong central authority over the military zones.

In some unspecified fashion adherence to these economic policies would lead to the growth of private enterprise and political democracy—both vaguely defined—inside Germany. Other variables, of course, would aid the development of a nonaggressive German polity. Although the military would preserve the essentials of the German administrative machinery, occupation officials would remove Nazi personnel. The Allies would foster training in democratic procedures for the Germans and education in democratic ideals. Finally, they would encourage political pluralism within a nontotalitarian framework. The end result would be a transformation of the German psyche and a commitment on an individual level to the democratic way of life.

In the period from 1939 to 1944 the American Department of State formulated this multilateral design, but it fought with other agencies and with the President, Franklin Roosevelt, for the control of policy. Moreover, much of the State Department's planning was contrived without considering that at the end of the war the Americans would suffer from new constraints, most importantly the destruction of the social fabric of Europe. But diplomats seemed little concerned with the actual course of the war, and concentrated on defining their vision of the future. Although this gives a scholastic flavor to the elaboration of State Department policy for Germany and to various conflicts in Washington, the policies that finally evolved were to have great influence in 1945 and 1946.

The conception of multilateralism and the assumptions bound up with its use form the basis of my analysis of U.S. policy for Germany. During Roosevelt's wartime administration these premises guided and justified much U.S. planning for Germany and gave it substantial continuity; in 1945 and 1946 the view dominated American international relations. But my goal has not been to give a complete account of German-American diplomacy. I have dealt only briefly with those political problems that had little significance for the future of Germany—such as wartime decisions concerning the role of the French. I have also given little attention to the wartime statements of principle made most prominently by Franklin Roosevelt—those concerns are at the focus of other accounts. Some analysis has been made of the intra-American squabbles occurring during this period, but, because it is so important, I have concentrated on the elaboration of the State Department position that became American policy in the spring of 1945. I have also devoted minimal space to many Allied frictions over Germany and have examined in depth only Russo-American antagonisms.

Within this framework I have developed three substantive arguments. First I shall attempt a reinterpretation of the "Morgenthau plan," which emerged in 1944 as a serious proposal for postwar control of Germany. Many historians have lamented its unrealistic and "pro-Communist" aspects. I shall argue that the plan can be called pro-Communist in only a frivolous and distorted sense and that it was as realistic as the view of the State Department; it preserved State's chief operative priority—the expansion of American commercial influence—and was in conception entirely consonant with U.S. interests.

My second argument is that the U.S. commitment to multilateralism was central in determining the American attitude to the critical question of reparations after the Yalta Conference. The triumph of State Department policies at this time inevitably led to a clash with the Russians. By August 1945, U.S. plans for Germany and the refusal of the Soviets to yield on reparations led the United States to devise a program that was, surprisingly, a prime determinant of the division of Germany. When American diplomats applied the State Department's multilateral principles at this time, they were confronted with an enormously confusing situation. They did not change their ideas, but the connection of these ideas to their deeds is undeniably complex. In understanding the relation of thought and action, it is essential to keep in mind a profound irony: in acting on multilateral principles U.S. decision makers ensured that a multilateral world would not be realized. But, overestimating their own strength and underestimating that of the USSR, the Americans basically did not understand what they were doing.

Finally, I shall attempt to show that the State Department's concept of a *world* politico-economic system precluded an American compromise on the German issue, where the United States was largely in control and where great-power agreement was perhaps possible. Instead, it forced American diplomats at the end of the war to ask for joint settlements in eastern Europe, where the Soviets would not cooperate, and contributed in a fundamental way to great-power hostility.

The conscious product of these compressed analyses of some areas of study and extended analyses of others is not, I hope, a distortion. My plan has been to delineate a strand of great-power conduct that typifies the diplomacy of the war and immediate postwar period. I am essentially interested in the premises of State Department thinking. My strategy in the first four chapters is to show what these premises were and how others perceived them; in the last five chapters, to analyze how the premises were acted on in 1945 and 1946.

To avoid misinterpretation I should add a disclaimer. The history of Depression diplomacy has been colored with our horror of Hitler and Nazi brutality. To say I share this horror is not, I think, to moralize. The history of the war and the peace has been shadowed by hindsight about supposed Soviet evil and perfidy. I am not a defender of the iniquities that are a part of the Russian system. But the task of the historian is not to praise or to blame, but to understand. The existence of wickedness should not prevent us from examining our own behavior soberly and realistically. U.S. diplomacy toward Germany showed an extraordinary continuity from 1939 to 1946 and proceeded on coherent and virtually unquestioned assumptions. American foreign affairs were *not* conducted in a "pragmatic" and unsystematic fashion as a response to the activities of others. The policies of the United States displayed a vigorous, dynamic thrust of their own and possessed well-defined and rigid characteristics. These essentials I have tried to set forth.

I have said that the concept of multilateralism can be used to interpret American foreign relations only during the war and immediate postwar period. To be sure, U.S. diplomats have always believed in the growth of commerce and liberal democracy. But in the 1939–1946 period the justification for these beliefs lay in a particular interpretation of contemporary history: the events of the interwar period provided a rationale for the actions the Americans took in the years that followed; and multilateral views are those essentially connected to this rationale.

This is not an esoteric phenomenon. Consider the interpretation of the history of the 1960's accepted by many liberals who came to political maturity during that time (and, indeed, by many other Americans). For them, John Kennedy's death was a tragedy of immense consequence for the American polity. After the assassination the United States seemed to have lost its bearings; Vietnam, racism, and the alienation of the young were all associated with this single senseless act. Yet, a belief in a corrupted republic is not new—many Americans in the past have had this concern. But for these liberals the belief is peculiarly attached to the events of the sixties and, most importantly, to Kennedy's murder.

For the American diplomats who made policy in World

War II, the same sort of thing was true; and if we are to understand multilateralism fully, we must examine the historical situation in which the view arose.

The third of Woodrow Wilson's famous Fourteen Points called for "the removal, so far as possible, of all economic barriers and the establishment of an equality of trade conditions among all the nations consenting to the peace." [1] This idea, along with all the others, did little to influence the events that culminated in a second world war, but Cordell Hull, a young congressman during World War I, committed himself to a Wilsonian ideal. Secretary of State from 1933 to 1944, Hull was the New Deal's leading Wilsonian; his intellectual biography typifies that of the diplomats who put the economic aspects of Wilson's thought at the center of American foreign policy during the mid-forties and used them to define multilateralism.

Hull regarded Wilson's presidential years as a turning point in his own life and in the history of his country. World War I had taught the Tennessee representative that "you could not separate the idea of commerce from the idea of peace," and he decided to announce and work for a liberal trade policy similar to Wilson's. From the time Hull formulated his creed, he never ceased to urge it on others; in 1948 he proudly recalled in his memoirs that he had pursued this philosophy with the same fervor as he had in his maiden speeches to the United States House of Representatives until his retirement twenty-five years later. Hull became convinced that "unhampered trade dovetailed with peace; high tariffs, trade barriers, and unfair economic competition with war." Although knowing that more was involved, he thought that with a freer flow of trade the vicious conflicts between nations would vanish and that the living standards of all countries would improve. Given less restrictive international commerce, the Americans might eliminate "the economic dissatisfaction that breeds war" and have a reasonable chance of achieving lasting peace.[2] Finally, Hull thought that if the United States were to maintain its "supreme position in world finance, commerce, and industry," the adoption of his proposals was imperative. Any other strategy would mean the "deathknell" of foreign commerce and "along with it our dominant position in the financial and commercial affairs of the world."[3]

During the twenties Hull felt himself the "Cassandra of Congress"—"my prophecies were having no more effect than those of the prophetess of the ancients." In 1927 he expressed his concerns in what he described as one of his most important addresses. He believed that the high-tariff protectionism of the Republican party was "the coarse and sordid doctrine of materialism" rooted "in selfishness and repugnant to the original ideals" on which America was founded. The most basic of his objects, Hull proclaimed on another occasion, was "the constant pursuit of human liberties."[4] The Depression made him an even more vigorous advocate of his policies, and he emphasized that the outstanding cause of unemployment was America's failure to develop foreign markets.

When Franklin Roosevelt became president of the United States in March 1933, he made Cordell Hull, by then an important senator, his secretary of state, a position Hull held longer than any other man. For the next twelve years his unbending commitment and zeal were officially representative of American diplomacy.

The coincidence of the Great Depression and Hull's accession to power had an extraordinary impact on American

foreign relations. To many, his proposals seemed like an
all-powerful remedy for the Depression, and the fear of
depression followed U.S. policy makers into the wartime
period when full employment returned. Diplomats became
convinced that if the United States was to avoid war and
economic instability, Hull's goals had to be achieved. Twenty
years after he took office, the aging Hull received a tribute
from another Wilsonian, the new secretary of state, John
Foster Dulles. "I feel unequal," wrote Dulles, "to the task
of living up to the great tradition you created." [5]

It would be an oversimplification to analyze American
policy during Roosevelt's first two administrations in terms
of multilateralism. Many other currents of opinion were important for diplomatic thinking, and actual policies were
influenced by survivals of protectionist thought and the pre-
vailing "isolationist" sentiment. More importantly, multilateral ideas would come to fruition only when they were confirmed by the outbreak of the European war in 1939. Nonetheless, Hull's beliefs were a significant component of U.S.
thinking on international affairs in this period.

The Secretary's direct effect on foreign policy varied over
the years. On many occasions he became despondent because his programs were sidetracked in one way or another;
yet, his influence was great. Under his leadership the United
States worked haltingly toward his ideal through the Reciprocal Trade Agreements Program and the series of treaties associated with it. By the "most favored nation" clause
of these treaties the two signatories agreed to grant to each
other all commercial benefits granted by either nation to a
third. The policy ensured that neither country discriminated
against the other, and it was hoped that eventually all nations would participate in the same plan.

Hull's influence was even more critical on diplomatic personnel. Of the men with whom he had close contact, those who accepted his ideas would move, in the course of time, into positions of great influence. Those who resisted his ideas—George Peek and Henry Morgenthau, Jr., to name two of the most famous—would eventually see their power wane and Hull's ideas triumph. During this time an entire generation of State Department decision makers was schooled in his policies and came to accept them without question. In the end, he established a constellation of political and economic beliefs that became the basic orientation of the State Department's inner circle. As Theodore Wilson has argued, Hull's commitment seems naive today, but during his tenure not only he "but almost all American diplomats viewed it as a universal panacea." [6]

There were many "internationalists" of various persuasions outside the State Department who regarded Woodrow Wilson as their hero and supported Hull's stewardship as secretary of state, but, more importantly, Hull's ideas dominated the State Department elite. Norman H. Davis held the unique rank of Ambassador at Large during the early days of the New Deal; he was Hull's closest associate and shared the Secretary's beliefs.[7] Breckinridge Long, who held many prestigious diplomatic posts in the thirties and early forties, was also one of Hull's intimate friends. Long was proud to have kept the "faith of Woodrow Wilson" throughout the years after World War I; he maintained that it was the "motivating thought of my political life for about thirty years." [8] George Messersmith, another highly regarded and perceptive career diplomat, was in "complete accord" with Hull "on all fundamental problems affecting our foreign relations." As Messersmith said in 1944, "There are those who

think that the conduct of economic policy can be separated
from political policy [but] political policy in our time has
to have its basis in economic factors." This could be denied,
Messersmith asserted, only by those "who do not know the
long history behind our foreign relations." Consolidating the
administration of the State Department around these ideas
"has been one of my principal preoccupations for over thirty
years." [9] Equally committed was Francis Sayre, a son-in-law
of Woodrow Wilson and a high-ranking department official in
the thirties. In negotiating with the Germans in 1935, he
claimed that "our whole program was built on the basis of
the most favored nation—that is complete equality of treatment." To achieve satisfactory German-American relations
there would have to be "a fundamental acceptance by Germany of our trade philosophy." [10] The views of William
Dodd, who became ambassador to Germany after Roosevelt's inauguration, were an unwitting parody of Hull's.
Dodd was "utterly loyal" to the Secretary's ideals—so much
so that even Hull called him "somewhat insane" on the
subject.[11]

There were also other illustrious and important diplomats
who responded as Hull did to World War I and the events
following it and who shared his ideological outlook, but who
were not personally close to the Secretary. Sumner Welles,
under secretary of state through much of the Roosevelt era,
was often personally at odds with his chief. Because he was
a White House confidant, historians have often regarded the
Under Secretary as the real power in the State Department.
His closeness to the President, it is said, made Hull's position
insignificant. But Welles "believed passionately in the ideals
of Woodrow Wilson"; Robert Divine has asserted that at the
beginning of World War II Welles was "the most eloquent

prophet of a new world order." [12] Henry L. Stimson, secretary of state under Herbert Hoover, achieved his greatest fame as secretary of war from 1940 to 1945. His experience in the State Department made him a determined opponent of economic isolation. During the thirties he became convinced that liberal political and economic internationalism was the "only sensible course" for the United States. Stimson believed that unless the United States had the extensive foreign trade envisioned in Hull's program, Americans faced "the compulsory government control of production and marketing; the suppression of our hereditary love of freedom; and, worst of all, the stifling of individual free thought and speech." [13] When Hull retired in 1944, Stimson wrote that one of his "chief pillars of support" was gone.[14]

Of course, Roosevelt was central to the conduct of U.S. diplomacy and scholars have documented his vacillation concerning Hull's goals. Although he had been assistant secretary of the navy in Wilson's administration, the new president at first reflected the feelings of many who were suspicious of the State Department's world orientation. But what has been termed FDR's "conversion" to some form of internationalism is equally well documented; indeed historians have pointed out that in the late thirties Hull's espousal of his doctrines was less vigorous than the President's innovative and flexible diplomacy. By this time Roosevelt generally supported the ideals the Secretary defended. As Willard Range has argued, Roosevelt embraced "what might roughly be called a global New Deal." He wanted "to export to all the world the economic and social goals and techniques that had done so much to raise standards of living, cultural as well as material, in the United States throughout her history." [15] Theodore Wilson has made the same point

more circumspectly, saying that FDR "was an advocate—
in theory, and sometimes in practice—of free equal trade
for all nations, but his advocacy varied with the circumstances." [16]

The start of World War II provided crucial confirmation
for the interpretation of recent history that Hull and like-
minded individuals accepted: World War I began a trend
away from free trade and toward economic nationalism; the
failure of the League of Nations accelerated the trend; in
the twenties various restrictions on commerce grew apace in
Europe and rising tariffs in the United States aggravated
the situation; countries that relied on foreign trade began to
suffer chronic unemployment, and worldwide depression
culminated an era of deeply misguided commercial policy;
economic misery brought the dictators to power in Europe,
weakened democracy around the world, and contributed to
the growth of autarchy and spheres of influence in international politics; now the frictions generated by opposed
groups of powers had plunged the world into another global
conflict.

This analysis of the interwar period provided the full historical dimension of multilateral beliefs. This was the set of
convictions at work from 1939 to 1944 when the American
State Department elaborated its program for the peace and
from 1945 to 1946 when the United States acted on this program.

1 Planning for the Peace, 1939–1944

As the United States and Germany moved closer to war, the administration began planning for peace. In September 1939, Secretary of State Cordell Hull appointed Leo Pasvolsky as his special assistant for postwar policy and, by December, Pasvolsky had submitted a proposal to establish an intradepartmental committee on problems of peace and reconstruction. In January 1940, almost two years before the United States entered the war, the Advisory Committee on Problems of Foreign Relations held its initial meeting. Like many of its successors, the committee was short-lived—it was defunct in two months. Hull mentioned it in his *Memoirs* "only to show how early we realized at the State Department the necessity for postwar planning and the equal necessity for the United States to take her full share in the peace and after." Hull's program was to be a "cornerstone" of this peace.[1] The economic subcommittee of the Advisory Committee survived longer than its parent; it became interdepartmental in scope and for the next year was the principal planning committee. But German war successes blocked its one positive proposal, that neutral nations consult to establish an international economic system. When the subcommittee became inactive, a Division of Special Research, created under Pasvolsky in early 1941, took over its functions and produced a series of studies dealing with all aspects of postwar policies.[2]

For the next four years the State Department would protect from all attacks the position these various committees worked out. The essential theme in the history of wartime planning is the Department's unwillingness to compromise its policies in the face of diverse opposition. State traded present effectiveness for the hope of a future victory. It resisted Roosevelt's initiatives; it defended its views against the War Department and the Treasury; and it engaged in skirmishes with the Russians and the British. The result of these battles was usually a refinement of the multilateral ideal in the State Department itself and in agencies that shared its outlook.

A striking expression of this orientation occurred at the high-level conference of August 1941, when the Americans tried to write multilateral policy for a defeated Reich into the first wartime statement of conviction, the Atlantic Charter. The fourth point of the original document was Wilsonian in origin. It called on Britain and the United States "to endeavor to further the enjoyment of all States, great or small, *victor or vanquished,* of access, on equal terms, to trade and to the raw materials of the world." The President urged the idea on Winston Churchill as a point of "very great importance" as "a means of assurance to the German and Italian people that the British and the United States governments desire to offer them, after the war, fair and equal opportunity of an economic character."

When Churchill added "with due respect for their existing obligations" to the U.S. memorandum, the State Department demonstrated the tenacity with which it would pursue these policies. For Under Secretary Sumner Welles this was "not a question of phraseology" but one "of a vital principle." If the powers could not establish this program after the war, "they might as well throw in the sponge and realize that one of the greatest factors in creating the present tragic situation" would continue. The American policy of "constructive sanity in world economics" was imperative; otherwise, Welles claimed, there would be no way to prevent the German practice of using trade and financial policies to achieve political ends. Roosevelt, however, was "entirely in accord" with the British redraft; it was "better than he had thought Mr. Churchill would be willing to concede."

Hull did not agree. Disappointed by the article, the Secretary secured FDR's approval and instructed Ambassador John Winant in England to protest to the British:

They must be assured and be kept assured that the fourth point holds out to all people a real prospect that defeat of the Axis will mean a post-war world in which all countries will not only have equal access to raw materials but . . . freer access to world markets, . . .

Winant was to "take the occasion, and every suitable occasion, to impress upon British leaders our view that the prosperity and peace of the post-war world" depended on these ideas. Anglo-American cooperation in the attainment of these goals, Hull stressed to Winant, was contingent upon complete English support of American policy.[3]

After the United States went to war, the State Department reformed its administrative structure again, and a new group of committees met to work out policy, specifically the

State Department position on the postwar control of Germany.[4] The official departmental historian of these groups relates that multilateralism served as a framework for their thinking, and that planners applied Hull's ideas to issues of the peace with little dissent.[5] Policy makers believed that the war's end would offer the United States its best chance to realize multilateral aims. Although Germany's internal economic structure would remain the same, the victors would integrate the defeated state into the new international economy. The Reich would continue as a strong industrial nation, but American experts would convert its manufacturing plants to peacetime production and destroy those industries capable of producing only for war.

Initially, this scheme was crudely developed. Because hatred of the Nazis generated demands for German partition, planners concentrated on elaborating a rationale that would prevent dismemberment: they thought that a group of weak German states would bring misery and lower standards of living to Europe—the very antithesis of what was to happen under multilateralism. The idea required a unified and industrially potent Germany. But opposition to the division of the Reich at this time also reflected a distrust of Russia and cognizance of European power realities. Isaiah Bowman, head of the group known as the Territorial Subcommittee, brought out this pattern of thought in an early discussion. Bowman argued that "if we proceed to fragment Germany," the United States would lose its only defense against the Soviet Union. "The only effective future check on Russia," he declared, "would be a strong central European unit." The view of Norman Davis, Chairman of the Security Subcommittee, best indicated the status of policy. After reflecting that the Americans might someday "beg

Germany on our knees to help us against Russia," he urged in April 1942 that in the postwar period the United States make Germany strong enough to be satisfied, but not strong enough to be offensive.[6]

As the war progressed, the Soviets became more easily accepted as an Ally and the specifically anti-Russian intent of planning disappeared. The victors would still reconstruct Germany on industrial lines, and the Department argued that this could be achieved only if the nation remained whole. But the reconstruction would take place in the framework of a new world system where the sources of war would vanish. To be sure, a unified Germany had *traditionally* been an enemy of Russia, but in the State Department's international order, this conflict would not occur.

By the end of 1942 the Department had fixed its position against dismemberment. Sumner Welles was the single opponent of the policy, and, as head of the Political Subcommittee, he attempted to have the group's members support partition; but in November 1942 he admitted that "the definite trend" was "toward retaining Germany as a unit."[7] When the State Department reorganized the committees in the late spring of 1943, only Welles's had a pro-partition history, and the tendency in the committee was away from dismemberment after the first months of discussion. The Security Subcommittee summary best articulated the policy makers' view: partition without effective economic controls would not be conducive to security, and with effective controls the need for partition disappeared.[8]

Many historians have argued that the departure of Welles in the fall of 1943 enabled the State Department to go ahead with plans for a unified Germany free of an antagonist who was close to the President and who often had Roosevelt's

support on partition. Scholars have implied that Welles advocated a program entirely at odds with that of the rest of
the Department.[9] But the Under Secretary backed Hull's
ends in Germany and did not veto his committee's views. In
1942, when planners' thought was explicitly anti-Russian,
Welles concurred that the Americans ought to create a
strong central European unit after the war. But he also believed that this goal was consonant with dismembering Germany for security purposes.

Those diplomats who were against partition assumed that
it would lead to economic ruin in central Europe; it would
also encourage German cries for unification and provide an
argument for a future war of revenge. Welles felt that
planners overemphasized the German urge for unity. More
importantly, he stated that if economic ruin would result
from partition, the Americans should avoid it. But he believed dismemberment would not cause such a catastrophe.
In his scheme the capacity for economic development in
each of the fragmented German states was "almost unlimited." Each one would have a balance between agriculture and industry, and, adhering strictly to multilateral
views, Welles went on to say that the Germans should be
granted equality of economic opportunity and those commercial arrangements that would ensure their prosperity.[10]
State Department thought before and after Welles was the
same; dispute concerned means, not ends.[11]

Although Roosevelt's opinions had not influenced the
early departmental consensus, the President had stated his
opposing position at least as early as March 1943, when
British Foreign Secretary Anthony Eden came to Washington. Recalling conversations with Joseph Stalin, Eden stated

that the Russian leader would insist on partition. Roosevelt shared Stalin's view. He hoped that dismemberment would occur because of a spontaneous German desire, but the President added that if this did not happen, the Allies must divide Germany by force. Dismemberment was the "only wholly satisfactory solution" to the German problem.[12]

Presumably the State Department's formulation of American strategy would incorporate into it the President's ideas, but this did not occur, and the Department continued to plan for a unified Germany. After another shakeup in July 1943 produced a different organizational structure, new committees wrote this policy into the documents Hull was to use at the Foreign Ministers Conference that was to be held in Moscow in October 1943.[13]

The Department first unanimously recommended that enforced partition be opposed. Since it was unlikely that the Germans would ask or want to have their territory divided, this position was tantamount to a commitment for a unified Reich. Germany would also have "a tolerable standard of living" and the victorious nations were to bring about her economic recovery and installation into a world commercial system.[14] Economic disarmament—the selected destruction of certain war industries—and the reorientation of German trade would make war and autarchy impossible and return Germany to "prosperous dependence" on overseas markets.[15]

Related to this economic policy was its concomitant political strategy. Economic measures would bring into existence the conditions under which Germany could become democratic and peace-loving; because economics so directly affected political consciousness in the American view, integrating Germany into an international economic community would eventually recreate the German psychology.[16] But the steps in this transformation were not clarified, and diplomats rarely elaborated the political structure for Germany they had in mind. If economic policy were intelligently articulated and carried out, political developments would follow of their own accord, and perhaps for this reason these developments were spoken of in vague, emotive terms.

Welles had expressed this view nicely. The construction of a viable postwar economic system, he said, was "almost as essential to the preservation of free institutions" as the winning of the war itself. A world commercial order was necessary for "the attainment of those three great demands of men and women everywhere—freedom, security, and peace." The key to peace after the war, he wrote elsewhere, was agreement on a basis for international trade that would afford "a fair and safe outlet to the peoples of the defeated Axis." More candidly, he claimed that "it must be a world in which the political, social, and economic forces that have their origin in other countries are canalized into channels that will permit us to attain our own objectives." [17]

But theorizing about global politics would prove useless unless State Department economic policies succeeded, and at this time FDR's desire for a punitive peace was a major obstacle. On September 1, 1943, Roosevelt wrote to Hull enclosing a copy of a letter to *The New York Times* that advocated dismemberment; FDR asked for State Department comment. Hull replied that "imposed partition would be little short of disaster both for Germany and for us." But if the Germans were assured of a place in a world political and economic system, the Americans "would substantially contribute to replacing German militarism with a constructive national spirit." [18]

A month later, in a meeting held to discuss the coming
Foreign Ministers Conference in Moscow, Roosevelt declared categorically that he favored the dismemberment of
Germany into three or more states. Confronted with State
Department arguments against partition, the President
countered that "we are inclined to exaggerate these effects."
He had traveled and studied in Germany, FDR continued,
and knew the country better than the men in the State Department. "He insisted that partition was the solution."
Roosevelt's opinion appeared irrevocable, but then, in a
rapid about-face, he expressed another aspect of his thought
that persisted until his death. "The whole transitional period," he said, "would have to be one of trial and error." "It
may well happen," he concluded, "that in practice we shall
discover that partition, undertaken immediately after the
war, may have to be abandoned." [19]

After this meeting Roosevelt was to argue confusingly
both for partition and for postponement of a decision. And
from this time on the President's desires did begin to influence the Department in a minimal way. Hull would at times
advocate delaying a decision. Although Roosevelt did not
give up his belief in dismemberment, the Secretary's tactic
was justified by what he could construe as FDR's ambivalence on the topic. Delay might also prevent a hasty decision
for partition by presidential whim.

The issue was still in dispute when negotiations took place
at the Moscow Conference in October and at the first Big
Three meeting of Churchill, Roosevelt, and Stalin, which
followed a month later at Tehran. The State Department
supported a unified German nation, which it considered essential to multilateralism, but at the conference, presumably

because it knew FDR would not go along, also urged further consideration of the problem. The President set in motion plans for partition.

Hull carried to Moscow the first comprehensive statement on the postwar treatment of Germany that the three Allies would discuss. The American paper was often ambiguous concerning the question of dismemberment and, where it was not, took a position favoring a single German state. The first paragraph declared that there was no indication that German defeat would promote a movement for political unity or one for fragmentation. "Certain vital phases of this question," it concluded, "continue under study." The next paragraph took a different view. The Allies would hold elections to create "a central German Government to which the occupation authorities would gradually transfer their responsibility." But the visitors would decentralize the government and encourage any indigenous movement "in favor of the diminution of Prussian domination over the Reich." [20]

After studying the proposal, Eden said the British favored dismemberment and would support separatist tendencies. But he added that there were different opinions within the British government on the desirability of imposing partition by force. Vyacheslav Molotov, Soviet commissar for foreign affairs, began the long display of Soviet caution on the subject and commented only that the USSR liked all ideas that would make Germany "harmless."

It is difficult not to conclude that a prime Russian motivation was obsessive fear of the Germans. Still fighting for their lives, the Soviets had not yet repelled the Nazis from positions deep in USSR territory. More than either of the Western powers the Russians wanted a weak and impotent

Germany. But the Soviets were also mindful of the history of Russo-German antagonism. Because they feared a future war of revenge, it additionally appears that they wanted strong Anglo-American sanction for any plan for the control of Germany: the Russians did not want to be held responsible for a harsh anti-German policy. The ensuing dialogue from the Moscow Conference illustrates what was to become the standard position of the USSR and the usual tactic of the State Department.

Eden wished to know the Soviets' feeling on dismemberment, particularly their view on the use of force to achieve it. Molotov answered that the U.S. draft was "in the nature of a minimum program which might be expanded." The Russians had come to the conference believing that the United States was willing to go further on dismemberment than the British, but from Hull's document the Soviet Foreign Commissar saw no evidence of that. When Molotov asked for specific proposals from the British, Eden said Churchill was interested in Russian views. Molotov agreed to reply but first wanted Hull's ideas. The Secretary said that the divergent Allied suggestions on the subject impressed the United States. Although American diplomats were still in favor of dismemberment, the trend had been toward keeping an open mind and exploring the question more fully. Molotov was at last put into the position of answering, and his ability to sidestep the issue equaled that of Hull and Eden. The Soviet government, he said, was behind its Allies in its planning for the peace. Although setting forth "correctly" the program the three should adopt, the American proposals were a minimum and not a maximum. On the one hand, because "Soviet public opinion" favored dismemberment, there were some who would not be satis-

fied by the U.S. plan; on the other hand, Russia must consider the "political advisability of any such step." In what
must be regarded as a diplomatic masterpiece, Molotov
closed by stating that the Soviets had come to the "definite
conclusion" that "the dismemberment of Germany was not
excluded." "The question would require further study." [21]

Both the Western powers and the Russians would defer
decision, but what was important for future Allied diplomacy was not the tacit desire to eschew commitment but
the dynamics behind the similar strategy of each power.
Checking FDR's inclination to partition, the State Department adopted Roosevelt's sometimes expressed policy of
delay. If the Allies made no commitment on dismemberment, perhaps they would avoid making one in the future.
The Russians were led to this tactic because they would not
back any program uncertain of tripartite support. A genuine
agreement to postpone final plans gave the appearance of
unanimity to conflicting attitudes.

At this point, the President was not concerned with the
subtleties of international economics but with his desire to
dismember Germany. Proceeding independently of the State
Department, he acted with little regard for the policy of
caution and delay he had emphasized.

On November 19, 1943, FDR discussed the Anglo-American invasion of Europe with his Joint Chiefs of Staff (JCS).
He argued that occupation zones should be equivalent to
the German states that would exist after partition. The Allies
would divide Germany into three or possibly five parts after
the war, and Stalin might approve this division. The United
States would occupy an enormous northwestern zone while
the British and the Russians would have truncated southern

and eastern zones respectively.[22] FDR did not inform the State Department about the policy decided upon at this meeting, nor about the decisions made two weeks later when the President took up dismemberment with Churchill and Stalin at the first Big Three meeting at Tehran.

At the initial session on November 28, Stalin "took the lead" about the German problem. Like Molotov before him, he stressed harsh measures but would not elaborate his own thinking. Charles Bohlen, a high-ranking aid to Averell Harriman, the ambassador in Moscow, wrote that Stalin seemed to feel Allied ideas thus far advanced were insufficient. Although appearing to favor partition, Stalin did not specify what he had in mind, and on various occasions induced his counterparts to go further in expressing their convictions. Stalin was "obviously trying to stimulate discussion and to ascertain the exact views of Churchill and Roosevelt" without stating his own proposals.[23]

When the Big Three later came back to German problems, Roosevelt turned their attention to the question of dismemberment. After Stalin indicated that they all "preferred" partition, FDR presented another plan for a five-part division of Germany and the internationalization of two areas. He had "thought it up some months ago." Churchill was against the idea and argued that the separation of Prussia and of some south German areas would suffice for security purposes. Neither of these proposals convinced Stalin: if the Big Three were to dismember Germany, they ought really to dismember the state; it was not a question of its division into five or six parts or into two areas.

It is unclear what the Soviet ruler had in mind, but goaded by the fear of Germany and satisfied by no proposal advanced, he remained unwilling to stipulate measures that

would satisfy him. When Churchill said that sooner or later
a divided Reich would be reunited and that the main thing
would be to keep Germany partitioned for fifty years, Stalin
agreed: no matter what was done, a strong German urge for
unity would remain; moreover, the Germans would ultimately dominate any "confederation" in which they might
be placed. This show of Soviet anxiety marked the last discussion of Germany at Tehran. At the end of the conference,
the three concluded that their proposals should be examined
more carefully; and they decided that dismemberment should
be studied by the European Advisory Commission, a tripartite body established by the Moscow Conference.[24]

When Churchill, Roosevelt, and Stalin left Tehran "friends
in fact, spirit, and purpose," the President had shaped American policy for the coming year. The uneasy agreement
among the Big Three would be kept intact because FDR's
severe opinions prevented the expression of State Department
views. Because he had not informed Hull of the negotiations
with the JCS and the other Allies, the State Department did
not consider his views in its own planning. Moreover, the
President displayed little interest in postwar Germany during the first eight months of 1944. As a practical question,
dismemberment receded into the background, and the Department had no desire to raise it. The State Department
historian of postwar planning has written that the Tehran
Conference proceeded with little concern for previous Department thought and did not affect this thought thereafter.[25] State's policies would be worked out along the multilateral lines that the Department had agreed on prior to the
Moscow and Tehran conferences.

During the early part of 1944, this program was, ironi-

cally, promoted through Roosevelt's lack of regard for the
State Department bureaucracy. As I noted, FDR had not
consulted with the Department before discussing dismemberment with his chiefs of staff in November 1943, and
afterward Hull remained ignorant of what had been decided. State did not learn of the President's desire for a
large northwest zone in Germany until February 25, and the
information came not from Roosevelt but from War Department personnel close to the JCS. At this time Hull still had
not received minutes of the Tehran Conference and er-
roneously connected the zonal decision with the negotiations of the Big Three; he did not know that the proposal
had resulted from FDR's talks with the American military
before Tehran.

The British, however, had found out earlier about the
President's idea from the Anglo-American Combined Chiefs
of Staff, who were planning for the invasion. Perhaps in
response, they had put forward another proposal at the first
meeting of the newly created European Advisory Commission (EAC) in mid-January of 1944. The State Department
representatives on the EAC knew nothing of FDR's diplomacy, and thus, even if they had wanted to do so, they were
in no position to oppose the British plan with the President's.
The English memorandum called for three zones, roughly
equal in size, under a control council and a joint occupation
of Berlin. After the Russians accepted a slightly modified
version of this proposal, the President's program was void.
There was little chance that the Soviets would support a
plan giving them less of Germany to govern. When FDR
learned that the British had brought up their paper in the
EAC, he acknowledged that the United States should not
even present his position formally, and he agreed that there

should be three zones of occupation—although the council's authority was vague—and the final status of the German state was left open.[26]

State lost little in this confusion, and probably gained in the demise of Roosevelt's scheme for partition. In fact, during much of 1944 it struggled with the other bureaucracies for the control of policy. Among proliferating federal agencies, only the War Department first threatened State programs. The War Department's position was that it wanted no "political" restrictions placed on the military. The commanders in the field would have autonomy, and Washington should leave policy to their discretion.

As early as 1942, the State Department had tried to circumvent the army on this issue and favorably considered a proposal for a truly joint occupation, with no "national sector" run by one country's troops; rather, mixed troops throughout all Germany would operate together under a single command.[27] For various reasons—among them military opposition—this idea received no serious attention, but State Department backing for it early in the war is simple to explain. National zones of occupation in the immediate postwar period, as agreed on in the EAC, certainly did not preclude the ultimate unification of Germany, but they were a step toward partition even if the occupying armies coordinated their policies. A joint occupation, however, would go a long way toward guaranteeing that the victors would not divide Germany. Hopefully it would also enable State to carry out its directives for *all* of Germany.

Because the State Department could not bring about the assimilation of the troops of the three powers, until the summer of 1945 it proposed a strong central ruling body to govern all the zones of occupation. If such a body could agree on coordinated policies, it would place the zonal military administrations in the role of "enforcement agencies." Maximal direction by this body would make the allocation of zones unimportant and ensure that the Allies would treat Germany uniformly and avoid dismemberment.*

But the military would permit no limitation on its freedom of action and vetoed all State Department attempts to restrict the authority of army personnel with detailed policy statements. Because the War Department believed that the sole duty of the army was to fight the war, it was adamant that the military be unencumbered by commitments concerning Germany's future. The occupation would also be brief and unsullied by politics.

State hoped to maintain liaison with the Joint Chiefs of Staff and the War Department and to receive clearance for its program through the Working Security Committee (WSC). The State Department created the WSC, composed of members from several agencies, to funnel interdepartmental recomendations to the EAC and to clear policy with interested American agencies; in the EAC the United States would coordinate this policy with that of the British and the Russians. For a host of reasons this program broke down. Roosevelt had little time for the EAC and felt that it was a minor body. At first even the State Department had opposed it, fearing that this London-based commission would put

* Diplomats argued that central direction was especially justified if the Americans were to counter Russian influence. If the Allies jointly determined policy and the zone commanders only implemented it, Soviet power would be minimized. See the State Department files, Washington D.C. (hereafter SDF), Lot 60D-224, Box 17, CAC Docs. 51–77, CAC 76, 7 March 1944; Box 20, CAC Reports, 37, 3 March 1944; Box 29, WS Docs. 1–45, WS 15-a, 27 January 1944, and WS 19, January 1944.

planning into British hands and that the regional policies
which might follow from a strong EAC would conflict with
plans for a world system. Eventually the Department did
back the organization when it found other avenues for the
consideration of multilateral policy blocked. But after it got
behind the EAC, State was leery of sanctioning the documents sent to London. As its name indicated, the commission was advisory, and any policy it approved had to be
approved again by the three great powers. Thus, American
papers often went to the U.S. delegation as "guidance" without formal authorization at all.[28]

The real problems for the State Department arose in the
WSC. At first, the War Department's representatives on the
WSC believed that only the army should formulate programs in occupied areas. The military could settle any policy
questions. Although this intransigence lasted only a short
time, it reflected the War Department's belief that the State
Department should not participate in occupation planning.
War did join in the functioning of the WSC thereafter, but
the committee was ineffectual and its failure contributed to
the failure of the EAC.

Although the War-State impasse had little to do with substantive matters, it had substantive consequences for many
committed to multilateral ideas. Hull and his associates did
not want the army to take steps that might compromise the
future establishment of a world order. If the army had its
way, the Department feared the Allies could not effect a
multilateral program later on.[29] From State's perspective its
strategy had to be part of the procedures of the occupation.

Nonetheless, the evils the State Department feared could
materialize only much later and only in a strange set of

circumstances. The autonomy of the American military could thwart civilian procedures only if the great powers agreed on the postwar treatment of Germany. Then, if the American army contravened the stated policies of its government and would not coordinate its actions with those of the other Allies, the military might contribute to misunderstanding and tension. In fearing the War Department's independent line, State was assuming that the Russians and the British would approve multilateral policies even if the U.S. military might not. Moreover, on a practical level, War Department thinking was consistent with that of State; in those areas under its jurisdiction before the end of the war, it actually implemented programs the State Department favored.

By April 1944 the Combined Chiefs of Staff had issued CCS 551, a Pre-Surrender Directive for Anglo-American use after the invasion of France. Serving as the basic document for Western military planning, it remained in effect until May of 1945, the date of surrender. The directive argued that the occupation should aid strategic goals, destroy Nazism, maintain law and order, and "restore normal conditions among the civilian population as soon as possible, insofar as such conditions will not interfere with military operations." Its "Economic and Relief Guide" required the maintenance of the production, collection, and distribution of food and agricultural produce. Leaving the German industrial plant intact, the military would repair utilities and coal mines; ensure efficiency in shipping and inland transport; re-establish the communication system; and revive export and import trade. Although the Americans would remove Nazi personnel, they would use the existing German administrative machinery to accomplish these aims and would continue rationing and the German regulation of wages and prices.[30]

In assuming that the army should not allow the occupation to hinder the fighting, the War Department assumed that the army would not compromise the German economy, and in the immediate postwar period, this assumption was a condition of the success of multilateral goals. The State Department planned that the German economy would remain much as it was before the war. The Reich would still be a formidable industrial state, even though the Allies would destroy its armament industry and reorient its commerce. Given this economic restructuring, Germany could become a peace-loving democracy. The War Department program would help to make these views viable and the new German political economy a reality. Of course, the Combined Chiefs' directive did not concern itself with the destruction of German war industries or the reorientation of German trade; nor did CCS 551 dwell on the subsequent democratization of the German political structure. But these were long-range issues, and in contrast to Roosevelt's harsh words, the military program was almost identical to the State Department's plans for the surrender period.[31]

However the State Department might view the situation, its disagreement was at this point a matter of *who* would execute policy and not of *what* policy would be executed. Moreover, on an operative level a disinterested multilateralist might have placed more trust in the War Department than in the State Department. Despite their complexity and internal consistency, State's voluminous policy memoranda sometimes had only a tenuous connection to reality. Hull and those who shared his vision had almost no idea of the chaos that would exist in the postwar period; they had no conception of the magnitude of the reconstruction task; and they paid little attention to how the victors would realize their programs, or how the United States would meet the enormous problems of a world devastated by war. The War Department provided an appropriate link between theory and practice.

But there was still no consensus on postwar plans. The War Department checked agreement within American ranks, and by August 1944 the U.S. government had no agreed policy in the WSC, and, consequently, had reached few agreements of import with its Allies. The conflicts in the WSC contributed to the failure of the EAC. Even negotiations on dismemberment came to a dead end. Here, as in other areas, the commission failed to function. As Paul Hammond has put it, the subject was "buried in subcommittee." [32]

Because of the stalemate within the American government there was little chance for the multilateral view to be modified by compromises; from the last months of 1943 and through the summer of 1944, within the State Department and in agencies that shared its perspective, multilateralism was endlessly refined and its most subtle implications spun out. Discussion on proposed economic policy covered a wide and interrelated series of topics, the most important of which were cartels, commodity agreements, foreign trade, and reparations. Innumerable papers prepared for the WSC and EAC spelled out the connections between these specific concerns and overall planning.

At this time multilateralism, as it applied to Germany, meant "a gradual and planned liquidation of that uneconomic expansion of German industry and agriculture that has taken place since the 1920's as a costly defense against wartime military blockade." This autarchical position would be unnecessary in the postwar, nonbelligerent order. The enemy nation would return to dependence on overseas markets and resources; it would export industrial goods and import foodstuffs and raw materials, "as a part of the program of expansion of world trade." At the same time the Allies would liquidate high-cost German "defense" industries as part of a program of "economic disarmament." During the occupation these policies would result in a "marked revival" of the German economy, an increase in national real income, and reparations for European reconstruction from surplus production.[33]

Although the theory may have promised peace and prosperity, the State Department's single-minded concern with constructing an international system prevented it from grasping other consequences of its proposals. These consequences become significant when the Russian position is brought into the foreground. The Soviets feared Germany and despaired of controlling the Reich in the postwar period; but they were determined that Allied policy should be the harshest one on which the Big Three could agree. A strong postwar Germany with a Western orientation was anathema to the USSR, and yet, when stripped of its verbiage, State Department plannning would create exactly that. To be sure, Germany would ideally not be a threat to the Russians in a new world order, but in assuming something like its old place in the European economy, Germany would be a formidable power. As one military official put it, "The main issue can be briefly stated in the question as to whether it is desirable to have a weak or a strong Germany." [34] Of course, these aspects of State Department planning might distress not only the Soviet but most of the American public. For this reason, another military representative on the WSC observed that "most of the Army probably agrees that the post-war promotion of a suspended German economy is not a desirable aim for this country to announce." [35]

It may have been lack of perception that caused the State Department not to recognize the anti-Soviet features of its multilateral vision, for there was in all of this planning an unrealistic aura that carried over into the postwar period. American diplomats were convinced that their policies would create a world political and economic system that reflected American moral ideals. They believed that both the Russians and the British would support or could be persuaded to support this scheme. They felt that the United States could easily accomplish the gigantic task of reconstruction; specifically, the Americans would readily integrate Germany into the multilateral system, and at the same time the new Reich would contribute greatly to reconstruction. We can best indicate the depth of commitment to this "millennial" view in the more detailed aspects of economic planning, particularly in what was to become the crucial area of reparations.*

The Americans understood reparations imperfectly. They had not been invaded and none of their industrial plant had been destroyed or removed. Yet, after World War I they had seen the issue cause dislocations in the German economy and had intervened to delay a German collapse. Early in the war, when the Russians had demanded compensation from Germany, the Americans had had little to say on the

---

* I have taken reparations as exemplary here because of their later importance, but American ideas on the future of German cartels and foreign trade are equally illuminating. See SDF, Lot 60D-224, Boxes 18, 20, 35 and 36.

problem.[36] At Moscow, Hull did make a guarded proposal on reparations and attempted to limit compensation in several ways. The Soviets had long expressed a desire for this form of aid, and Molotov's dissent from these U.S. suggestions was to be expected. But neither Hull nor Molotov explored the matter in any depth.*

The Soviet position became more clear at the end of 1943 when a semiofficial article by Russian economist Eugene Varga became available to the State Department. Varga argued that because of deterioration and destruction, reparations in the form of removals of German industrial plants and capital equipment would be insignificant. The chief source of reparations would have to be consignments of goods from German current production after the war, that is, year-to-year deliveries of German manufactures for which there would be no payment. German industry would not be moved to Russia, but would remain in the enemy country and produce for the USSR. The USSR, Varga concluded, would find it "absolutely essential" to receive reparations of this kind in order to revert to a peacetime economy and to reconstruct.[37] Around the same time Averell Harriman, American ambassador in Moscow, felt that the Soviets and Americans would disagree on the amount to be collected; and in the summer of 1944 he informed Hull that the Rus-

* Foreign Relations of the United States, 1943, I (Washington, 1963), 666, 740–741 (further references to this series of volumes will be cited as FR followed by the volume number and date of publication). The general proposal that Hull presented on the treatment of Germany at Moscow conflicted with the U.S. reparations document he presented. The former paper expressed no reservations and argued that the "principle be recognized" that Germany pay "reparations for the physical damage" inflicted by its armed forces. Such reparations would have represented a fantastic sum, and policy that espoused them would be much less cautious than that spelled out in the reparations paper (722).

sians also thought Soviet-American views on the issue would diverge.*

Actually the U.S. position on reparations was unclear during this time, but beginning in late 1943 and during the next year both departmental and interdepartmental committees were set up to formulate the American program. During this period the Americans made the distinction between the two forms of collecting reparations. They gave little thought to the removal and transferal of industrial capital equipment from Germany to the victorious nations. Although the Allies would make some removals of this sort to accomplish what the Americans called economic disarmament, the procedure would net only a small amount. Even large-scale removals would not provide extensive reparations and, much more importantly, would leave Germany economically impotent and unable to participate in multilateralism. Rather, in addition to exporting goods, Germany was to make year-to-year deliveries of current production of her industry, although maintenance of a minimal German standard of living was to have precedence over reparations. The State Department justification of the reparations program was that free German goods would aid in the reconstruction of the rest of Europe; the Allies would use the compensation as a means of rebuilding devastated Allied economies and it would decrease the need for reconstruction loans. The Germans would be punished in the initial period and their needs—above a bare minimum—made subordinate to those of the rest of Europe; but in making the German industry work for others, the Americans would also ensure

---

* FR, 1943, III (1963), 591; 1944, IV (1966), 895. There was a tension in the Soviet desire for security *and* its desire for reparations that would entail the maintenance of some German industry. I take this up in the next chapter.

that the Germans would ultimately have some industrial strength.[38]

The State Department also discussed limiting reparations to what existing German industry could produce. If German industrial potential remained in its immediate postwar state, diplomats were uncertain whether the victors could integrate Germany into the new global system and obtain enough production for the reconstruction of Europe. Although the three powers should not make Germany too potent economically, the agreed solution was that Germany should be rebuilt so that it could contribute substantially to European restoration.[39]

The problem considered at greatest length was the relationship between reparations and multilateralism. The Department recognized that conditions would be chaotic in the immediate postwar era. This would be an interim period in which the Allies would repair the economies of various nations. Although the victors could extract more if they delayed reparations until Germany recovered from the war, they would not be extracting reparations when most needed. Moreover, heavy reparations payments in the later period would compromise the international system. In effect, these reparations payments would build up German exports and create markets for the defeated nation so that it might become an industrial threat. If reparations were heavy at first and tapered later, only temporary markets would accrue to Germany, and American long-range plans would remain unimpaired. Early deliveries would also punish the nation by retarding its reconstruction, but would not restrict German productive capacity.[40]

This consensus in the State Department on the relation of reparations to multilateralism did not preclude a difference of opinion within the committees discussing the problem.[41] One group of policy makers was opposed to reparations entirely, but felt that the damage done by the Germans and the insistence of the ravished nations would make the program necessary. Their concern centered around specifying an exact sum, but does not seem to have flowed from a belief that the Allies could not extract a large amount. In a mild way some in this group also thought that reparations would make it more difficult to achieve multilateral goals, but, primarily, they saw no compelling reason to make an American commitment to collect goods from the Germans.[42]

The other group of policy makers did not share this attitude. The first draft of the final report on reparations worked out two plans based on three-power control of a united Germany and moderate war damage. One, providing for maximal payments over ten years with small initial reparations, would yield $30 billion. The other plan—which was consonant with multilateral views—provided for larger payments during reconstruction with a tapering off in reparations at the end of the collection period; it would yield $21 billion. The last version of the final report dropped all figures. But they were considered throughout, and their excision on what appear to be grounds *other than* disbelief in the possibility of collecting the sum is an illuminating commentary on the State Department's outlook.* (By July 1945,

---

* SDF, Lot 60D-224, Box 7, PWC Docs. Nos. 221–230, PWC 226, Part IV; PWC 226a, Part IV, 10 June 1944. The figures were apparently dropped because policy makers saw no good reason to make an American commitment to collect a specific sum from the Germans. In late December, the Office of Strategic Services of the State Department still argued that under similar assumptions reparations might total $6.5 billion a year and could be doubled (OSS Research and Analysis Report 2350, "Problems of German Reparations," SDF).

just a year later, the State Department thought that *no* current production reparations were possible. All reparations would come from the capital removals contemplated in the economic disarmament program and were estimated at $3.5 billion.*) It is of course true that State Department officials finally dropped the mention of a figure, but the drafts of the report were evidence that their view of the Reich's place in the postwar world was based on extraordinary optimism. Germany would make enormous contributions to European recovery; international reconstruction would take place rapidly; and the world political economy would quickly become a reality.

By August 1944 the State Department and other likeminded agencies had completed their studies on postwar policies for Germany; with little understanding of the chances for the acceptance of the work, Hull was making arrangements to submit it to the President for final approval.[43] At lower levels the military veto that had frustrated War-State discussion and produced the crystallization of multilateral policy was still effective, and work in the WSC and the EAC remained snarled. But as August passed, the focus of discussion shifted.

---

* *FR*, Potsdam II (1960), 892. I have arrived at this figure by doubling what the Allied Reparation Commission representative, Edwin Pauley, said was available from the *western* zones under a zonal reparation plan. It is therefore something of an *overestimate* of what the Americans thought was available. Even under a plan that would treat Germany as a unit—something not contemplated in July 1945—total reparations were only to be in the range of $5 to $6 billion. Both the $3.5 and the $5 to $6 billion figures were themselves later to prove too high. See the discussion in Chapters 8 and 9, and the conclusion.

2 Morgenthau, Roosevelt, and the Russians

At the end of July 1944, Under Secretary of State Edward Stettinius dined with Secretary of War Henry L. Stimson and Stimson's Assistant Secretary, John J. McCloy. Stimson wanted to know who was to be responsible for demobilizing Germany and dismantling her munitions after the war and who was to decide on dismemberment. Neither McCloy nor Stettinius could give him an answer; they felt there was a "missing link" in the War and State Department plans.[1] When the Treasury intruded into postwar planning for Germany, this "missing link" appeared in a way that threatened both departments. The embroglio that resulted constitutes the best known and best documented series of events occurring in Washington during the war. In this chapter, I shall avoid a detailed retelling of the development of the "Morgenthau plan" for the "pastoralization" of Germany; I shall concentrate instead on the significance of the plan in illuminating eventual American postwar policy.

Because the War Department wanted autonomy, until early August 1944 it had been the principal agent in delaying decisions; then a new analysis of the war made it alter its position. With the advance of the Western Allies, army officials recognized that they would need directives soon.

The military also believed that perhaps it could not prevent the collapse of the German economic and political structure, and Dwight Eisenhower argued that the Pre-Surrender Directive (CCS 551), calling for military responsibility for the rehabilitation of Germany, was no longer applicable.[2] If Germany were to collapse, he said, the army should not be given the impossible task of saving or controlling the country's economic structure, and American Chief of Staff George Marshall shared some of Eisenhower's fears. Although civilians in the War Department did not take so bleak a view, some policy decisions had to be forthcoming.[3] Even if the military government were to exert itself to prevent collapse, policy was imperative, and the War Department became interested in obtaining agreement on policy throughout August.

But in mid-August, at a time when the State and War Departments might have come to terms, Secretary of the Treasury Henry Morgenthau traveled to Europe. Until this time the Treasury had played a passive role supportive of the State Department, and Morgenthau had not interested himself in the German issue. Now the Secretary and his assistant, Harry Dexter White, discussed the German problem with Eisenhower and high-level British and American officials. By the time Morgenthau had returned, he had concluded that the planning which had taken place expressed the ideas of "experts" who wished to build up a strong Germany.[4]

Morgenthau's views were connected with the interdepartmental reparations proposals that the Treasury had initially supported and that Hull wanted FDR to approve. Although the State Department planned that some heavy industrial equipment would go to the victors, it did not stress this

form of reparation because removals would leave Germany
weak and unable to participate in the new world system.
Moreover, the dollar value of these reparations would be
minimal. The final interdepartmental reparations document
of August 1944 stated that the "great bulk" of reparations
would come from annual deliveries of German manufactures. Current production compensation would not harm
Germany's industrial plant and would ensure that the Reich
could pay, "in absolute terms, a very substantial amount." [5]

White explained to Morgenthau that this memorandum
envisioned a reconstructed Germany upon which Europe
would be dependent for goods, and Morgenthau made the
memorandum the basis for his disagreement with State
Department planning. When the Treasury Secretary first
expounded his ideas, White commented that what they
wanted from Germany was "peace not reparations." According to the two Treasury officials, reparation (the Treasury
preferred to call it "restitution") should take the form of
dismantling, executed on an immense scale. They justified
this policy in several ways. The removals would aid Allied
recovery, and the impotent German state that remained
would not endanger European security. The Treasury also
argued that the scheme would aid the British. Extensive dismantling would eliminate Britain's "chief continental competitor" for international trade; Britain's future would be
safe, and she could take over some of the Reich's export
markets.[6]

The rest of Morgenthau's plan evidenced his harsh attitude even more. As White and his associates initially
drafted the plan, it called for the Allies to reconstruct Germany on agricultural and light industrial lines, substantially
contracting German heavy industry. The Big Three would

partition Germany and internationalize the Ruhr, which would retain some industry; but the Allies would not allow this industry to contribute to the remaining German states. The military government would take no steps to secure a German economic revival and would eschew responsibility for German internal affairs in the short occupation envisioned.[7]

White put together this first sketch of Treasury policy after Morgenthau's "spasmodic" exposition of his feelings.[8] But two weeks after his return from Europe, Morgenthau had decided that White's views were not tough enough, and the Treasury staff prepared a second, more drastic, plan. Instead of calling for the internationalization of the Ruhr, Morgenthau urged that the victors "deindustrialize" the area, close down its coal mines, and flood them.[*]

Morgenthau did more than prepare policy statements; he also saw the President, informing him that no one was acting on FDR's plans for a severe treatment of Germany. When this discussion failed to provoke Roosevelt, Morgenthau saw the President for a second time on August 25 and took with him a handbook on military government for Germany that he had acquired on his trip. Calling for the rapid reconstruction of the German economy, the handbook ac-

* Henry Morgenthau, "Our Policy Toward Germany," *New York Post*, 28 November 1947. Morgenthau was consistently more extreme in his proposals than his staff, including the influential White. For the running battle between the Secretary, who wanted to destroy all of the Ruhr industrial complex, and his aides, who were more inclined to be selective in the removal of industry, see the *Morgenthau Diary (Germany)*, 2 vols. (Washington, D.C., 1967), published for the Senate Subcommittee to Investigate the Administration of the Internal Security Act and Other Internal Security Laws of the Committee on the Judiciary, pp. 460–462, 483–494, 497–502, 590–596, 876–877, 882.

corded with the Pre-Surrender-Directive; it reflected the
army viewpoint *prior* to August, when the fear of German
collapse was altering military ideas.[9] In this meeting with
FDR, Morgenthau succeeded. If Roosevelt did not read the
handbook, he was angered enough by excerpts culled from
it to send them to Stimson in a withering letter about the
army's policies. FDR ordered the War Department to revise the handbook and return it for his inspection.*

* *Morgenthau Diary*, I, 440–445; *FR*, 1945, III (1968), 390–391.
Although it is not relevant here, the subsequent history of the handbook is important for an understanding of future U.S. policy. The
War Department immediately suspended its distribution, but on September 15, after the military found it impossible to block out the
passages that called for the reconstruction of Germany, the army
issued it with a disclaimer in the flyleaf. The disclaimer stated that the
handbook applied to the presurrender period only and that reconstruction should *not* take place beyond that necessary for military
purposes (Paul Y. Hammond, "Directives for the Occupation of Germany: The Washington Controversy," in *American Civil-Military Relations*, ed. Harold Stein [Birmingham, Ala., 1963], p. 356). As one
historian who served with the U.S. Political Division in Germany put
it, the military published the handbook "unofficially" for use by military personnel "after a few minor changes." In addition, the German
Country Unit, the planning staff that had written the handbook,
issued several other manuals. The Country Unit's plans were considered "constructive," recognizing the "futility" of revenge and were
designed "to get [the] German economy back on its feet" (Harold
Zink, *The United States in Germany 1944–1955* [Princeton, 1957],
pp. 20–21). As another American adviser recalled, the policies for
Germany that the Country Unit devised were similar to State Department plans (E. F. Penrose, *Economic Planning for the Peace*
[Princeton, 1953], p. 242). General Lucius Clay, the American military governor in Germany in the postwar period, thought that the
manual contained policies that differed little from the U.S. policy
"first" proclaimed in September 1946. At that time the Americans
publicly adopted a program designed to win German support and
achieve economic reconstruction in the enemy nation (Lucius Clay,
Decision in Germany [Garden City, 1950], p. 8).

In addition to berating his Secretary of War, Roosevelt formed a "Cabinet Committee" composed of his personal aide, Harry Hopkins, Hull, Morgenthau, and Stimson to thrash out the German issue. The major dispute in what was to become a long and bitter quarrel among policy makers concerned the Treasury and State Department means of controlling Germany. A victory for Morgenthau meant economic misery in the Reich and a decline in central Europe's ability to export and import. In short, the Treasury was attacking central doctrines of multilateralism, and, indeed, all of the memoranda previously worked out by the State Department and like-minded agencies were set aside in the new policy battle.

These circumstances are sufficient to confuse the picture of American policy making, but Hull's attitude made the situation more difficult to comprehend. The Secretary was ill and soon to retire, but in a manner that even Morgenthau found inexplicable, the patron of multilateralism at first agreed with the Treasury position. "Sacrifices at home" might be necessary "to make the Germans suffer," Hull said at one point—a "sacrifice in a little of our trade." [10] During the first weeks of the dispute, Secretary of War Stimson became the chief defender of multilateral ideas. By mid-September, when Hull again defended his old position, he seems to have opposed the Treasury on idiosyncratic grounds. He was more anxious to assert his prerogatives over those of Morgenthau than to see his policies implemented.

There is only a lame explanation for the position Hull took. He was sick, and his associates found him difficult to deal with. Apparently his attitude must be attributed to these personal factors; indeed, in his memoirs Hull denied that he at first favored Morgenthau.[11] By December 1944, however, he had retired, and during much of the period under discussion Under Secretary Stettinius was in charge of the Department.

Roosevelt's behavior was equally complex. Although he took a severe position on Germany, the President also wanted to keep his options open and counseled caution and delay, perhaps consciously keeping his Secretaries off balance. He could lecture his Secretary of State: "Now of course, Mr. Hull, you and I together for the last fifteen years have stood for increased trade and increased prosperity and peace and so on. And I am sure you agree with me that we have got to do that in Germany." Then, three days later on September 9, he said he wanted to "put Germany back as an agricultural country." [12] But as Stimson reported, Roosevelt did not support Morgenthau's revised and harsher proposal. The President was attracted to Morgenthau's arguments about Britain, and in fact made them his own. A weak Germany, FDR thought, would mean a strong Britain. The Ruhr would supply raw material for the British steel industry to help the English, who were "broke," and the three powers would curtail Germany's exports to expand English markets.[13]

On September 13, in the middle of these discussions, Roosevelt went to Quebec to confer with Churchill. Morgenthau was present, and the results of the meeting appeared disastrous to State Department planning.

Reasoning that if Germany were weakened Britain would receive the European steel business after the war, Roosevelt backed the Treasury proposal. Although not persuaded that Morgenthau's plan was in Britain's interest, Churchill accepted it in exchange for at least an implicit understanding that the Americans would settle Lend-Lease matters in favor of the English.[14] The result of these exchanges was an extraordinary document embodying Treasury ideas. Initialed by Roosevelt and Churchill, it called for the removal of the metallurgical, chemical, and electrical industries in Germany and the conversion of Germany into a country "primarily agricultural and pastoral in its character." [15]

Because the *quid pro quo*'s exchanged were antithetical to multilateral goals, the memorandum represented a formidable challenge to State policies. The Department did *not* want to twist Britain's arm to obtain Anglo-American agreement for the harsh treatment of Germany. Instead, the Department had wanted to trade American concessions on Lend-Lease for assurance that Great Britain would commit itself to multilateralism.[16]

In addition to this Treasury threat, State was still disputing with the War Department. War needed to have policy settled one way or another, but its position was unclear. Assistant Secretary McCloy, who was responsible for many policy matters, shared Stimson's views and disliked Morgenthau's program, but he desired occupation directives that would give the military the greatest possible discretion. Sharing his desire for autonomy were those in the army who wanted to manage the occupation only as they saw fit but who wanted no responsibility for German collapse.[17]

In a sense the army's policy was contradictory: it wanted autonomy to do what it wanted, yet did not want responsibility for what might be done. The result of these conflicting commitments was effective War Department support for the Treasury. Even though Stimson and McCloy opposed Morgenthau's economic and political views, Morgen-

thau endorsed military autonomy, and the Quebec memorandum did ensure that the civilians would not hold the
military responsible for maintaining the German economy
in the first months of occupation. This authority without
responsibility did not displease some in the army: chaos was
almost "planned," and in fact had Roosevelt's sanction.
There is also evidence that War was willing to grant the
Treasury verbal concessions—concessions that might mean
little in the occupation. McCloy himself watered down the
most severe aspects of "deindustrialization" and argued
that the Treasury plan would be "most difficult" to implement because by "training and instinct" the military would
proceed on different assumptions.[18] When a State Department memorandum on Germany was drafted at this time,
McCloy felt that War and State were nearly agreed on the
proposals.[19]

Despite this similarity of view, the State Department
could not support the military desire for freedom of action
in occupation areas. Morgenthau could; an independent
American position in its zone would contribute to the partition that Treasury thought imperative. Even after the military regained its confidence in its ability to control and
rehabilitate the German economy, the issue of autonomy
remained paramount, and War and Treasury developed a
tenuous alliance that lasted until the following spring.

By the end of September the bickering had produced the
first of a series of ambiguous American directives for U.S.
military authorities in which the Treasury had a hand. Like
its successors, the version of September 22 was supposedly
"interim" in nature, for use only in the immediate surrender
period, and it supposedly dealt only with short term military
objectives—the complete prevention of German return to

belligerent status—and not long term political and economic ones. In its economic section, on the one hand, the directive seemingly called on the military to take no steps in the rehabilitation of Germany; on the other hand, there were clauses which would allow the military, under varied circumstances, to exercise control of the German economy. The overall intent of the directive and those coming after it was negative, but the documents also contained loopholes: the various versions all attempted to compromise irreconcilable means of controlling Germany. The Morgenthau plan influenced all of them, but they also incorporated disparate views of the State Department; all were based on an uneasy War-Treasury coalition. As long as the Treasury was powerful, the United States might execute the severe intent of the directives, but should Treasury influence wane, the loopholes made them susceptible to varying interpretations.[20] Fighting over these memoranda—all known as JCS 1067—continued inconclusively through the spring of 1945.

In the meantime, and more importantly, the State Department took up the matter with Roosevelt. On September 25, Hull sent a memorandum to the President asking that the Americans seek *tripartite* consensus before acting on the Quebec agreement. This procedure was vital, Hull claimed, if there was to be an understanding with the Soviet. Hull also pointed out that the British War Cabinet might not support Churchill on deindustrialization. Later the Secretary saw FDR, reiterated these arguments, and gained the impression that Roosevelt was not committed to the Treasury position.[21]

Responding to this document, FDR indicated what was his more-or-less-constant position, as far as it could be called

a position at all, until his death in April 1945. The President
commented that tripartite discussion would secure no purpose at this time; certainly this discussion should not occur
in the EAC, which was on a "tertiary" level. He went on to
say that the "real nub" of the situation was to keep Britain
from bankruptcy; the Allies could not permit Britain to
collapse while they reconstructed Germany. The victors
could control the industry of the Ruhr and Saar but no one
wanted it eradicated. And Roosevelt implied that the Russians would pursue a policy of dismantling in its zone; even
were the American government to oppose dismantling, it
should not protest if its protests had no chance of meeting
with success.[22]

With the vacillations that appeared as the President am-
plified his views in the future, it is plausible to say that he
had no view at all except an inclination to treat Germany
severely and a desire to avoid a final decision. His priorities
were mixed and often, I think, frivolous: he wanted to
prohibit Germany from having aircraft and was much concerned to ban parading and uniform-wearing.[23] But he did
espouse a reasonably coherent economic view that was at
the center of his thinking on Germany.

Roosevelt conceived of a nonexporting German state
with an internally balanced economy sufficient for its own
needs. Industry would remain to produce for the Germans
but not for the world. But the President did waver here. On
the one hand, he wished to see a curtailment of German exports and British takeover of former German markets; alternatively, he desired shipments of raw material from the
Ruhr to Britain, and British production of steel for Europe.

Morgenthau often made the connection between British
prosperity and his proposal the prime selling point with the

President. What FDR particularly liked about the Morgenthau plan was that it would "help put England back on its feet." Morgenthau commented that both Roosevelt and Hopkins immediately were drawn to the plan when the benefits to Britain were mentioned. "That appeals to them right away," Morgenthau explained to his staff.

FDR's conception of a future German economy was a far cry from Hull's industrial exporter that would take its place in a global political economy. Specifically, Roosevelt was against reparations in the State Department sense of annual deliveries from German current production, but like the Treasury, he favored extensive removals of capital equipment. He supposed that the Russians would be interested solely in these removals and would approve his plan. Elements of this policy came up consistently over the next several months. In fact, Roosevelt's perspective was similar to that put forth in the original Treasury plan that Harry Dexter White had drafted; and at one point the President apparently indicated agreement with this Treasury policy. His continuing concern was and would be the status of Britain.[24]

In late September and early October, FDR expressed these ideas to Stimson. Although he wanted to prevent England from becoming a pauper, Roosevelt did not "really intend" to pastoralize Germany. Some of the raw materials from the Ruhr could be used by the Germans while others would be turned over to Britain in order for her to make manufactured articles for increased exports.[25]

With the President apparently retreating from Treasury policy, the State Department pressed its advantage. In another long memorandum, Hull urged that American plans be coordinated with both Britain and Russia and intimated that Morgenthau's proposal would not be agreed upon. The document outlined State Department thought that had been "developing" on this matter. The United States should postpone decisions on both partition and the collection of year-to-year recurring reparations. The Department was attempting to achieve its goals by delay. In espousing no commitment on reparations (i.e., current production), it would forestall Treasury plans for reparations (i.e., removals of industrial plants and machines) and leave the German economy uncompromised. "The primary and continuing objectives" of State Department policy were to make Germany incapable of waging war and to eliminate its "economic domination of Europe." The United States should destroy all plants incapable of conversion to peacetime production and abolish German self-sufficiency. The Reich would become "dependent on world markets," and the Americans would establish "controls over foreign trade and key industries." [26]

Roosevelt's reply was not so much a retreat from the Morgenthau plan as it was a retreat from all commitments. Because FDR disliked "making detailed plans for a country which we do not yet occupy," he felt that "Speed on these matters is not an essential at the present moment." Directives drawn up in conjunction with the other Allies—especially in the "advisory" EAC—should not be elaborate. The President concluded with a paragraph on State's "primary and continuing" objectives. "I agree with it in principle," the President wrote, "but I do not know what part of it means." Much of State Department thought was "dependent on what we and the Allies find when we get into Germany—and we are not there yet." [27]

By November, Hull had ceased to take a part in the activities of the Department, and although he did not retire until a month later, its real head was Under Secretary Stettinius. Most important about Stettinius' brief tenure in office —he was replaced in eight months—was his commitment to his predecessor's work. Immediate wartime objectives were, of course, the support of the armed forces and the prevention of the resurgence of Axis militarism. But on foreign policy the new Secretary's often repeated aim was agreement on measures to promote expansion of U.S. foreign trade and productivity. This program would enable America to maintain full employment and to enter, together with other Allies, an era of greater prosperity and higher living standards.[28]

In November, Stettinius approached the President many times to advocate these policies. On the eleventh he sent Roosevelt a memorandum supposedly setting forth the American position as it had evolved since September and had been reflected in a conversation the day before with the President. Stettinius began by indicating that Britain and Russia would not accept plans like the Treasury's. Although Britain feared German competition, it did not want to see Germany "pastoralized." Rather, it wanted selected German industry destroyed and the rest controlled, so that it could take over some of the German export markets. The State Department presumably designed this argument to combat the President's idea that the Morgenthau plan would help the British economy. On their side, Stettinius continued, the Russians did not fear German competition, but were interested in obtaining goods for reconstruction and development. Although they would want some reparations in the form of capital removals, they would rely primarily on reparations from current production. Stettinius probably set forth this argument to combat the President's idea that the

Russians would approve of Treasury dismantling. Both of the other Allies would desire controls over the German economy and would oppose "sweeping deindustrialization." The United States, pursuing the aims shared by Britain and Russia, was in an excellent position to mediate their differences. More confident, the Department no longer favored delay on reparations. As it had in the past, it wanted a short heavy program from current German output to aid in reconstruction.

The program contemplated in the occupation was a broader one of longer range, but it conformed to the "general economic foreign policy" of the United States, and Stettinius concluded by spelling out almost ritualistically the overall multilateral view.[29]

When Stettinius saw the President four days later, Roosevelt conceded after some discussion that the memorandum was sufficiently severe. He was pleased that "it did not dot all the i's and cross all the t's." Although FDR wanted a *tough* civilian view on the Allied Control Council that would govern occupied Germany, he was willing to have the document sent to interested agencies as a statement of his policy.

Immediately thereafter, Roosevelt changed his mind again. When the State Department sent him the letter of transmittal to other departments to accompany its latest document, the President replied that he would redraft it. A week later, on November 22, Stettinius sent him a helpful letter to use in the redrafting.[30] Nothing happened. Morgenthau, however, seems to have had little to do with this shift in presidential attitude, and FDR's son-in-law, John Boettiger, appears to have caused the vacillation; failing health made the President rely on the family in developing policy.

The War Department, again willing to assume some responsibility for German political and economic structure, influenced Boettiger. Disliking the substance of Morgenthau's approach, Boettiger favored a positive military program that was, nonetheless, free of State Department control. He thought his ideas intermediate between those of State and Treasury.[31]

Whatever the details, the State Department seems to have blamed Morgenthau for the President's inconstancy. In advising FDR on the redraft of its memorandum, State gave the guise of Treasury severity to its own proposals without altering their content. Allied policy was to be "severe"— underlined—and Germany was to have a "rock bottom" standard of living. The military might remove capital equipment (the Treasury's method of exacting reparations) but only so far as was consistent with maintaining a minimum economy. The United States should not destroy German industry but convert it to peacetime production for German needs and for recurring reparations. If there was an effective international security organization, deindustrialization would be unnecessary. If there was no such organization, Germany would rebuild and deindustrialization in the long run, that is, in about twenty years, would be useless. Because it was logically impossible for the Treasury program to work, the United States should avoid it. Instead, the Americans must integrate Germany into a liberal world economy, and the State Department conjured up all its arguments on this point.[32]

Throughout this period FDR was literally barraged by brief messages from Stettinius pointing out the impracticality of Treasury views,[33] but the President would not embrace State's approach. He reiterated what was in effect a pro-Treasury position along with his desire to avoid a final decision.

The State Department waited months for a "redraft" of its long November statement, and on March 6, 1945, FDR returned the proposal. Accompanying it was a note indicating Roosevelt's resistance to Stettinius' commitments. "I have read your memorandum of November eleventh on economic treatment of Germany," the President wrote. "Frankly I do not understand it and I think you had better bring this with you and talk with me about it some day." [34]

In the meanwhile another curt note had gone from Roosevelt to the State Department on December 6. In it FDR adhered to the first and milder version of the Treasury position that Harry White had expounded. There were several things State Department planners should "keep in the linings of their hats." The Allies could allow Germany to come back industrially "to meet her own needs, but not do any exporting for some time and we know better how things are going to work out." This statement in effect destroyed the *sine qua non* of State Department policy, an exporting German state that would participate in a world trade system. Roosevelt's hostility was further revealed in the next statement: "we are against reparations." Germany would not have industrial goods to export, nor would it supply reparations in current products. But Morgenthau and White did conceive of reparations from removals of industrial plants. The capital equipment taken to "deindustrialize" Germany would go to the Allies so that they could reconstruct. But the Treasury usually called these reparations "restitution." [35] Roosevelt had read the original Treasury memo "very carefully" and had taken another memo to bed with him on the night of September 13 at Quebec.[36] There are thus some grounds for

believing that he had picked up the Treasury idea of "restitution." The President's next instruction was that "we do
want restitution of looted property of all kinds." [37]

Although Roosevelt's ideas were congruent with the Treasury plan written under White's direction, Morgenthau disagreed with them just as he had disagreed with White. Having read FDR's memorandum, Morgenthau told Stettinius
that if Germany was allowed to have enough industry to
meet its own needs, it "can make anything under that." That
part of the President's letter "set me [Morgenthau] back on
my heels." [38]

It would be foolish to argue that the short letter reflected
Roosevelt's fixed perspective. The President consistently
favored the milder of the Treasury positions, but his conceptions were too ill defined to be considered final. And
throughout December, Stettinius continued to negotiate
with him and gained a commitment that in the first instance
FDR would work out German problems with State.[39] What
this meant is unclear because Roosevelt did not change his
strategy and continued to frustrate the State Department.
More significantly, as the dialogue between the departments
took place, the Treasury developed an alternative approach
to establishing a postwar order well within a framework
oriented to the United States. It is important to investigate
this approach.

As some policy makers realized earlier, State Department
plans for Germany had anti-Russian aspects. Philip Mosely,
an American political adviser in the EAC, reiterated these
thoughts when Morgenthau first enunciated his brain child
in Britain. Mosely argued that the Treasury plan would
drive the Germans to the USSR, and, he recalled having

said, the United States did not fight two wars in order to turn Germany over to Russia.[40] Nevertheless, these anti-Russian features may be best, if not adequately, described as "overtones" of the State Department design. The total plan envisioned a strong Germany *and* a strong Russia in a completely reconstructed world. The Americans would eliminate the frictions that led to war, and mute the traditional hostilities between both countries.

In one sense the plan could be construed as anti-Soviet (as distinct from anti-Russian) because it insisted on democracy and not Communism in Germany. But during the war this issue was defined too abstractly to enter discussion concretely. In a more important sense, the plan could be construed as anti-Soviet *and* anti-Russian: whatever it looked like in theory, in practice American policy might lead to a vigorous, Western-oriented Germany, inimical to Russia. But diplomats never considered that the consequences of executing the plan might be different from what they intended; indeed, they thought Moscow would embrace multilateral goals because they were in the Soviet interest; and the State Department certainly never understood that others could see untoward consequences in its ideas. The Department's political and economic view was not *in intention* anti-Soviet (or anti-Russian) but it might very well be so *in fact*. Morgenthau's proposals exposed these aspects of State planning to those who did not share the Department's version of the postwar world.[41]

But Morgenthau's idea was not "pro-Soviet" in a way detrimental to American interests. Like the State Department, the Treasury was concerned with the growth of U.S. commercial and economic influence. In fact, the Treasury feared that the current production reparations contemplated by the State Department might hinder U.S. trade expansion. These reparations would "considerably reduce export market possibilities in the world for Allied industries." [42] In the postwar period European nations would receive free goods in reparation, and their need for other sources of supply would be minimized. If Germany gained an advantage in world markets under these circumstances, and many countries became dependent on it, such a situation would decrease the chances for the maximization of Anglo-American exports.

In this respect, Treasury views apparently derived from those of long-time presidential confidant Bernard Baruch. Baruch advocated before Morgenthau that the Americans strive *not* for a general increase in trade and competition that would benefit the United States—as Hull argued—but for the elimination of competitors like Germany.[43] If Germany could no longer supply Europe, the Treasury claimed, not only Britain but also the United States would "enjoy expanded foreign post-war markets." [44] To be sure, Morgenthau was unsure of the truth of this claim. He once stated that the elimination of Germany as an industrial nation might *reduce* American markets. But he also thought his scheme would help to solve American and British domestic problems after the war in the vital but underemployed coal and steel industries.[45]

Morgenthau's ambivalence is explicable if we realize that security was most important to the Treasury view of the Reich. Revenge may have personally motivated the Secretary, but he despaired of controlling German war potential. Because nothing could guarantee the development of a pacific democracy in Germany, the Allies must keep the nation weak. For example, a Germany from which current production reparations would come could easily be industrially strong; consequently, they had to be curtailed. As the Treasury saw it, American goals for commercial expansion had to be achieved without the military threat of a reconstructed Germany.

The other significant aspect of the Treasury program was its plan for the Soviet Union. By January 1945, Morgenthau formulated a scheme "for comprehensive aid to Russia during her reconstruction period." This aid would not be Lend-Lease but "an arrangement that will have definite and long range benefits for the United States as well as for Russia."

The Treasury proposed a $10 billion credit to the USSR for the purchase of reconstruction material in the United States. Although the USSR would repay partly with Soviet trade profits, gold, and the normal Russian dollar supply, it would pay the Americans back chiefly from "strategic raw materials in short supply in the U.S." An important feature of the loan was that it would enable the United States to conserve "depleted natural resources by drawing on Russia's huge reserves for current needs of industrial raw materials in short supply here." "We would be able," Morgenthau told Roosevelt, "to obtain a provision in the financial agreement whereby we could call upon Russia for whatever raw materials we need without giving commitment on our part to buy." [46]

At Morgenthau's request, Harry White had obtained the specific information on the raw materials involved in March 1944. White argued that because the USSR had a state-controlled and planned economy, it would be possible for the United States "to influence the Soviet pattern of anticipated national surpluses and deficits" in the repayments of raw materials.[47] Expressing a basic American commitment, Morgenthau indicated to the President that a program of commercial expansion connected with the Soviet "would be a major step in your program to provide 60 million jobs in the post-war period." [48]

The Treasury scheme was related to Morgenthau's desire to extinguish the German military threat and exact revenge. But as Treasury planners now conceived their idea, the weakening of Germany would not occur at the expense of the United States. With the other part of the plan, an enormous credit to the Soviet Union, Russia would be integrated into a Western politico-economic system in a position subordinate to the United States: it would supply the Americans with raw materials. Increased trade to Russia and eastern Europe would match any trade that the United States and Britain might lose to a nonindustrial Germany. America would become the major source of industrial and manufactured goods to all of Europe.

Treasury ideas were radical and unrealistic. The Treasury itself believed that the fate of Germany could be decided "without reference to the economic consequences upon the rest of Europe." As the State Department contended, Morgenthau's proposal would bring about extensive and important changes in the European economy as a whole. The Treasury agreed: implementation of its program would mean that "the whole balance of industrial power in Europe will be shifted." [49]

On conception the Treasury plan was an alternative method for achieving postwar goals also fundamental to the State Department: the expansion of American trade and commercial influence, the preservation of democratic institutions, and freedom from the scourge of war. Even in early September 1944, when the interagency dispute was most bitter, Stimson noted this aspect of the disagreement. "Our

discussions relate to a matter of method entirely," he wrote
Roosevelt, "our objective is the same." [50] Five months later a
State Department official made the same point. There was
"full agreement" on the objective, and "a difference of emphasis . . . regarding the economic measures appropriate
to that objective." [51] Moreover, Morgenthau's program *was
no more unrealistic* than the State Department aim of multilateralism. The Treasury thought that the United States had
the power to reorient the entire European economy away
from Germany. In an equally delusive manner the State
Department thought that it could destroy the sources of
conflict all over the globe. The difference between the two
plans lay in what might be the results of the failure of each.
If Treasury preconceptions were acted upon and failed, a
resurgent Russia would dominate all of Europe. If State preconceptions were acted upon and failed, a renascent and
reconstructed Germany would once again hostilely face the
Soviet.

In this respect the attitude of the Russians is crucial for
the analysis of Allied policy. Subsequent historians have
assumed that the USSR immediately supported the Morgenthau plan because of its uncritically pro-Soviet aspects.[52]
But the State Department urged *abandoning* the Treasury
proposal because it could never gain the support of the
USSR. The Russians, the State Department claimed, would
want substantial reparations from current production and,
therefore, an industrially reconstructed Germany.[53] Actually
neither of these views adequately explains what appears to
be a more complicated and ambiguous Soviet aim.

Both Molotov and Stalin displayed extraordinary caution
in disclosing Soviet ideas about Germany. Throughout the

early stages of the war Stalin repeatedly said that the Allies should not destroy Germany. In March 1943, Eden suggested that Stalin wanted British and American troops "heavily in Europe" when the German defeat came. This was fixed Russian policy because Stalin did not desire full responsibility for what would happen at the collapse. Because the Russians did "not wish to take any responsibility for the well-being of the German people," Ambassador Harriman in Moscow thought that the Soviets had no intention of "fostering communism in Germany."[54]

Even if the Soviets did not wish a miserable or Communist Germany, they did want their traditional enemy weakened as a military threat. Both Eden and Harriman believed that the Russians would insist on a partitioned Germany, and in 1944 the British government was convinced that the USSR would "maintain its determination to keep Germany weak" for a much longer time than the Western Allies.[55]

These appraisals were in line with the circumspect views expressed by Molotov and Stalin. The Russian leaders were single-minded in their dread of a German resurgence and determined to prevent one; but they also wished to avoid a vengeful peace which would ultimately unleash itself on them. Apparently for these reasons the Russians were unwilling to commit themselves on their plans for Germany without a commitment from Britain and the United States to behave similarly. F. T. Gousev, the Soviet representative in the EAC, stressed the importance of joint occupation policies to prevent the Germans from playing politics with the three powers.[56]

The Soviets' desire for heavy reparations conflicted with their goal of military security. In 1943 the Russian economist Varga had urged large reparations, and Harriman warned that the Russians wanted enormous reparations.[57] Because transfer of industrial equipment would not provide a large amount, reparations would have to include materials from year-to-year German manufacture, and this would require that much German industry be left standing. If the Allies implemented this program, the Russians might soon face a strong Germany. Morgenthau's proposal that a large credit be given to the Soviets is perhaps evidence that their attitude was ambiguous. Should the Americans accept the Morgenthau plan, they would have to persuade the Russians. Morgenthau could accordingly offer a loan: assured of American dollars, the Russians could go along with the Treasury idea of industrial removals but no current productions reparations.

USSR planning consequently appears to have been undetermined when the American dispute over the Morgenthau plan became public in the fall of 1944. At least when U.S. decision makers discussed the subject with Soviet diplomats, the Americans received contradictory views of Russian policy.

In September an American official in the EAC reported that as far as Gousev had expressed Soviet ideas on Germany, they coincided with State Department notions.[58] Pasvolsky, Hull's special assistant, also received this impression from A. A. Sobolev, the Vice Chairman of the Soviet Delegation at Dumbarton Oaks. He told Pasvolsky that he did not quite understand the furor over the Morgenthau plan, but "he was certain that Mr. Morgenthau's type of thinking was not acceptable to the Soviet Government." [59]

A few weeks later Harry White saw Russian Ambassador Andrei Gromyko, who had just returned from the USSR.

High Soviet officials had not informed Gromyko of their plans for the future of Germany, but he thought his superiors stood "very close or closer" to the Morgenthau plan.[60]

Ivan Maisky, recently appointed Assistant Commissar for Foreign Affairs, confirmed this position in a January interview with Averell Harriman. The USSR was concerned with security and *not* current production reparations, although Maisky added that the Russians had reached no conclusions on details and that he was only stating their present attitude. Harriman also noted that Maisky was more willing to talk about "preliminary views" than any other members of the Soviet Foreign Office. Soon after, Winant reported that this view was definitely not that of the Russians in the EAC.[61]

In the period before the Yalta Conference, both American *and* Soviet plans for Germany seem to have been ill defined. The policy of the American government was an amalgam of contradictory proposals whose connections were extraordinarily intricate. The basic argument was the clash between State and Treasury over the strength of Germany, and was illustrated by their divergent plans for reparations. But the desire of the military for freedom of action also had implications for high policy. Ironically, although the army's economic program was that of the State Department, the War Department's need to ensure its administrative integrity drove it to an alliance with the Treasury: Morgenthau's goal of partition and McCloy's of autonomy coincided. Presiding over the bickering was FDR, maintaining a position he conceived to be "between" those of the Treasury and State Departments. Yet, if Roosevelt took a consistent stand, his idea of a nonexporting German state that would promote

British welfare was never worked out in any sophisticated manner; and it had no basis in the realities of European economics.

As Stimson reflected later in an exaggerated fashion, the problem was not one of coordination, but rather that the policy of FDR himself was unknown, unclear, or even contradictory.[62] On its side, the Soviet Union perhaps wanted a plan that was impossible to achieve, but would probably not support any position the United States adopted.

Although neither government was ready to commit itself, some agreements appeared necessary if only because Nazi defeat seemed near. With the German problem in mind, the Big Three initiated the dramatic diplomacy of 1945.

3 Yalta and
Its Aftermath

The Yalta Conference took place at a time when significant clarifications could have occurred in great power relations; and, to be sure, it has come to have major symbolic
significance. But so far as Germany and the problems associated with it were concerned, the outcome of the meeting
was a further delay of decisions—temporizing appears to
have been Roosevelt's conscious strategy. Indeed, the development that took place in one area—reparations—was
apparently the result of ignorance and inadvertence: FDR
and Stettinius, who conducted the Yalta reparations negotiations, seemed unaware of the issues at stake and consequently permitted a further definition of American policy.
After the conference, however, U.S. decision makers were
again caught up in the Washington controversy. From the
end of the Crimea meeting in early February until Roosevelt's death, the main interest of the German problem is its
connection to the State-War-Treasury fight. It clouded some
of the basic issues of Soviet-American relations in regard to
Germany and occupied the energy of diplomats; only after
the President's death would there be a clarification of great-
power relations.

When the Big Three took up dismemberment at Yalta on February 5, Stalin opened discussion by asking whether Roosevelt and Churchill still adhered to their belief in dismemberment. *If they were to partition Germany, Stalin inquired, would there be three separate governments?* Churchill concurred on dismemberment "in principle," but he said a final decision concerning its manner could not be made at the time. FDR interposed that this did not settle what Stalin had brought up: "Are we going to dismember or not?" In one of his customary attempts to compromise, the President added that both Stalin and Churchill were talking about the same thing, namely, should they not "agree in principle . . . on the principle of dismemberment." Passing over Roosevelt's suggestion that the foreign ministers "submit a recommendation" on methods for studying dismemberment, Stalin pressed "to ascertain exactly what the intentions of the three governments are." If they were going to partition, he wanted the foreign ministers to work out the details. Rather than answering, the President asked Churchill if the word "dismemberment" should be added to the surrender terms. The Prime Minister consented, but, closing discussion for the day, Eden qualified this approval by stating that it would be sufficient to elaborate "some other formula to make dismemberment possible." [1]

The next day the foreign ministers debated the question along the lines Eden proposed. Secretary Stettinius made two suggestions: the first favored dismemberment by the powers "as they deem requisite"; the second, dismemberment "to the degree necessary" to safeguard peace and security. Eden and Stettinius preferred the first draft, considered the weaker of the two. But Stettinius was willing to support Molotov, who preferred the second. Eden was not so amenable to compromise and was adamant in arguing that the British could commit themselves only to the first proposition. In demanding the stronger version and urging additional phrases to clarify the intent of the Big Three, Molotov was less circumspect than Stalin, and the meeting ended in an Eden-Molotov standoff. At the plenary meeting that afternoon, however, Molotov withdrew his reservations. That Stalin raised no objections is evidence that he, as well as Churchill and Roosevelt, was agreeable to delay. And when the foreign ministers met to create a committee of the EAC to study dismemberment, Molotov claimed that the subject under discussion was the "study of procedure for dismembering Germany and not the actual dismemberment or detail thereof." At this point Eden considered Molotov's conception of the commission too weak and thought the body should "go further than merely studying questions of procedure." [2]

A State Department survey on "Post Yalta Developments" described the Russian negotiations perceptively: the USSR desire to discuss partition "apparently stemmed from a wish to probe more deeply into . . . long-range views of the post-war position of Germany." The Soviets, the document stated, had made no decision to advocate partition; [3] the fragmentation of Germany was a step that no one of the three powers felt compelled to take. [4]

Although the Allies resolved the problem of dismemberment by temporizing, they could not circumvent the problem of reparations in a similar way. Reparations were the key to the Soviet position on Germany, and "Assistant President" James Byrnes recalled that they were the "chief interest" of the Russians. [5] On this issue they did want a decision.

The USSR was determined to receive a sum large enough to enable it to begin reconstruction, but it was unclear how the three powers would collect this sum. Reparations from current production and dismantling each had disadvantages. Moreover, dismemberment was ambiguously tied to reparations. While serving security interests, partition, like dismantling, would give the Germans a motive for revenge and limit current production reparations. A number of little Germanies did not have the economic, and therefore reparation, potential of a united Germany.

We do not know how the Soviets resolved these conflicts in their own minds. But the miscellaneous forms of the reparations program they put forward indicate that their main concern was receiving an amount of reparations. On February 5, Stalin brought up the question and had Ivan Maisky, assistant commissar for foreign affairs, present the USSR plan. Maisky proposed that the Allies remove 80 per cent of German heavy industry—iron, steel, electrical power, and chemicals—within two years; they would remove 100 per cent of the specialized war industry. In addition, the Germans were to make deliveries from their current production for ten years. Maisky concluded by saying that the USSR would want not less than $10 billion from both sources.

Churchill demurred, and the first of many sharp exchanges occurred between him and Stalin over reparations. Although Roosevelt remarked that the United States had no wish to repeat the mistake of the last war and subsidize Germany, he asserted nonetheless that "he would willingly support any claims for Soviet reparations." Adumbrating the first version of the Morgenthau plan with which he was in sympathy, FDR continued that the United States would help

Great Britain expand her trade and the USSR "retain" reparations. The victors, it seems, would deindustrialize to provide manufacturing plant for the Russians. Enough industry would be left so that Germany would be a self-supporting, although not an exporting, nation; then Britain could take over her markets. "In rebuilding," the President concluded, "we must get all we can but we can't get it all. Leave Germany enough industry and work to keep her from starving." [6]

Whatever Roosevelt's concerns, the major issue was the Soviet demand for $10 billion, and the unsettled discussion of the plenary session was transferred to the foreign ministers' meeting. Evidencing a lack of concern for the details of the Soviet program, Molotov put forward a different plan. He dropped the mention of 80 per cent destruction of German heavy industry and added another $10 billion to go to the British, the Americans, and all others. Maisky commented that half of the total of $20 billion would come from removals, half from current production. [7]

Eden had pointed out the conflicts in the Russian proposal to obtain reparations from both deindustrialization and current production. [8] Indeed, when Maisky presented his plan for removing 80 per cent of German heavy industry, he contended that with the remaining 20 per cent the Reich would have enough industry "for [the] real need of the German economy." [9] If this statement were true, it is difficult to see how Maisky could argue in the next breath for current production reparations. After Molotov put forward the revised Russian plan, Maisky made a similar error. He said that after removals were made, Germany would still have enough industry to secure central European living standards; then, without computing the loss that would ensue because of deindustrialization, he calculated that the

German national income would yield $1 billion yearly in
current production reparations.[10] When Eden questioned
the effect of dismemberment on reparations from current
production, Maisky most clearly expressed the Soviet position. When the Big Three decided on the practical form of
dismemberment, they could "adjust" the reparations plan,
although $1 billion annually would be possible after the con-
templated removals. "If Mr. Eden had any doubts the easiest
way out was to accept the [Russian] formula . . . and to
raise the British proposals . . . [later] on this basis." [11]

Eden did have doubts, and so did the Americans. After
consulting with the President, Stettinius set forth another
plan two days later on February 9, and attempted to water
down the Soviet proposal.[12] A reparation commission, which
all agreed would be formed and which would meet in Moscow, "should take into consideration in its initial studies the
Soviet Government's suggested total of twenty billion dollars from all forms of reparations." Both Molotov and Maisky
argued that this section should contain the additional phrase
"as the basis." Although "the final figures arrived at by the
Commission might be a little more or less than $20,000,000,-
000," the Soviet delegation urged "that this figure be accepted as the basis." Both Eden and Stettinius were unwilling to set $20 billion "as the basis." Stettinius maintained
that the figure should be set by the commission and offered
that the Soviet Union receive 50 per cent of the total.
Molotov did not object, but claimed that the figure might be
a little more or less than 50 per cent; the important thing
was to name an amount. Finally, "after some discussion" the
Soviet and American delegations agreed. The Reparation
Commission "should consider in its initial studies as a basis
for discussion" the Russian suggestion of $20 billion, one-

half of which was to go to the USSR. Eden could not consent, and negotiations turned to another point.[13]

The Protocol of the conference stated the results of this day's agreements and disagreements on reparations: the United States and the Soviet would concur on the $20 billion "as a basis for discussion" while the British refused to agree. Clearly the Americans yielded as they did as a compromise, and then they did not assent to an exact figure. But it is also true that they agreed that the total reparations bill would be vaguely "around" the Russian amount. As Stettinius recalled the accord—apparently quoting Molotov —the figure might be a little more or a little less.[14]

The dynamics of the reparations negotiations reveal an ancient principle of bureaucratic logic: if the Soviets could set the agenda for the Reparation Commission and have discussions begin at the $20 billion level, they would be in an excellent position to achieve what they wanted in the normal give-and-take of negotiations. In acquiescing to the Soviet demand, the Americans committed themselves to serious bargaining with the Russians over a substantial monetary figure. The USSR could expect to get several billion dollars in reparations for itself.*

The following day Stettinius sided with Molotov in an attempt to win British support for the Soviet-American agreement. The Secretary pointed out to Eden "that the ten-year period [for reparations payments] was merely mentioned as a basis for discussion. It might result that all capital movements could be affected in seven years." [15] Stettinius' meaning is not clear. He may not have understood that the

---

* I have usually summarized this understanding by speaking of the commitment to be vaguely or loosely around $20 billion, one-half to go to the USSR.

suggested ten years of reparations were to be in the form of current production and not removals. Alternatively, as FDR's mouthpiece, he may have been indicating that he favored only reparations in terms of removals. But in pointing out that it could take seven years to fulfill an agreement to take ten years "as a basis for discussion," he implied what the Soviet reparations figure would be like.

Neither the United States nor the Soviet Union, Stettinius went on, was committed to ten years or $20 billion. In later arguing that the Americans did not promise the Soviet Union $10 billion, Stettinius approvingly cited Maisky's understanding of the discussion: the Russian plan "did not commit the Allies to the exact figure." The United States did not consent, Stettinius recalled, on $10 billion as an "agreed amount." [16] Here, he undoubtedly conceived the U.S. commitment to be not simply *to discuss* $10 billion as the Soviet share but *to base* the reparations figure on it. The USSR was to get a definite amount in reparations somewhere near $10 billion. [17]

At the plenary session the same day neither FDR nor Stalin grasped the issues, and Churchill led the discussion by asserting that the British would recognize no figure whatsoever. Roosevelt was afraid that if a sum were mentioned, the American people would believe it involved money and not material "in kind." Although FDR may really have wanted to avoid naming an amount, no evidence points in this direction. Even Churchill, who wanted support at this time, regarded Roosevelt's reasoning as irrelevant. As H. Freeman Matthews of the State Department's Division of European Affairs wrote, "The President made it clear that what he feared was a system of reparations paid in money"; and Stettinius later told Stimson and Forrestal that

FDR backed the Soviet program.[18] When Stalin asked if the Americans withdrew their approval to take the $20 billion as a basis of discussion, Roosevelt replied that he was "completely" in agreement; but because reparations meant money to so many people, they should add the phrase "in kind."

This was done, and having secured FDR's acquiescence, Stalin turned to the British and spelled out the meaning of the accord. When Eden asked what was the value of a figure if there were no commitment, Stalin answered that the commission could change the basis and modify it in any way. The sum was not "sacrosanct" and could be "reduced or increased"; the Russians were prepared to discuss it. Churchill remained adamant, and, relenting, Stalin proposed that the commission be instructed "to consider the amount of reparations." Both the Prime Minister and Roosevelt acceded, and the issue seemed settled.[19]

After the meeting, however, the Russians reminded Roosevelt that he had not backed up Stettinius' agreement on reparations and had sided with the British. In response, FDR made it clear at dinner that he did not assent to the English idea of mentioning no figure at all. The Protocol on Reparations was changed again, and its final wording reflected the Stettinius-Molotov compromise. The British were put into the position of dissenting, while the Soviet and American delegations concurred that $20 billion in kind be taken as a basis of discussion, one-half to go to the Russians.[20]

Both Herbert Feis in his *Churchill, Roosevelt, and Stalin,* and Gabriel Kolko in *The Politics of War,* narrate these events in a distorted way, and therefore misunderstand the nature of the reparations compromise.[21] One reason for the confusion surrounding this agreement may be precisely the informal way in which it was made. When the State Department later circulated copies of the reparations discussion at Yalta, no document recounted this final decision or indicated that a firmer commitment had been given at the dinner conversations. The State Department itself may have been confused about the extent to which the United States was committed.[22]

Although the accord was vague, it embodied more than U.S. diplomats admitted later. While they were not committed to an exact sum, the Americans were committed to a figure loosely around $20 billion. To be sure, the commitment was made by Roosevelt, whose knowledge of the German problem was superficial, and by Stettinius, whose abilities were doubted.[23] But the Americans were bound: they did not go along with the British, who *were willing* to consider "an amount" of reparations, although not a specific sum. As Hopkins wrote the President, "Let the British disagree if *they* want to—and continue *their* disagreement in Moscow." [24] This contrast with the English position is crucial to comprehending the American posture. If the United States committed itself to "discussion," why did the British refuse to go along? Or, to put the question another way, if only "discussion" were at issue, why didn't the Americans support the British and refuse to name an amount? In this matter as in so many others, FDR wished to avoid any binding agreement, but a lack of concentrated thought allowed him to reach an accord that proved embarrassing to his successors. The British saw the points at issue: as Eden said, "rightly or wrongly, the British Government felt that even the naming of a sum as the basis of discussion would commit them." [25]

Although the State Department had prepared two lengthy "Briefing Book Papers" on the postwar treatment of Germany, extended negotiations on this question did not occur at the conference. But the documents taken by the Department to the Crimea talks showed how few compromises it had made with War and Treasury. Against War, State called for centralized control of the German economy; against Treasury, it called for the conversion of German manufacturing plant to peacetime production and not its destruction. Although there would be disarmament and control of war potential, the State Department would not contemplate "sweeping measures of industrial impairment." Coming from current production, reparations would consist of the surplus above the industrial production needed to maintain a minimal standard of living and other prior charges. Deliveries would be of short duration so that they would not interfere with the export trade of other countries or entrench Germany in the markets of the claimant states. From the beginning of the occupation, the Allies would carry out all policies in the light of long-range objectives. Military rule should not prejudice "Germany's ultimate place in the projected world order."

Here again was reference to the *sine qua non* of State Department planning, its conception of multilateralism. The Allies would abolish German self-sufficiency and eliminate its instruments of economic aggression. These two goals indicated the central idea that guided policy. Abolition of self-sufficiency required "the removal of all protection and subsidies to high-cost domestic production." Elimination of the instruments of economic aggression required "the prohibition of all discriminatory trade controls, clearing agreements, and international cartel arrangements." Demonstrating the consistency of its German policy from the thirties, the Department aimed at "the assimilation—on a basis of equality —of a reformed, peaceful, and economically non-aggressive Germany into a liberal system of world trade." [26]

At Yalta the Big Three passed over these questions on which the State Department had such strong views. Even when the conferees accepted a U.S. draft of the communiqué on the meeting, the State Department made its public program more ambiguous. Only by reading between the lines would one discern the position that the Department had taken to the Crimea. The relevant passages on Germany read:

we are determined to . . . remove or destroy all German military equipment; eliminate or control all German industry that could be used for military production . . . and take in harmony such other measures as may be necessary to the future peace and safety of the world. It is not our purpose to destroy the people of Germany, but only when Nazism and Militarism have been extirpated will there be hope for a decent life for Germans, and a place for them in the comity of nations.[27]

Although Roosevelt was opposed to State Department policies, his inattentiveness led him to acquiesce to a Soviet reparations demand that the State Department would initially support. As State Department planners recognized, reparations would take the form of transfers of German current production, and Germany would be returned to the status of an exporting country.[28]

There has been some misunderstanding of this question. John L. Snell has written that "Stalin made Morgenthau's principles his own at Yalta." [29] But the essential element in the Soviet plan was the $10 billion demand, which meant that Germany would keep at least some industry, and Maisky was quick to drop his suggestion that the powers remove 80 per cent of German heavy industry. Snell also writes that any discussion of reparations signified a commitment to de-industrialization. But as the State Department had noted in 1944, a heavy program of current production reparations could build up the German economy inordinately. Thus, as Snell does claim, the reparations discussion was a clear-cut defeat for the Quebec agreements of September 1944 but not, as he argues, because the Soviets got no commitment. It was a defeat for Quebec because the commitment the Soviets received meant a measure of industrialization.[30]

After the conference, with this argument in mind, the State Department renewed its attempt to gain control of postwar planning.[31] Although Stettinius was away, Under Secretary Joseph Grew and James Dunn of the State Department set to work on a general policy statement based on what they felt was the intent of the Yalta Protocol; the statement could be used to clarify the ambiguities of the military directive JCS 1067. In addition, on February 21, Grew met with Leon Henderson, former head of the Office of Price Administration. Henderson, who had returned from a trip to Europe sponsored by the Foreign Economic Administration (FEA), was bitter in his condemnation of American European policy and of the lack of State Department authority. James Perkins, a member of the Henderson mission, wrote the report on the trip. He argued that the present vague American policy could not deal with the elimination and control of German war potential, the handling of a system of reparations, and the prevention of serious disease and unrest. U.S. plans would make it possible for the Germans to rebuild and escape their responsibilities for delivering reparations. Perkins recommended that the United States revise JCS 1067 to provide for "the basic objectives" of the occupation—industrial control and reparations.[32]

The view of the FEA impressed Grew and Dunn; at least it expressed enough of their own predilections to form the basis of the new set of proposals. But the real justification for creating this document lay in the fact that the Department was willing to use the Russian desire for reparations to have its policy statement approved. On March 2, commenting on Henderson's trip and the Russian demand for reparations, Stimson summarized various plans that had been discussed for the treatment of Germany. The last alternative he described as "the changed plan produced by Russian demand for reparations which necessitates, according to Henderson, complete economic control of Germany—rationing, prices, wages." [33]

On March 10 the State Department presented this new document to the President. The memorandum provided for all those things that War and Treasury had consistently vetoed. State ensured centralized control of Germany by the "paramount" authority of the proposed Control Council and the "enforcment" function of the zone commander. The unitary economy resulting was to yield "substantial reparations" from current production; Germany would discharge this obligation within ten years. The Department might have endorsed the Soviet demand in order to justify this program, but at the same time it hedged on reparations by arguing that the maintenance of a minimal standard of living had priority over them as a claim on the German economy.[34]

The State Department appears to have been secretive about the Crimea Conference, and McCloy and Morgenthau were ignorant of the Yalta decisions until at least March 10. Within the next five days, however, they learned what had transpired, and on March 15 they also found out about the new directive. Morgenthau, McCloy, and their aides concurred that this State Department document relied on the Yalta decision "that recurrent reparations were to be made." [35] Morgenthau believed that the Yalta Protocol was subject to interpretation and that it could be made congruent with JCS 1067. McCloy agreed, but even though he was willing to back the Treasury to gain autonomy for the military, the substantive similarity of view between the State and War Departments could not be hidden. McCloy wanted no part of Treasury plans for deindustrialization. Like the State Department officers, he used the Yalta reparations decision to forestall dismantling, and told Morgenthau that JCS 1067 would suffice—"At least with the slightest modification, you may have reparations here and there." [36]

Morgenthau and his staff went to work on a criticism of the March 10 directive. Although admitting that the State Department could make a case, they argued with some misgivings that the Yalta Reparations Protocol could be interpreted so that JCS 1067 could still be implemented. One of them commented that "the reparations documents which they signed at Yalta and the parts on reparations in the State Department directive look good, but everywhere else is chiseled." Morgenthau protested that the Yalta commitment was "in the form of a proposal." He wrote Stettinius that it was perhaps "being used as an excuse to argue that in order to collect reparations in the future it is necessary to assume control of the German internal economy." This was a consistent tactic on the part of the Treasury, but both of the other departments, of course, urged that the agreement required revision of some parts of JCS 1067.[37]

Although Roosevelt seems to have concluded that the victors should not dismantle German industry as Morgenthau wished, the dying President had to create harmony. McCloy, Boettiger, and William L. Clayton, assistant secretary of state for economic affairs, testified that FDR did not want to "eliminate" German manufacture; he did not hold "extremist" views on this point. The President had no objection to Germany's having substantial industry as long as the Germans "used their industries for their own internal needs." McCloy quoted Roosevelt as saying, "I want to have German industry maintained to the fullest extent necessary to maintain the Germans so that we don't have the burden of taking care of them." "I think that means a very substantial degree of preservation of the German industry," FDR continued, "but I am very leery of their exports." [38] The President had not altered his idea of a nonexporting German state whose excess capital equipment would be removed for reparations.

Roosevelt was also adamant in opposing the centralization that the State Department emphasized. Again his son-in-law Boettiger appears to have influenced the President. FDR felt he was taking a "moderate" position on centralization— mid-way between the State Department and the Treasury.[39] When the State Department attempted to convince the President of the necessity for economic controls "in light of the reparations that were determined on at Yalta," FDR was unclear. When McCloy saw him, Roosevelt hedged: "Well, maybe so. Of course, we did agree to reparations." [40]

Nothing would sway Morgenthau. He urged that "the

maintenance and rehabilitation of [the] German economy" were "a German problem"; the United States should not undertake these tasks "in order to collect reparations or for any other reason except the security of the occupying forces."[41] Unfortunately for the Department of State, its desire for economic control required the priority of Allied Control Council authority over that of the zone commander, so that, for the immediate future, the War-Treasury alliance was reestablished in opposition to central control. But in all other matters the War Department was closer to State than to Treasury. A draft directive on Germany by the War Department provided for current product reparations, opposed by the Treasury, and substituted for State's minimal living standard clause the more flexible "disease and unrest" formula.[42] If War and State could settle the zonal question, they would agree on German policy.

The upshot of the infighting was another document, approved on March 23. Like the versions of the directive for the American military (JCS 1067), the U.S. policy memorandum of March 23 was an amalgam of conflicting ideas: its program for the control of Germany was negative in intent because of Treasury influence; but State Department additions made the document subject to varying interpretations. By means of this new series of proposals the President hoped to end interdepartmental conflicts, but the unfulfilled goal of State for strong inter-Allied controls and of Treasury for deindustrialization meant that the agencies resolved their disputes in a typical Rooseveltian fashion: by putting all elements in a "tenuous balance."[43] Bickering did not end but shifted to a fight over the meaning of various clauses. Although the State Department had suffered a defeat, policy makers responsible for the discarded March 10 document were optimistic. James Dunn, who had spent much time on the first document, told Stettinius that the new directive "was only different in language and not in spirit" from the old.[44]

The importance of the short-lived memorandum of March 10 is its reflection of the reparations commitment to the Russians. The commitment was first diluted when War and Treasury persuaded the President to repudiate the document that the Crimea accord justified. The policy statement of March 23 returned intra-American matters to their ambiguous state; the first three months of 1945 had ended with no resolution of U.S. policy problems. The writing of the March 23 directive reasserted the War-Treasury threat to multilateralism; indicated the similarity of the State and War positions; and manifested Roosevelt's role as adjudicator and his own mediating position.

As Stimson wrote on March 29, "this poor subject has had a hard life for the past six or eight months owing to the President's indecision. . . . Never has anything which I have witnessed in the last four years shown such instance of the bad effects of our chaotic administration." There had been "a tumultuous and fantastic history of six months vacillation."[45]

FDR's acceptance and later repudiation of the State Department's March 10 directive displayed, as did his earlier actions, his inability to concentrate on the German problem and his desire to avoid any binding decisions. He does not seem to have understood the issues involved in the American bickering. The belief that the Allies treat Germany as a nonexporting economic unit in order to aid Britain is the one continuity running through his short memoranda. But

Roosevelt's tactic of delay was also a studied maneuver that he hoped would enable him to step in at the right moment and exercise his masterly power of improvisation. Then, with internal and external opposition off-balance, he might have executed a program that he deemed politically suitable. But this state of affairs did not come to pass, and when the President died, there was no American policy. State Department programs would quickly become predominant.

4 Contours of Soviet-American Relations, 1943–1945

The debate in Washington over Germany had an extremely abstract quality, and it is sometimes difficult to believe policy makers were aware that the armies of the great powers were slaughtering one another around the world and that the fabric of European civilization was being ripped to pieces. Nonetheless, the consequences of the five years of planning were critical for the decisions made in 1945 and 1946. To understand the connection between wartime plans and postwar decisions it is necessary to survey some broad aspects of Soviet-American diplomacy during the latter part of the war, and place some of the preceding discussion in perspective. Although, in regard to the future of Germany, decision makers in Washington were caught up in the interdepartmental quarrel, this quarrel must also be seen in the context of American thinking about the postwar position of the USSR. We are initially faced with the fact that in appraising Russian intentions, we often lack evidence on which to base an attribution of motivation. In those cases where we possess documentation, I have been impressed—as are most historians—by what we have come to call Soviet "realism." But this kind of analysis is not on its face consistent with the belief of many in the Russian leadership's

93

fanatic devotion to Communism and world revolution. I
also believe that any understanding of Soviet diplomacy
must consider its ideological underpinnings; but I am as un-
happy with juxtaposing realism and fanaticism in Soviet
diplomacy as I am with juxtaposing politico-economic interest and morality in American diplomacy. Nonetheless, I
am at a loss in offering an alternative in the former case,
and my tentative discussions hopefully allow more adven-
turous students to reach whatever more complete explanations may be available. I have been content simply to note
that however we are to grasp the motivation of the Russians
in these instances, they always seem to have judged the
limitations of their power correctly and suited what they
said to these judgments.

In those other situations where we have little documentation about Soviet policy making, the problem is more acute.
Some historians have accepted the evaluations of Soviet intentions that Western diplomats put forward. I cannot see
that this is very helpful. George Kennan's appraisals of Russian motives made during his 1945–1946 service in Russia
still carry weight as *historical* appraisals.[1] Accepting his authority, many historians have maintained that the Soviets
consistently attempted to transform the world in their own
image. Because the Russian archives remain closed, this
kind of assessment must be made with great circumspection.
I think we also have *prima facie* reason to treat it with suspicion because of its source: I wonder how much credence
historians would give to evaluations of American intentions
if delivered by a leading Soviet diplomat. The great wealth
of evidence available concerns U.S. intentions; and oddly
enough—as has been argued—Washington's view *was* one
dedicated to reshaping the world in an American image.

There is no satisfactory solution for extrapolating the aims of the USSR from negligible sources; but in one case I have found it necessary to make an important judgment about the Soviet Union. What did it want—at the end of the war—in regard to eastern and central Europe? I have answered this question by accepting, for the sake of argument, the views of Arthur M. Schlesinger, Jr. Writing in the semiofficial *Foreign Affairs* in 1967, Schlesinger urged that

it is not unreasonable to suppose that Stalin would have been satisfied at the end of the war to secure what Kennan has called "a protective glacis along Russia's western border," and that, in exchange for a free hand in Eastern Europe, he was prepared to give the British and Americans equally free hands in their zones of vital interest, including nations as close to Russia as Greece (for the British) and, very probably—or at least so the Jugoslavs believe—China (for the United States). In other words, his initial objectives were very probably not world conquest but Russian security.

Schlesinger added that the Russians may have considered it legitimate to stir up trouble in a "Western zone," but were willing to have the United States and Great Britain take anti-Communist action there. In turn, they expected a free hand in eastern Europe.[2] Briefly, Schlesinger's analysis maintains that the Cold War originated in the clash of this "sphere of influence" approach with what he calls American "universalism"—roughly the political aspect of multilateralism. Unfortunately, he does not explore the social context in which his "universalism" exists; and does not appear to realize that for many who did not share its premises, it was a plan for worldwide U.S. supremacy.

Although we may debate the merits of Schlesinger's con-

ception of universalism, much of the evidence we have sup-
ports something like his understanding of Russian goals. In
all likelihood, the aims of the Russians were more complex,
governed by their appraisals of the varying political, economic, and strategic importance of each individual eastern
European country, and their calculation of Soviet strength
in each. But Schlesinger's stance is a useful one to adopt: it
makes the most plausible case for a vigorous and expansionist Russian diplomacy in the immediate postwar period.[3]
Whatever these complexities, we must investigate some of
the evidence we have for determining Soviet intentions and
place it in the context of developing American strategies
for the peace.

During the latter part of 1943 and throughout 1944, Washington based its evaluations of the USSR largely on the reports of Averell Harriman, ambassador to the Soviet Union.
As Admiral William Standley recalled, Harriman's role was
more than that of a "mere ambassador." Standley, his predecessor in Moscow, pointed out that Harriman had a
"unique assignment" and that there was "nothing during the
war quite like it." "He was the overall coordinator of both
civilian and military matters in Moscow. The military representatives, General Deane, and the civilian agencies, such as
the Office of War Information, the War Production Board,
the Lend-Lease Administration, the War Shipping Administration, and even the Office of Strategic Services reported
to Harriman."[4] Sometime presidential representative Joseph
E. Davies agreed in this assessment. Davies urged on Harriman "that he was one of the key men whom history would
ultimately hold responsible. . . ."[5] George Kennan has reflected in his *Memoirs* that Harriman pursued "Rooseveltian"

foreign policy—for Kennan a version of Schlesinger's universalism—"with a dedication, a persistence, and an unflagging energy and attention that has [sic] no parallel in my experience." [6]

By 1945, U.S. policy makers could judge events for themselves and did not need to rely on theories about what the Soviets might do, but Harriman remained one of the foremost diplomatic authorities on the USSR, constantly sought out for his opinions. We shall see that in a measure his views were reflected in the development of U.S. thinking about the Russians; in turn, this thinking will illuminate the crystallization of American strategy after Roosevelt's death.

During his service in Moscow, Harriman had, of course, many concerns, but one of the most important was his attention to postwar Soviet-American economic arrangements. In the formation of his complex perspective four factors evolved simultaneously. The first was an understanding of the link between American economic assistance and the alliance with the Soviets both during and after the war. Second was his idea of the effect reparations to the USSR from defeated nations would have on this economic assistance. Third was a determination of the importance of trade between the two countries to their respective domestic economies and an evaluation of the part that a loan to the Russians would play in encouraging the trade. The last was an opinion on the role the U.S. government should play in making any economic plans.

Harriman's first concern was evident from the beginning of the war: U.S. economic strength in the form of Lend-Lease to its allies was critical to the battle against Germany. The aid to Russia was designed to fulfill a twin purpose: it would keep the USSR in the war and, in so doing, enable the United States to husband its resources. As General John Deane, Harriman's military attaché, stated, "We should be honest with ourselves and admit that our most compelling motive in sending supplies to Russia was to save our own skins." [7] Since the *quid pro quo* for Lend-Lease was Russian lives, during the early part of the war the Americans rarely if ever attempted to combat displays of Russian intransigence by withholding Lend-Lease. The fear that the Soviet would make a separate peace precluded this kind of action. As Admiral Standley, the ambassador in Moscow in 1942 and 1943, recalled, "we had a pretty good 'or else' in those days, although I had very little success in persuading our government to use it." [8] Harriman recounted later that the "primary objective" at the time was to keep the USSR in the war as an effective fighting force.[9] Even in March 1944, General Marshall pointed out to FDR that "if Russia were deprived of it [Lend-Lease], Germany could probably still defeat the U.S.S.R." "Lend-Lease," Marshall argued, "is our trump card in dealing with [the] U.S.S.R., and its control is possibly the most effective means we have to keep the Soviets on the offensive in connection with the second front." [10]

After Harriman took over in Moscow and it became apparent that the Allies would win the war, talks began concerning the status of Lend-Lease at the war's end. Would Lend-Lease cover goods having a definite postwar value but shipped near the end of the war? What would happen to Lend-Lease material "in the pipe line" at the war's end? Would some sort of Lend-Lease be forthcoming after the war to enable Russia to reconstruct? As planning concerning the Soviet Union developed, American diplomats agreed that the United States would phase out Lend-Lease in some way; policy makers would consider a loan to aid in reconstruction. This loan would require that the American Export-Import Bank expand its facilities and that Congress repeal the Johnson Act, which forbade loans to countries defaulting on World War I financial commitments.

Any loan would contain provisions that the Soviets purchase reconstruction equipment in the United States and pay off the credit in Russian goods, primarily raw materials. But the Americans questioned whether the Russian economy could supply enough in trade to meet repayment demands. In late 1943, Elbridge Durbrow, the State Department's economic expert on eastern Europe, raised this problem. He said it was in the American political and economic interest to assist the USSR in rehabilitation. But careful studies made by an interdepartmental committee showed that it would be "most difficult" to increase Russo-American trade to give the Soviet the purchasing power to pay off this credit.[11] In April 1944 members of the State Department Division of Commercial Policy and Agreements were discussing how they could curb the "extravagant and unrealistic" claims about postwar trade between the two countries.[12] The Division of Trade Agreements did estimate that gold exports might add several hundred million dollars a year to USSR purchasing power although a credit might impose a burden on the Soviet balance of payments when it was paid off. Joint effort might increase Soviet exports to the United States, but, another official calculated, they would be inadequate for the servicing and liquidation of the credits and loans that the USSR would need and want to obtain. Harriman was still optimistic after studying reports of this sort: if the United States adopted import policies enabling it to take advantage of the situation, substantial trade could occur.[13]

The second factor of import to him was the relation of

trade problems to reparations. After the Moscow Conference in November 1943, he cabled Roosevelt that if America
had difficulties with Russia over Germany, they would arise
from an economic problem: Moscow's attitude was tougher
than that of Washington, "particularly in regard to the magnitude of reparations." Later he based his optimism about
increased trade on the fact that the Russians' need for U.S.
equipment would be enormous *despite* their "receiving substantial imports from Germany in reparations." [14] When Eric
Johnston, president of the American Chamber of Commerce,
came to Russia in June 1944 to discuss future trade between
the two countries, Harriman made the point again to Hull.
Johnston recognized that the extent of German reparations
to the USSR might be a factor "in determining the amount
and character of capital goods which would be desired from
the United States." [15]

In August 1944, Ambassador John Winant in England
linked the questions of trade and reparations. He urged the
United States to consider ways of aiding the postwar Soviet
economy and of tying this aid to "a satisfactory settlement
of the problem of German reparations and of the most important political issues." The Soviets would be "particularly
eager" to get reparations. But because the major part of the
industry they wanted would be in western-controlled zones,
Winant favored a joint plan to avoid an undue burden for
the United States.[16] A month later, during the early development of the Morgenthau plan, Roosevelt made the same
connection. Misinterpreting Russian intentions, FDR believed the Soviets would unhesitatingly favor the pastoralization of Germany. The President wrote Hull that they
would do "more or less what they wish" in their zone. The
Americans could not afford to get into a position of re-

cording protests against Russian dismantling unless there were some chance that the USSR would heed them. Then the President curiously concluded that he did "not intend by this to break off or delay negotiations with the Soviet government over Lend-Lease. . . . This, however, does not immediately concern the German industrial future." [17]

These complications did not change the U.S. position: Harriman and other American policy makers were inclined to press for increased trade with Russia. His third concern was the connection of this trade to American domestic prosperity. The United States had emerged from the Depression only with the war, and all diplomats feared that peace would bring a return to this abysmal condition. In his initial talks with the Soviets, Harriman had been frank in indicating the connection he saw between increased foreign commerce and domestic prosperity. In November 1943, he had told Anastas Mikoyan, Russian Commissar for Foreign Trade, that "aside from the sympathy of the American people it would be in the self-interest of the United States to be able to afford full employment during the period of transition from war-time to peace-time economy." During the early part of 1944, Harriman conveyed these thoughts to Hull. He telegraphed the Secretary that reconstruction aid to the Soviet would "be of enormous value in cushioning the shock from war to peace"; the United States must be ready to put Russian orders into production after the cessation of hostilities. The Soviet orders would be of value in relieving dislocations.[18] As talks progressed, the USSR began to press the Americans for concessions on the terms of postwar assistance. The Russian policy makers gained the impression that "U.S. industry was in large measure idle in types of equipment the U.S.S.R. wants. . . ." The Soviets indicated that the American government was "most desirous of giving business to American firms to help tide them over from a wartime to a peacetime basis." [19]

With all of these matters at issue, Harriman's fourth conviction became most significant: he believed that Washington should play a role in credit negotiations. When Donald Nelson, chairman of the War Production Board, visited Stalin shortly after Harriman was appointed, Nelson argued that a group of American businessmen should finance postwar Russian loans. Although Stalin agreed, Harriman urged that the American government carry out discussions. Next to the war, the Soviets considered reconstruction to be "the most important political as well as economic problem that confronts them." Consequently, "our participation in reconstruction is an important and integral part of our diplomatic dealings with them and it is therefore to my judgment essential that the negotiations be handled under the direction of those dealing with our overall relations with the Soviet Union." Hull took up this idea also, reiterating that reconstruction assistance should "form an integral part of our over-all relations." [20]

Throughout 1944 these four elements of Harriman's thought often came together in articulate statements of policy that other policy makers would eventually pick up. Increased Russo-American trade would benefit the American domestic economy. But because the USSR valued American cooperation in this field, Harriman argued that there should be governmental control of postwar aid; it should not be treated "in its purely commercial and economic aspects" but "in the fabric of our overall relations." As a start in this direction he suggested that an initial loan

go to purchase U.S. goods and that the United States retain
control of the unallocated balance. The credit should not be
used for purposes "incompatible with United States interests" or extended unless "our relations are developing satis-
factorily in other directions." [21]

The State Department had begun to reflect on Harriman's
perspective during the early part of 1944. Durbrow, soon
to become chief of the State Department's Eastern European Affairs Division, submitted a lengthy memorandum on
Soviet policy. He stated that some Soviet leaders wanted to
establish in eastern Europe or at least in the Balkans "more
or less complete Soviet hegemony." This strategy to establish "their own *cordon sanitaire*" was based on their need for
security. The Russians' fear of the weakness of their country
after the war was the best "lever" that the United States had
to convince them to go along with American policies "if they
want our aid and cooperation." The United States should
make it clear that it would be "impossible for us to give our
wholehearted full cooperation and aid to them if they insist
on taking unilateral actions which are not in conformity
with . . . [our] basic principles." [22]

After Harriman had digested Durbrow's memorandum,
he cabled Hull his fullest outline to that date (March 1944)
of a coherent policy toward the Soviet Union. Harriman was
impressed that economic assistance was "one of the most
effective weapons at our disposal to influence European
political events in the direction we desire." Using this
weapon, the United States could "avoid the development of
a sphere of influence of the Soviet Union over Eastern Europe and the Balkans." Washington should grant economic
assistance "in accordance with our basic policy"; Washington should withhold it "if individual countries do not con-

form to our standards." In dealing with the Russians, economic assistance was "one of our principal practical levers for influencing political action compatible with our principles." Harriman then concluded that the United States subordinate to larger political interests those domestic needs that increased Soviet trade might satisfy.[23]

By the fall of 1944 the issues became more practical than theoretical as the Red Army moved into Rumania and Hungary; in control in these countries, the Soviet Union displayed every intention of exercising a large degree of economic and political influence. The consequence might easily be the antithesis of what was to happen under multilateralism, a Soviet bloc that would have discriminatory commercial arrangements and would practice antidemocratic politics. Indeed, Harriman and those who shared his views became most concerned with their view of an expanding Russian police state that made systematic use of terror to achieve political ends. The war had suppressed over twenty years of American hostility to the Soviet political system; in 1944 and 1945, Russian policies quickly stirred up the deep U.S. suspicion and fear that the forced alliance had muted. The British, in a much weaker position than the United States, came to terms with Soviet power in the famous Stalin-Churchill "spheres of influence" pact of October 1944. British Foreign Secretary Anthony Eden made the "flat statement" that the British were obliged to make concessions to the USSR to get concessions for themselves in areas in which they were interested.[24]

Soviet-American relations were never put on such a footing. To be sure, the Soviets were signatory to wartime documents that expressed the grand political aspects of multilateralism, but there is little evidence that they took seriously these documents concerning "freely elected," "democratic" governments. In fact, they signed them with reservations.[25] As Harriman recalled later, Stalin would not allow free elections when he knew that governments hostile to the Soviet would result.[26] In operative terms Moscow acted on the practical premise that Britain and the United States established in the Italian surrender of 1943. The Western powers precluded Soviet influence there, and using this example, the Russians followed the same program in the countries they occupied.[27]

On their side, the Americans adhered to a Rooseveltian strategy of delay and did not commit themselves to the acceptance of Russian policies, as the British had. Harriman did cable Hull of Moscow's attitude shortly before the Churchill-Stalin agreement: "Molotov has on a number of occasions indicated to me that he considered that after they had put us on notice of a Soviet policy or plan and we did not at that time object, we had acquiesced in and accepted the Soviet position." [28] Harriman also recalled to Hull the position the Soviets took at the Moscow Conference: while the USSR promised to keep Britain and the United States informed on affairs with its immediate neighbors, it would make no further commitments.[29]

In September 1944, Harriman outlined in a cable to Hull what he thought the American attitude should be to Soviet policies in eastern Europe. Hull had wired Harriman that recent Russian decisions raised serious doubts about USSR plans. He sought Harriman's advice on "how to meet this change in Russian attitude" and wanted his "estimate of the present trend of Soviet policy." The Secretary closed by saying that "I need not tell you that questions of the highest import to the future peace of the world are involved and that I look forward to your reply with the greatest interest."

Harriman replied by saying that he felt "that the only way we can eventually come to an understanding with the Soviet Union on the question of non-interference in the internal affairs of other countries is for us to take a definite interest in the solution of the problems of each individual country as they arise." "If we give them a free hand with any one country the precedent will be established," the Ambassador continued, "whereas if through our influence we can temper Soviet domination in each situation, I believe we have a chance to lead them to a behavior in international affairs that is compatible to our concepts." He was not recommending interference in the affairs of other countries but "quite the reverse, insisting that the Soviets do not unduly interfere in exercising their responsibilities as the occupying power."

Harriman ended his cable with an evaluation of the Russian nation. The Soviets, he concluded, "have little understanding of the real concept of Western civilization." "They are always conscious of the fact that they are a backward country materially and culturally" but take great pride in their military strength. The United States "should be understanding of their sensitivity" and yet "oppose them promptly with the greatest of firmness where we see them going wrong." In these cases, Harriman said, "there can be no compromise or indecision if we are to build a sound foundation for future relations with this strange country." In matters of importance "we should make it plain that their failure to conform to our concepts will affect our willingness to cooperate with them." On those occasions they should be made to feel "specific results from our displeasure." "On matters that are vital to us . . . ," he wrote, "I believe we should make them understand patiently but firmly that we cannot accept their point of view." [30] As the Ambassador had aptly put it earlier, the problem was to get the Russians to "play the international game with us in accordance with our standards." [31]

A month later he followed this long appraisal with an analysis of Russian aims supportive of Schlesinger's viewpoint. Hull asked the Ambassador for information on "ulterior economic motives" of the Soviets. Harriman doubted that ulterior economic motives would explain Russian policy. Destruction in the Soviet Union was severe, he commented, and the Soviets were determined to get everything they could out of Germany and its satellites to make good at least part of their losses. The Russians eventually wanted "to see economic stability in central Europe" and would not deliberately "pursue a policy of economic disruption in these countries." For the moment, however, their "main preoccupations" were "military and political rather than economic." They were aware that if economic distress resulted from the policies they pursued, this would not be to their disadvantage: "it would result in a reduction of the industrial and military potential of the countries in question" and "would reduce the standard of living to something nearer the Russian level." Finally, Moscow's overall policy "would undermine the economic position and thereby the influence of the wealthier and more conservative classes," and "contribute to the establishment in power of groups entirely friendly to the Soviet Union." [32]

From the end of 1944 through 1945, Harriman's conception of Soviet policy changed with the shifting Russian re-

sponses to the events that occurred in the period, and he
was sometimes confident that the Soviets would willingly
cooperate. But however he and other diplomats conceived
the precise nature of the Soviet purpose, they were determined that the USSR should not accomplish its aims at the
expense of multilateralism. The states of eastern Europe as
well as Germany were to be reoriented to a global political
economy; and if the Soviet purpose was to establish a
sphere of influence with totalitarian political rule, Harriman
believed the United States could prevent this development.
He also believed that there would be a satisfactory basis
for postwar relations between the two countries only if the
Soviet could be persuaded to go along with American proposals.[33] The question for Harriman became *how* to achieve
American goals. What means were the Americans to use to
make the Russians come to terms? Harriman was not im-
mune to strategic considerations. In October 1944 he argued
that the "basic weapon" of the United States should *not* be
the threat to withhold economic assistance but to refrain
from cooperation in the maintenance of a general security
system.[34] Nonetheless, this line of reasoning does not, to my
knowledge, appear at any other time, and from the fall of
1944 through mid-1945, Harriman repeatedly specified
economic measures which might achieve multilateralism.[35]

He had wired Harry Hopkins in September that the United
States must change its conciliatory attitude in the face of
Russian intransigencies. In order to get the Soviets "to play
a decent role in international affairs" it would be necessary
to take "a firm but friendly *quid pro quo* attitude." [36] At the
end of 1944 he wanted Stettinius, the new secretary, to raise
the issue of Lend-Lease in order to get concessions: the
Americans might explain that lack of cooperation on eastern

Europe reparations issues then at stake had to affect the final Lend-Lease settlement "adversely to the Soviet interest." [37]

Although the Secretary would not use Lend-Lease as a lever at this time,[38] Washington did not compromise Harriman's long-range objectives. By 1945 many U.S. decision makers based their perception of events on their understanding of a Soviet bid for eastern Europe. Of course, they saw this effort as the expansion of an evil politico-economic bloc, a belligerent threat to multilateralism that only an aggressor could contemplate. And as time passed, diplomats accepted Harriman's ideas, or came to similar conclusions on their own.

In the first months of the new year, talks with the Russians over the phasing out of Lend-Lease and over postwar assistance became stalled. The Soviets were to repay Lend-Lease items they would use after the defeat of Germany by long-term credits. In reality these items would be the first the USSR would acquire by reconstruction aid, and negotiators did not reach accord about them. Working on the supposition that the Americans would subordinate political aspects of the loans to the need for peacetime trade, the Russians overreached themselves: they demanded better terms than the United States was willing to give. When a Lend-Lease agreement was signed in April 1945, the matter of reconstruction goods was left hanging.[39]

While these negotiations were proceeding inconclusively, the Russians asked for a $6 billion reconstruction credit. The Soviets made their request slightly before the Treasury proposed its $10 billion loan to the USSR in January 1945, and the State Department reacted negatively to both plans. A Treasury official participating in the discussions told Morgenthau that the State Department wanted "important political quid pro quo" before the United States would make the loan. The issues the State Department wanted settled were the Kerenski debt, American claims during the Czarist period, and Soviet political dealings with Bulgaria, Poland, Rumania, and the Baltic states. Harriman commented on the Russian proposition that the Soviets "should be given to understand" that "our willingness to cooperate wholeheartedly with them" would "depend upon their behavior in international matters." [40]

Harriman and Clayton concurred that credit was "the only concrete bargaining lever" that the United States could use in settling political and economic problems with the Russians. Clayton was suspicious of the Soviets' ability to increase their trade to the extent needed to repay the larger Treasury credit. There was also concern that financing might require congressional approval and the repeal of the Johnson act.[41]

With all of these factors in mind, policy makers decided three weeks before the Yalta Conference to give no thought to the Soviet request for $6 billion until the two nations completed Lend-Lease arrangements. Roosevelt said that the Americans would hold back "until we get what we want." [42] Toward the end of January, the FEA also advised the President that economic strength was still the top bargaining power of the United States at international conferences. The Americans, the FEA said, could not surrender it.[43] The status of the Soviet loan may be inferred from Grew's remarks to James Reston of the New York Times, who attempted to gain information on the Russian proposal. Reston said his main purpose was "to understand the whole picture"; Grew replied that if Reston "understood the nature of a picture I would be justified in saying that there was no picture." [44]

The effective State Department veto of the Treasury loan was a crucial victory for multilateralism. Morgenthau wanted to make the loan to obtain an economic concession for the Treasury plan—Russian agreement on dismantling. As he put it, the Russians were intelligent and reasonable men. There was "a good chance of their going on with us [on no current production reparations], providing we offer something in lieu thereof." [45] But this credit would have deprived the United States of leverage in gaining political concessions on multilateral ends from the USSR. Accordingly, the loan decision was a triumph for Harriman's strategy. As he urged, the Americans had to adopt "a more positive policy of using our economic influence to further our broad political ideals." [46]

At this point the issue central to this narrative entered discussion. In January, Grew and Clayton argued that the rate of Soviet reconstruction was tied both to the aid it could expect from the United States *and* to reparations deliveries from Germany.* Presidential Assistant Lauchlin Currie took a different line in a statement prepared for Yalta. "The needs of Russia," Currie wrote Roosevelt, "are so

---

*FR, Yalta (1955), p. 322. This memo noted that $2 billion in credits would only speed up Soviet reconstruction three to four months and that therefore Washington's attempts to coerce the Russians with a credit might have little effect. It is important since this seems to be one of the few times that the Americans recognized the limitations of their power. Harriman, of course, disagreed (FR, 1945, V [1967], 995), and Clayton apparently changed his mind (p. 845). Truman was later to agree with Harriman (Truman, *Memoirs,* I [Garden City, 1955], 71).

enormous that reparations need not interfere with large reconstruction credits from the U.S." [47]

Currie's view had little influence in the Crimea. At the
first foreign ministers' meeting Molotov told Stettinius that
the USSR "expected to receive reparations from Germany in
kind and hoped that the United States would furnish the
Soviet Union with long term credits." [48] For the Russians,
reparations were bound up with the reconstruction of the
USSR. But Molotov's specific conjunction of the questions at
Yalta got no results. Stettinius replied that the Americans
would discuss the problem at any time, but nothing more
was said during the negotiations. [49]

As we have noted, from the Crimea meeting to FDR's
death, discussion of the problem of Germany in Washington
still centered around the interdepartmental dispute. Nonetheless, Harriman in Moscow continued to advance proposals for general American strategy on eastern Europe and
aid to the Russians (including reparations). His views did
not yet reflect American policy, but their impact was grow-
ing. The belief that the Soviets would willingly adopt U.S.
policy was changing to one that they would and could be
persuaded to do so.

As one reprisal against a minor Soviet intransigency, Harriman suggested in mid-March that "we cut off some of
their Lend-Lease products that conduce directly to the
war like sugar and industrial tools." Two weeks later he and
General Deane advocated that the United States ship
Lend-Lease by slow route because the Russians had again
been uncooperative. [50] On the same day, April 3, Stettinius
recorded the content of Harriman's most recent cable in his
departmental diary: "we should tie closely our economic
assistance in Europe to our political problem with the Sovi-

ets." With Britain, Harriman continued, the United States should reestablish the European economy and counteract the Soviet program. In the next few days Harriman responded twice to State Department requests for policy guidance and stressed that Washington use its economic policy "to assist countries naturally friendly to us." In view of the Soviet reluctance to implement Crimea decisions, the United States should be slow in making commitments on reparations, a "subject in which the Soviet Government has shown much interest." Harriman "regretfully" concluded that the United States should be guided "by the policy of taking care of our Western Allies and other areas under our responsibility first, allocating to Russia what may be left." On April 11, he disputed Stettinius' remark that the Soviets might not need American aid; on the contrary, Harriman declared, they needed it very much.[51]

When Roosevelt died, there were two strains of American diplomatic behavior that are significant for interpreting future U.S. policy for Germany. On the one hand, the interdepartmental dispute left the United States without any agreed policy on Germany: the U.S. program was a mixture of conflicting ideas. On the other hand, State Department decision makers such as Harriman, Clayton, and Grew were developing with increasing clarity an overall position that the United States should take toward the Russians: the Americans ought to use economic sanctions (like the withholding of reparations) to make the Soviet Union comply with American politico-economic aims. In the four months after FDR's death, German policy would be defined in conformity with the State Department's general position, and this position would emerge as American policy.

5 American Consensus, April–July 1945

The development of American diplomacy in the late spring and early summer of 1945 is enormously complex. Without abandoning a chronological presentation entirely, I have found it easier to present four important series of events separately, the first two dealing with the victory of State Department views on Germany; the last two with the coordination of these views with an overall scheme of conduct. First, without FDR's backing, Morgenthau's plans lost out to those of the State Department. Second, events occurring in Germany minimized the administrative dispute between the army and the State Department. Third, the Americans decided to adopt the comprehensive policy that I outlined in the last chapter and made their plans for Germany consistent with it: economic coercion would resolve the international political and economic problems the USSR presented to the United States. For the first time—without having to contend with the obstacles that Rooseveltian ambivalence created—the Americans were able to translate their multilateral theory into a concrete practical policy. It placed reparations, Lend-Lease, and financial aid to the Russians in one framework. The views of the State Department had had an involuted history throughout the twelve years of Hull's tenure. Six months after his retirement, in a most crucial period, they were in the ascendancy. Finally, and most importantly for this monograph, the end to inter-departmental quarreling and agreement on general policy made definition of the reparations issue possible and enabled the United States to put forward a coherent position in the negotiations that the powers conducted in June and July.

Under the aegis of the State Department, the Informal Policy Committee on Germany was formed in mid-March as an interdepartmental clearing house for occupation directives. On the basis of the March 23 policy statement, the committee worked out further revisions of the military directive JCS 1067. On May 11, the new president, Harry Truman, approved them. Like the March 23 document, this version of JCS 1067 incorporated some Treasury proposals. Nevertheless, the State and War Departments watered down its harsher aspects or made them ambiguous. That the Treasury was able to exert influence was due more to the position it had developed over the preceding months than to the popularity of its policies. Even before Roosevelt's death, the Treasury had reported that the "State Department supported in most instances by F.E.A. [Foreign Economic Administration] and War, is bent upon establishing widespread controls of large sectors of the German economy." [1]

Although the latest military directive remained in force for over two years, diplomats making policy almost immediately interpreted its clauses to bring the document into line with State Department priorities. McCloy recalled that in Germany General Lucius Clay did "precisely what the War Department expected him to do" in solving occupation problems: he whittled away "the unworkable clauses of JCS 1067 empirically and piecemeal." *

On June 8, Grew wrote Stimson that there was "no longer disagreement" about the need to ensure the economic controls in Germany necessary to achieve the occupation's aims. These aims included the rehabilitation and the maintenance of a minimal German economy, the financing of occupation costs, and reparations.[2] A State Department memorandum later forwarded to the July Big Three meeting at Potsdam also declared the shift in policy: "Whatever forms of language had been used," the American goal was not deindustrialization. Despite "certain public statements" that Washington had accepted this policy, the memorandum continued, the Americans had adopted another alternative. This alternative read:

If we are not prepared to destroy the German nation, and if we are not prepared to occupy or police Germany *permanently,* we have no choice but to attempt to change the German character . . . we are occupying Germany for the purpose of changing the inward character of the German nation and the German people to such an extent that Germany can be trusted at some future time with independent existence as a nation in a world in which weapons will be more destructive and more difficult to control than they are today.

In exaggerated form this statement reflected the American view that economic means could be placed in the forefront in achieving noneconomic ends. In some unspecified way foreign economic policies would result in the re-creation of

---

* Quoted in Walter Dorn, "The Debate over American Occupation Policy in Germany in 1944–1945," *Political Science Quarterly,* 72 (1957), 501. For an analysis of military policy in Germany see Chapter 8.

the enemy psyche and produce a wholesome democratic psychology compatible with that of the Americans.[3]

The symbolic triumph of this vision as policy occurred on July 5. Sometime before this date President Truman had told Stimson that he (Truman) had opposed the Morgenthau plan even before he became vice president. As President, Truman said, he felt even more strongly. On July 5, when Morgenthau inquired about his uncertain status in the new cabinet, Truman did not reassure him. Morgenthau offered to resign, and Truman accepted.[4] Admiral William Leahy, chief of staff to both Roosevelt and Truman, thought the new president's action "very significant." Truman said emphatically that "the Treasury proposals for the treatment of Germany are out."[5] Indeed, Leahy had predicted this nearly nine months before: he had told Morgenthau in November, "You will never get your program through on Germany."[6]

The President and the Treasury no longer threatened the hegemony of the State Department, but there was still tension between War and State. During the late spring of 1945, however, the dispute concerning the authority of the zonal commander had receded into the background. Faced with the actual devastation in Europe, State did not press for immediate commitments on long range issues. In agreement with War's practical economic policies, State was more amenable to McCloy's insistence that current policy directives should be "interim."[7]

At this point the War and State Departments pursued joint policies that revealed an emerging consensus. By June the State Department was attempting to rehabilitate western European economies; it also desired a German contribution to their recovery. Europe was particularly desperate for coal, and Truman and Churchill jointly ordered the occupa- tion authorities to maximize German production for export. This policy would have two important effects. In the first place, it would subordinate the revival of the internal Ger- man economy to that of the rest of Europe. The State De- partment reparation program always contemplated the pri- ority of European over German reconstruction, and coal pol- icy served the same goal. The export of German coal would take precedence over "the use of coal for industrial produc- tion and civilian purposes within Germany." This might "cause unemployment, unrest and dissatisfaction among Germans of a magnitude which may necessitate firm and rigorous action." In the immediate future the occupation would punish the Germans. The newly appointed secretary of state, James Byrnes, wrote that *"during the period of critical coal shortage* [this program] will delay the resump- tion of industrial activity in Germany." In the short run the Reich would suffer. But as military officials increased coal production, they would put mines back into action, import coal mining machinery, restore transportation facilities, and reinvigorate other aspects of the German economy con- nected with the coal industry.[8] As the British historian of this aspect of Allied strategy remarks, "That the official Al- lied policy at this time was still to undertake no economic rehabilitation of Germany scarcely touched this situation." [9] In the long run Germany would be assured of industrial strength.

One consequence of the Truman-Churchill directive caused War-State trouble. At the beginning of the occupa- tion, the money for a program of western European re- habilitation would come from the United States. Assistant Secretary Clayton believed that American financing should go beyond meeting the needs of occupying forces, displaced persons, and German civilians; the Americans, Clayton felt, should pay for "all imports which serve the purposes of the United States government in Germany," i.e., should pay for European rehabilitation. The State Department claimed that it was the War Department's obligation to finance these imports. Although War agreed with State's programs toward Germany and shared its desire to rehabilitate Europe, the military did not want responsibility for the financing of imports without instructions from the President. Because the War Department refused to commit itself without higher direction, the dispute dragged on until the end of July. At that time the President issued the needed authorization in response to a proposal from both Byrnes of State and Mc-Cloy of War.[10]

In other areas the War Department supported multilateral goals. When the various departments were completing the May 11 revision of JCS 1067, the War Department urged that the American zone commander be given discretion to waive the prohibition of the manufacture of synthetic rubber and oil, magnesium, and aluminum. If the Americans were to avoid import burdens, discretion of this sort was an imperative. In fact, the military argued that the United States should allow Germany to maintain these facilities until the Allies worked out the minimal requirements for the economies of Germany and the liberated areas. Because this program ensured the integrity of the German industrial plant, it was congruent with State Department policy, and Stimson sanctioned it in May over Morgenthau's protest.[11] When policy makers discussed the matter with Truman, the President said "in this respect he entirely disagreed with Mr. Morgenthau." [12]

Of greater importance was the outlook of Stimson him-

self. This respected elder statesman had always been against
a "harsh" German policy. After Roosevelt died, the Secretary of War quickly informed the new President of his
views. Stimson would resist, he told Truman in May, any
plan that would deprive Germany of the chance for a contented, nonmilitaristic civilization; any program Stimson
could support would entail some German industrialization.
At the beginning of July the Secretary advised Truman that
it was necessary to exclude all idea of punishment from
American programs and to implement constructive measures
for German rehabilitation. In his diary the next day Stimson also wrote that the views of new Secretary of State
Byrnes "entirely clicked" with those of the War Department.[13] Stimson's conception of the postwar international
system was most significant. The Secretary was inclined to
agree with Hull that economics was central. Stimson believed that "America must so organize her trade and her
foreign finance that the world might achieve the economic
stability which had never been approached after 1918. In
long-range terms, this meant a constant effort to expand
American foreign trade, and especially American imports,
by the kind of policy so valiantly begun by Mr. Hull twelve
years before." [14]

A final clarification of overall American strategy had occurred simultaneously with the decline of Treasury power
and with the State-War agreements. After Roosevelt's death
Harriman had been flown back to Washington to participate in a series of high level meetings. On April 20, he
urged ranking State Department officials that there was a
"basic and irreconcilable difference of objective" between
the USSR and the United States. The difference lay in the

Russian "urge for its own security to see Soviet concepts extend to as large an area of the world as possible." [15] The Ambassador now seconded Clayton and Grew that Washington had great economic leverage in dealing with the USSR; at first the United States ought to take stands on minor points "to avoid giving the Russians the idea we had made a major change in policy"; similarly, negotiations on a loan should begin promptly, although it would be satisfactory to let them drag along. [16]

At the same time Harriman told Truman and a top group of advisers that a "barbarian invasion of Europe" faced the United States. The Americans had to stand firm because the USSR, in need of reconstruction assistance, had no wish to break with the United States. [17] On April 23, the Americans held another top policy meeting, and officially decided to take a "firm" general approach with the Russians. Long in favor of this policy himself, Admiral Leahy reported that the consensus was that "the time has arrived to take a strong American attitude toward the Soviet." Truman's feelings, he went on, were "particularly pleasing to me."

A few hours later the American policy received its most forceful and explicit expression. In an interview with Molotov, Truman bluntly warned the Russian that U.S. economic assistance would depend on a positive American appraisal of Soviet policy in eastern Europe. *

"All men who have dealt with Russia," Harriman had concluded, "know of the Russian attempt to chisel, by bluff,

* William Leahy Diary, Library of Congress, 23 April 1945; Gar Alperovitz, *Atomic Diplomacy* (New York, 1965), pp. 19–40. Stimson still urged caution, but by the end of the summer, he too had come around. In order to live in amity with other freer nations, he came to believe, the Russian system would have to change (Elting Morison, *Turmoil and Tradition* [New York, 1964], p. 529).

pressure, and other unscrupulous methods, to get what they wish." "While we cannot go to war with Russia, we must do everything we can to maintain our position as strongly as possible in Eastern Europe." The Soviet was building a "tier of friendly states there" and the American task was "to make it difficult for her to do so, since to build one tier of states implies the possibility of further tiers, layer on layer." "Our whole position . . . the one advantage we had was to stand firm on our position in Eastern Europe." [18]

Immediately after the German surrender in May, Truman cut off Lend-Lease, and ordered ships at sea carrying materiel to turn back. Three days later the President modified the order to enable the ships to continue and to permit the United States to complete hastily stopped loadings. There is debate over the purpose of American policy about this issue.[19] But in the context of decision making at the time, it is clear that the Americans viewed Lend-Lease as an economic weapon. On May 11, the day Truman signed the order, the State Department's Staff Committee discussed the matter. Clayton said, "It was the view of all concerned that the lend-lease program for the USSR should be so flexible that it could be cut off at any time." Lend-Lease, Clayton himself maintained, "could be stopped whenever the Department should decide that that action was necessary." Although he underestimated the number of weapons the Americans had, Acting Secretary Grew was more blunt: "Lend-lease assistance," he argued, "is this Government's only leverage against the Soviet Union." [20] By early June the State Department's thought was that the Soviets would get very little Lend-Lease or its equivalent "without strings attached"; the Americans would use any aid "for our own ends and not just Russian ends." [21]

There was much confusion in the development and clarification of the U.S. position on reparations in the spring and summer of 1945, but it would be a mistake to believe that the strategy that eventually evolved was merely the product of a series of accidents: reparations policy took its place within the larger American program.

At Yalta the three powers had decided to create a reparation commission, which was to meet in Moscow after the Crimea meeting. Under the influence of the Treasury, the Informal Policy Committee on Germany had drafted a set of principles reflecting Morgenthau's ideas for the American delegation. Opposing any reparations plan that would "promote or require the building up of German economic capacity," the instructions called for reparations from capital removals in the heavy industries "to the maximum extent possible." Morgenthau had referred to this clause as "the guts" of the document.[22] The Americans would agree on current output reparations only if they became necessary for political reasons; even under such circumstances, they were to be as small as possible in relation to capital removals and would not entail maintenance of the German war potential. But the clauses calling for dismantling that would weaken Germany were hedged by concessions to the State Department. The reparations negotiators were to reject any plan directly or indirectly forcing the United States or any other country to finance Germany. The victors were ultimately to leave the Germans "with sufficient means to provide a minimum subsistence standard of living without sustained outside relief." [23]

One might think that with the decline of Treasury power, Morgenthau's opponents would have used the document's escape clauses to emphasize current production reparations, but the State Department shifted its policy on this. As issues besides the Reich's economic position became intertwined with reparations, the dominance of multilateral policies was felt in a more subtle way. The bias against reparations from current output continued, although on a basis different from Morgenthau's. Ernest Penrose, economic adviser to Ambassador Winant at the time, has analyzed this shift in policy explicitly. It became necessary to check "Russia's exorbitant demands on Germany and her efforts to get a foothold in the Ruhr." Britain and the United States realized that if they poured money into Germany, the defeated nation might be forced to use it to pay off the Soviets. This knowledge provided a basis for following a Treasury policy "originally advocated on grounds now unacceptable." [24]

The economic havoc in Europe at the war's end was great enough to make a concrete, practical impact on the Americans: Germany would not easily take her place in a multilateral order if she were to pay substantial recurring reparations. Moreover, the Americans had become clearly aware of a Soviet threat to their global design. The United States would finance the Germans if its money promoted the establishment of a multilateral world; but the Americans would not aid the Reich so that it could compensate the Russians. Some capital removals would take place in accordance with the State Department's desire to "disarm" Germany economically; the victors would dismantle the Reich's war industries and bring her economy into line with the multilateral ideal. Although not on the scale Morgenthau envisioned, these removals might serve as reparations. But the Allies would extract current production reparations only insofar as they did not interfere with the new Germany's participation in mulitlateralism.

Immediately after Yalta, the State Department had argued that its plans for the Reich's economy were essential if Washington were to meet the Soviet demands for reparations. With the Treasury no longer a threat, the Department did not need to support the Russian view; it could back the Treasury demand for strictures on current production.

This new constellation of factors enabled reparations policy to maintain its outward Morgenthauist form while serving the interests of the State Department. Some aspects of its new position on reparations were clarified by Emil Despres, the Department's expert on German economic matters. At an interdepartmental meeting of April 25, Assistant Secretary Clayton remarked that "the total German reparations have been agreed upon." Although there was some confusion on the matter, subsequent discussion revealed that the $20 billion figure was being "discarded" by the United States as a basis of discussion. Serving both on the Informal Policy Committee on Germany and on the committee working out reparations principles, Despres explained the situation:

The thought hasn't been to drop that [commitment in regard to $20 billion] in the sense of ignoring the commitment or the proposed basis of discussion that was arrived at at Yalta, but we have had the feeling, frankly, that twenty billion dollars was likely to exceed Germany's capacity to pay, and we would like to de-emphasize it. . . . As it stands now it says—I don't know the exact words—but it says that the reparations shall be limited to an amount. The outer limit will therefore be such as to leave Germany with enough resources to provide a minimum subsistence standard of living.[25]

A month before his death, FDR had appointed White House economist Isador Lubin to head the American dele-

gation of the Reparation Commission. In response to advice
from Harriman in early April, Roosevelt informed Lubin
that Harriman suggested caution. The President also instructed the new minister to refer back to the White House
any proposals the Russians presented.

Harriman had wanted more than caution in dealing with
the Russians: he urged that Lubin delay his arrival in the
Soviet Union. A week later, on April 10, he recommended
that Lubin remain temporarily in Washington. Harriman's
position was that the United States should temporize until
economic and political problems with the Soviets were "settled to our satisfaction." [26] Although Roosevelt apparently
had no more to say on the question, the State Department
was not convinced that the Americans should delay the
meeting. On April 7, the Department informed Harriman
that Lubin's mission would leave about April 15; it wanted
the Russians to know that "preparations are complete and
that final scheduling of the departure awaits only the determination of an approximate starting date for the discussions in Moscow . . . we do not feel that a useful purpose
would be secured by delay in beginning discussion of reparations." [27] On April 12, the Secretary of State cabled Ambassador Winant in Britain that the United States was concerned about the British attitude toward convening the
Reparation Commission. The English were stalling, and
Washington desired "a definite decision" made on the selec-
tion of the United Kingdom representative and "a more or
less definite date" made for the representative's departure to
Moscow.[28]

Nevertheless, the difference between official State Department policy and the harder line pushed by Harriman was

one of degree. Officials deleted the following sentence from the cable to Harriman: "It would be unfortunate if the Russians gained the impression that difficulties . . . had altered our readiness to begin reparations discussions." [29]

The Ambassador soon triumphed. Almost coincident with Roosevelt's death on April 12, policy shifted. On April 13, Lubin had the State Department wire Harriman that he would not leave until the Ambassador decided it was advisable.[30] During the next two weeks—the period in which agreement was reached on the policy of economic coercion —Truman backed Harriman even more strongly. On April 18, the Department asked the new President if Lubin's rank were to remain "minister." Truman did not answer the question, but he did make his priorities clear. The President replied: "I don't want him to go at this time." [31]

Although Lubin kept his rank as minister, on April 27, Truman appointed Edwin Pauley as *ambassador* over Lubin. Pauley was an independent oil man and Democratic fund raiser whom FDR had been considering for a future position as Secretary of the Navy, and the significance of this change was not lost on the press. The *United States News,* now *U.S. News and World Report,* argued that Pauley's appointment was evidence

of this country's changing attitude toward Russia. . . .[When Lubin was made minister], this country's interest was confined primarily to making certain that Germany is so stripped of productive capacity that she will be unable to go to war for many decades to come. Dr. Lubin, a quiet, capable, and clearheaded statistician and economist, was considered well chosen for the job he was expected to do. . . . But, as matters have developed, bargaining among the victors is expected to be a principal characteristic of the reparations settlement . . . so President Truman replaced Dr. Lubin with Mr. Pauley, the shrewd, practical oil operator.[32]

Truman, who described Pauley as "a tough, mean so and so," later believed that only the oil man's toughness produced any reparations policy at all. Truman also indicated that the Russians had some idea of a change. When Pauley arrived in Moscow in June, the President recalled, the Russians greeted the new Ambassador with the broadcast of an attack on "U.S. industrialists who are doing their utmost to restore German heavy industry." [33]

Truman and Pauley were not the only new American policy makers. From April 17 to June 26, Secretary of State Stettinius was at San Francisco setting up the United Nations, and Truman named Under Secretary Joseph Grew acting secretary of state. No one would consider Grew a friend of the Soviets. His biographer writes that he always believed in peace through diplomacy—with one exception. "He saw no value in engaging in diplomacy with Communist nations. Communism, in his view, made diplomacy impossible. He held that view from the time of the Russian Revolution and maintained it into retirement." [34] Grew's own thought at this time was that "as soon as the San Francisco conference is over, our policy toward Soviet Russia should immediately stiffen, all along the line." [35]

When Stettinius did return from San Francisco on June 27, he was appointed "personal representative" of the President—Truman did not want him as secretary of state. The President named Grew secretary *ad interim* until James Byrnes received the top position on July 3. But Secretary Byrnes left straightaway for Potsdam, and Truman reappointed Grew acting secretary of state until Byrnes returned. With all of this shuffling it is difficult to ascertain who was responsible for policy. Pauley, who did not get to Moscow until June 11, almost always sent his messages to "the secretary of state," but they were either answered by Grew directly or rewired by Harriman to Grew. Although Pauley accepted State Department premises, he acted independently. Considering himself responsible to the President, he developed an acrimonious relationship with Department policy makers and related to Morgenthau that he had told the State Department "to go to hell." [36] Grew and his associates feared a return to the diplomacy of the Roosevelt administration, in which FDR's representatives sidetracked departmental plans. In this instance Pauley did act on his own initiative, but the substantive difference between his policy and that of the State Department was that Pauley carried out more aggressive policy. As Truman recalled, he appointed the abrasive businessman over Lubin because he wanted someone as tough as Molotov.[37]

One reason Harriman had given for deferring Lubin's departure was the issue of French representation on the Reparation Commission. The Yalta Protocol had called for Big Three participation only, and the Russians were eager for talks on this basis. Before Roosevelt's death, the Americans had been dickering over the commission's membership, although they had been willing to go to Moscow to dicker. After Truman's order that Lubin was not to leave, the United States stand became stronger: at the end of April the Americans made a solution to the quarrel over membership a condition of their going to Moscow at all.

Despite this hard line, the admission or nonadmission of France was a minor matter. Essentially, Harriman wanted no further commitments given on reparations until the United States decided on "over-all policy" for the Soviets. The commission's status was a bargaining counter to be used to temporize with the USSR while the Americans defined their position. In early May, Eden and Pauley decided that only the Big Three would discuss reparations in Moscow. In effect the Americans reverted to Roosevelt's strategy: negotiation would take place but the United States would be "cautious" in its commitments. A worried George Kennan, the chargé in Moscow, expressed his fear to Harriman that even a large U.S. delegation in the Soviet capital would be a victory for the USSR. Harriman's answer defined the American tactic. "I feel we have nothing to worry about in regard to the size of the reparations delegation," Harriman said. "The principal point is that Mr. Pauley's instructions are very firm." "While we may not reach any agreement," the Ambassador reassured, "I have no fears about us giving in." [38]

Although the Americans consented to go to Moscow, the USSR would not hurry them.[39] When Harry Hopkins arrived in Russia at the end of May on a special mission for Truman, the commission had yet to meet, and Stalin argued that the United States position on France was contrary to the Yalta accord. Hopkins told the Russian leader that only the three powers would meet in Moscow and that the United States would probably not be unyielding on the question of French admission.[40] Hopkins settled nothing that the Americans had not decided before, and finally, during the second week of June, the Soviet Union received the reparation ambassador.

Although the State Department still wanted to use the issue of French representation, Pauley had little time for it. On July 2, Grew instructed him to attempt to get a place on

the body for France. The Ambassador was to avoid proposals that would strengthen Big Three membership because the United States desired equal French participation.
Pauley believed this was impossible: the Russians stood on
the Yalta Protocol, which stipulated tripartite negotiations.[41]
But in addition to showing a concern for the Crimea agreements, Pauley concentrated on a matter of economic importance.

The new ambassador saw the connection between reparations and the industrial futures of the Reich and the Soviet
Union. Impressed by the American reparations documents
of April and May, he was determined to avoid the dangers
to the United States in recurring payments or large scale
dismantling. The United States would not furnish the
wherewithal for the Germans to pay off the Russians; nor
would it allow capital removals that would threaten the
German economy.

On June 26, Pauley took the first steps to ensure that the
U.S. representatives on the Reparation Commission would
clear any removals the Allies would make from the American zone. Removals might take place only if the United
States could ascertain in the future whether they would be
considered reparations of some sort *or* German exports. If
Germany could not meet reparations payments without
indebting itself to Great Britain or the United States, neither
country need consider these initial removals reparations;
Britain and the United States could claim them as export
goods that the countries receiving them would pay for.
Pauley also forced the commission away from naming a
fixed figure. Twenty billion dollars was "wholly unrealistic," [42] i.e., it would result in America's footing the reparations bill.

Independently of the State Department, Pauley pursued

similar ends. But his refusal to grant the Russians a definite sum arose from different sources than those that contributed to the Department's dilution of the Yalta commitment. The Reparation Ambassador had not been at the Yalta conference and had received his information about it secondhand, particularly from Admiral Leahy, who gave Pauley the "general import" of the accord from notes and memory. Leahy was an unfortunate choice because he appears to have had only a confused understanding of the Yalta reparations discussion.[43] Indicating that he had not even read the protocol closely, Pauley also believed that Churchill, in addition to Roosevelt and Stalin, approved of the $20 billion as a basis of discussion. The position Pauley took did not stem from the influence of the State Department. Indeed, Department officials were not willing for the moment to go so far as Pauley. On July 2, Grew wired him that "the Department is not opposed to the discussion of an amount of reparations." To be sure, it considered $20 billion too high a sum, and one "approaching" $12 or $14 billion would be "more appropriate." But Pauley could adopt $20 billion "as a starting point for exploration and discussion." This position was still surprisingly in line with the Yalta formula: the Russians were to get a substantial sum—several billion dollars—which could be loosely construed as half of some figure "around" $20 billion.[44]

Despite the Department viewpoint, Pauley would not talk about an amount. His mission made no attempt to negotiate, and many of its members spent their time "junketing." Richard Scandrett, a minority voice in the American delegation, noted that the tenets on which Pauley intended to proceed "were contrary to the actual agreements which Roosevelt, Churchill, and Stalin had made at Yalta"; many of the staff members were openly antagonistic to the Russians; and Pauley's initial moves "clearly indicated to the Soviets that what he really proposed was to renegotiate the Yalta agreements." [45]

On June 19, Pauley had proposed to Grew that the United States endorse a plan allocating reparations on a percentage basis and not mention a sum. The Big Three would divide the total amount among themselves, with 55 per cent to go to the USSR, 22½ per cent to the British, and 22½ per cent to the United States. They would then invite other nations to make claims and would give up proportionately from their own shares to meet any other reasonable demands. On July 3, Pauley wrote to Ivan Maisky, acting as head of the Russian delegation and, contrary to his instructions of July 2, told Maisky that the Americans could only set percentages of the total reparations bill.[46] When the negotiations ended in mid-July, Pauley retreated from this position only to the extent of increasing the Soviet cut by one percentage point.[47]

Maisky would not elaborate on the view the USSR had expressed at Yalta. He simply repeated the proposal for $20 billion, collected through two years of capital withdrawals and ten of current production. As one American policy maker put it, Maisky's position throughout these meetings was characterized by "extraordinary hesitancy" to present data for the Soviet program. By now, if not earlier, the Russians evidently realized that their suggestions for heavy deindustrialization and current output reparations were opposed. The Soviets reminded the Americans of their commitment and seemed content to let them come up with a program to implement it.[48]

In addition to putting forward a proposal for a percentage

allocation of reparations, Pauley attempted to have the commission work out a set of conditions for the exaction of reparation. He set forth the following principle, which became the crux of disagreement between the Russians and the Western powers and reflected in itself the American conception of the postwar world: "In working out the economic balance of Germany the necessary means must be provided for payment of imports approved by the governments concerned before reparations deliveries are made from current production or from stocks of goods." [49] In short, Great Britain and the United States wanted Germany to pay its bills before reparations were taken from it. This was the "first-charge" principle. Exports from Germany were first to pay for essential imports; only thereafter could the United States consider the exports as reparations.

The United States had adhered to this position before. The Briefing Book Paper prepared for the Yalta Conference had stated that payment for necessary imports into Germany should receive priority "ranking above reparations." In Pauley's original instructions Washington opposed any plan that entailed American financing of reconstruction in Germany or of reparation. [50] These considerations had previously functioned on an intellectual level, but Pauley concretely introduced them into diplomacy. He told Maisky his government stood firmly on the principle, and was sure the United States would not recede from it; Pauley felt so keenly about the condition that he could not recommend its compromise. His staff then composed a draft of a proposed letter from Truman to Stalin and Churchill in which Truman insisted on the principle's acceptance. [51]

The fullest exposition of the rationale behind the first-charge idea appears in a letter from Pauley to Maisky. There could be no current production reparation from Germany, Pauley stated, unless the Germans shipped more goods out of the country than went in; that is, there must be a large export surplus. Reparations were not to cause Germany to have a balance of payments problem. But, he went on, the Allies would not achieve an export balance in Germany to be used for reparations unless there were some indispensable imports needed for the production of reparations. If exports did not pay for these imports, Pauley concluded, the United States or some other power would have to pay for them. The United States refused to do what it had done after World War I. It would not loan Germany money (ostensibly to pay for imports and prevent its economic collapse) while some other power drained off exports in reparations. The first charge on Germany's exports must pay for the imports needed for what the Americans called a minimal peace economy; thereafter, the Russians could take the excess as reparations.[52]

The Americans, then, claimed that there was a direct relationship between the ability of the German economy to meet the reparations burden and to pay for needed imports. If this relation existed, there was reason in the United States demand that it not be forced to funnel money into Germany at one end while someone else took it out at the other. Before the Germans made reparations deliveries, their economy should be healthy enough to pay its debts. At this time and in the future the United States made this argument to the Soviet in a way calculated to display the outrageousness of USSR proposals.

But *was there* a direct relationship between the ability to meet reparations payments and the ability to export? The American Briefing Book Paper used at Yalta indicated that to avoid certain difficulties in the collection of reparations goods, the goods should be those "that Germany is able to deliver *and* the claimant nations are willing to receive." In a similar paper prepared for Potsdam, the American program for German exports also contained *two* conditions: the first concerned "the types and quantities of equipment and supplies which Germany would have to make available on reparations account"; the second, "the types and quantities of goods which Germany would have to export in order to make payment for such imports as are essential to the German economy." [53] The German economic structure might be vigorous enough to produce reparations goods; because they were free, these goods would be accepted by all claimant nations. But other countries might *not* be willing to trade with Germany; they might not be willing to pay for, with suitable imports of their own, whatever exports Germany produced. This situation might occur because of restrictive trade agreements, because of Germany's supplying the same goods free as reparations, or because of any number of other variables. The condition of postwar Germany was such that just this stress might exist. German industrial potential, from which reparations would be paid, was much stronger than Germany's ability to enter the international export market competitively. Many factors would affect the ability to export more than production for reparation: the concentration of war damage, the loss of key foreign trade items, the confiscation of liquid assets and shipping, the sundering of export connections, and the disrupted world economic system. [54]

The fundamental point of the first-charge principle was that Germany be able to export successfully and so meet an important requirement for participation in a multilateral political and economic system. But in the world commercial system as it then existed, the principle meant more than this. Only the United States was in a position to pay for exports from Germany, and since the United States was actively attempting to rehabilitate the western European economies, in all likelihood they would next be able to trade with the new Reich. If the principle were realized, Germany would be geared to the immense productivity of the United States, and it would trade with its key traditional importers, western Europe and the United States. Finally, the Americans emphasized that trade had to be conducted in a nondiscriminatory manner. On a practical level, the principle was almost equivalent to the whole of the U.S. politico-economic position: the Americans would deny Russia reparations until they integrated Germany into a multilateral order.

The principle embodied more than a concern that the United States would have to finance the German economy. Whether it paid reparations or not, Germany would need monetary support in the near future because of the chaotic postwar world. The Americans believed that all the European economies would operate at a deficit for the next two years, and, as I have noted, the Americans were willing to aid these economies; that is, they were willing to finance the Germans. The United States would not, however, allow the Germans to produce reconstruction material for the USSR until their exports were acceptable in international markets. The United States would compromise only after its grand scheme were realized. When the Americans proclaimed to the USSR the sanctity of the first-charge principle, they were saying they would finance German multilateralism but not aid Soviet Allies.

We should also note that this U.S. position entailed payment in foreign exchange (i.e., in gold or convertible currencies), as the Germans had made reparation in the twenties, rather than "in kind" (i.e., in goods and services). The first-charge principle implied just that: if the surplus of foreign currencies derived from export-import operations were a real one, it would reduce to some form of gold, or currencies convertible with gold or dollars.[55] This fact might be of little interest if it did not mean that Washington was contradicting the position agreed on at Yalta: there Roosevelt had stressed that the Germans had to pay reparation "in kind" to avoid problems the World War I reparation settlement created. Reparations had allegedly broken down in the twenties because the victors demanded them in money; only reparations in kind would obviate this difficulty, and Roosevelt's notion, supported by Stalin and Churchill, became tripartite policy.[56]

Pauley paid no attention to this argument until he described his interim negotiations to the new secretary of state. Byrnes was a domestic politician fresh to the job and could not be expected to be conversant with the subtleties of foreign economic policy. Pauley told Byrnes that the United States must avoid naming a reparations sum because of the reason FDR had given at Yalta: the American people would think that Germany was paying in money and not in goods, and because they remembered the twenties they would disapprove. But the point of this argument was not to prevent naming a sum, only to ensure that a sum be paid in kind. The use of the argument by Pauley—who did not even support in kind reparations—to Byrnes almost smacks of duplicity.[57]

However we interpret Pauley's intention, he saw the dangers of in kind reparations; Pauley thought that only monetary reparations would give the United States the necessary control over the situation, and these would be subject to the first-charge principle.

The American commitment to multilateralism involved in the first-charge principle is connected to another problem that we ought to analyze separately. Suppose the Americans capitulated to the Soviets on the reparations program; suppose also, as appeared likely to occur, that in the near future Germany produced goods for reparations but not for export. Bilateral economic relationships would develop between the Russians and the Germans: Germany would become the supplier of heavy industry to the USSR and might be drawn into a Soviet economic orbit.

By the early summer of 1945 many top American decision makers—Truman, Leahy, Clayton, Grew, and Pauley most specifically—had been persuaded by Harriman or had concluded for themselves what U.S. policy for the Russians was to be: economic sanctions would be used to gain Soviet compliance to American goals; the United States could apply these sanctions merely by delaying various decisions. This general position reinforced American concern about German reparations. In any event they would complicate multilateral policies. Now it additionally became expedient to put economic pressure on the Russians by procrastinating on commitments on various kinds of economic aid. The consequence for reparations policy was clear: the Soviets would get little cooperation from the Americans on this form of reconstruction help.

In May, Leo Crowley of the FEA, who was handling the Lend-Lease negotiations, had tied all the aspects of American strategy together for Reparation Ambassador Pauley:

Confirming our brief conference this afternoon, I want to re-iterate my firm opinion that it is absolutely essential to the best interests of our Government that you be kept in close touch with the Russian Lend Lease program and any economic aid which may be contemplated in that connection. Hence, you may be sure that before any negotiations are completed or any economic assistance given you will be fully advised so that we may have your reaction.

I am anxious to cooperate with you to the fullest extent to the end that you will be placed in the strongest possible position so far as your own negotiations are concerned.[58]

As Pauley told his staff in July, because the Americans would not support "the Soviet position on the dollar evaluation of reparations," they would adopt another tactic. The reparations plan would be "more limited in scope" and defer "a number of important details." [59]

When the Americans went to the Potsdam Conference in July, they were aware that reparations were not a secondary issue on which they could compromise. A policy of low reparations, or a strictly controlled reparations policy, became an operative part of a multilateral program—a plan for bringing about a politically and economically rehabilitated Germany, oriented to the United States.

6 The Economics of
the Potsdam Conference

The Americans responsible for formulating policy at Potsdam in July and August 1945 were a distinguished and intelligent group committed to the multilateral ideal—Pauley, Clayton, and Harriman. Pauley participated both as the U.S. representative on the Reparation Commission and as a member of the important Sub-committee on German economic problems. The chairman of the American group in this Sub-committee was Assistant Secretary of State Clayton.[1] After Hull's retirement, former cotton manufacturer Clayton became the most dedicated and articulate proponent of the former Secretary's ideas. On his appointment at the end of 1944, Clayton asserted that he was an "outspoken and consistent advocate of Cordell Hull's philosophy."[2] Clayton shared Hull's beliefs in the primacy of economics, that "the international economic policies of nations have more to do with creating conditions which lead to war than any other single factor."[3] He wrote his mentor that Hull's belief was "so thoroughly ingrained in my system that I shall always work and fight for it."[4]

Averell Harriman attended the conference in his capacity as ambassador to the Soviet Union; as I have tried to show, the Ambassador was the most sophisticated thinker on

141

Russo-American relations.[5] He was informed on the Moscow reparations discussions, supported Pauley's decision to reject the $20 billion Yalta commitment, and attended the strategy meetings of the U.S. reparation delegation.[6]

The new secretary of state, James Byrnes, was a domestic politician with little knowledge of foreign policy. Although eager to assert his own authority, Byrnes became the spokesman of Pauley, Clayton, and Harriman, often, it appears, without knowledge of the positions he took. But the Secretary also espoused multilateral ideas in a simplified form. In January 1945 he had written FDR:

We must export goods if we are to provide jobs for all of our workers. We cannot export goods unless others have the dollars required to pay. These dollars can be secured only through credit arrangements and through the import of goods into this country. When we raise barriers against imports we restrict our outlets and reduce job opportunities at home.[7]

During his first few months in office, as Gaddis Smith has observed, former Secretary Hull powerfully influenced Byrnes.[8]

With some success, a few scholars have advanced the argument that Byrnes as well as Truman were the leaders of an anti-Russian movement that developed after Roosevelt's death. There is little evidence for this contention. Sumner Welles singled out Byrnes for criticism at Potsdam because he "least of all" possessed "either knowledge, understanding, or experience in foreign relations." Welles went on to say that Byrnes was a man with a profound ignorance "of even the rudimentary facts of international life."[9] E. F. Penrose has written that Byrnes initiated little of the play at Potsdam.[10] Special Ambassador Joseph Davies worried because Byrnes and Truman were the only ones at Potsdam who were *not* violently opposed to the USSR; they were "surrounded" by people "actively hostile" to Russia. Davies feared that a "palace intrigue" was closing around the President.[11]

Truman's lack of qualifications for the office he assumed is well known but often forgotten. Leahy did not see how the "completely inexperienced" President could carry out U.S. foreign policy.[12] One scholar has commented that although Truman's touch was unsure through much of this period, the new President sometimes acted on impulse to appear no less decisive than his great predecessor.[13] The official British historian of wartime diplomacy has lamented that Truman added to the Potsdam difficulties by "his incomplete understanding of the importance of European issues."[14]

What seems to have happened is that State Department policies, which were in one respect always anti-Soviet, became American policy after Roosevelt's death. One can only speculate whether the U.S. government would have implemented these policies had Roosevelt lived; but they did have a large, committed, and influential group supporting them. The new President made it all the easier for them to be carried out and, incidentally, provided a figure who could be held responsible for the development of American diplomacy.[15] These speculations aside, there was effective unity on multilateral goals for Germany at Potsdam. But this agreement made decisions no easier for the Americans. In attempting to protect their program, they were forced into tortured and complex negotiations that increased their difficulties.

When U.S. diplomats arrived in Berlin, the Russians confronted them with a *fait accompli* in the Soviet zone; Clayton and Pauley related to Byrnes that the Russians were stripping the eastern zone of Germany of all removable equipment—in fact, the Soviets had taken material from the U.S. zone of Berlin to the USSR zone of Berlin until shortly before the American diplomats arrived there.[16] Truman noted the voracious nature and irrationality of the Russian policy. The Soviets, he said, had taken everything out of industrial plants, loaded it into flatcars, and then in many instances allowed it to remain on a sidetrack. "The material was rusting and disintegrating," Truman wrote. "Very soon it would be of no use to anybody." [17] The Russians started this process earlier, and it had reached its height in May. Former Soviet officials have argued that the USSR carried out dismantling in the absence of overall direction; the single aim was to ship the greatest amount of equipment out of Germany and Berlin in the shortest time, before the Allies established a joint administration and a planned reparations program.[18]

At this point the American dilemma was clear. The USSR had a critical need for reconstruction equipment and goods, and the Western powers had accentuated this need by their unwillingness as yet to aid Soviet reconstruction. Before the Allied Control Council in charge of the military occupation of Germany began to function, the Russians were determined to take everything they could from Germany. As the Americans saw it, the problem was to prevent the Soviets from sabotaging U.S. plans and at the same time to preserve Allied unity in Germany.

On July 17, Truman presented a United States memorandum on Germany to the first plenary meeting. When the foreign ministers brought it up the next day, Byrnes suggested that they form a subcommittee on German economic problems. Molotov and Eden agreed, and to this committee Byrnes appointed Clayton and Pauley. At its initial meeting the Americans introduced two commitments—related to the problem outlined above—which they tried to keep delicately in balance. The first concerned multilateral policy for Germany and advocated the first-charge principle as a basis of negotiations; the second concerned Allied harmony and called for the treatment of Germany as an economic unit. Maisky, now a member of the Economic Sub-committee, responded to the Western powers the next day that reparations should be the "first-charge" on exports. "Capitalists," he said, "want to have profits from foreign trade and don't care about reparations for those who suffered." A regulated economy could meet both reparations and export requirements. The quadripartite military Allied Control Council—the three had given France a hand in the rule of Germany—for whom the diplomats would draw up instructions would govern Germany under a comprehensive program. But, Maisky concluded, if there was a conflict between reparations and exports, the latter must give way. Of course, the Americans would not go along. In a manner reminiscent of what had gone before and presaging much to come, Clayton stated that the American people would not subsidize the German economy as they had done after the last war.[19]

The U.S. delegates appear to have seen little hope of reaching agreement in terms satisfactory to them. The USSR demanded reparations from Germany, and although the Americans could prevent removals from the western zones, there was nothing the United States could do to hinder the Russians in the east. In their initial reflections on the Sub-committee impasse the Americans were ready to abandon four-power agreement for the immediate future and leave the problem to the military forces that would govern Germany. U.S. diplomats discussed among themselves a proposal allowing the zone commanders to handle reparations matters as they saw fit, "subject only to such general agreement as they may wish and be able to reach in the Control Council." Each zone commander would limit the program of removals so as not to prejudice his government's conception of the occupation. In effect each power would apply its version of the first-charge principle to its zone: the military authorities would set aside the necessary means to pay for "imports approved by the Governments concerned" before they made removals of current production and stocks of goods. The United States would "proceed with operations in its Zone without regard to reparations as such." The American military would remove whatever plants, equipment, and material "as it desires to remove," assuming "that the other occupying powers will do likewise." [20]

These proposals appeared only as United States delegation "working papers," but they symbolized the abandonment of four-power cooperation in Germany. For the present, the United States and at least Britain would deal gently with the German economy while the Russians went their own way. As Stimson commented on July 22, the "oriental" Russian policy on war booty was "bound to force us to preserve the economy in western Germany in close cooperation with the British." [21]

The Control Council would give a façade of unity, but the American plan would limit the treatment of Germany as a whole. Nonetheless, the United States did not view the situation in precisely this light. The idea was to protect multilateral policies in the western zones by not giving the Russians any influence there. Isolated in the eastern zone, the Russians could ultimately be persuaded to agree to American goals for all of Germany. U.S. decision makers at Potsdam thought their diplomatic position was strong enough to win Soviet acquiescence. As we shall see, however, the British, the Russians, and American experts at home were more perceptive: the U.S. stance at Potsdam ended great power unity in Germany.

Although the Americans incorporated the fundamentals of their zonal plan into U.S. policy, they softened it for formal presentation. By July 22, Clayton had formulated the rudiments of a revised plan, and on July 23, Byrnes presented them to Molotov.[22]

As the official U.S. report on reparations later stated, the American suggestion "radically altered" Allied diplomacy toward Germany.[23] Although it stipulated that in all other matters the Allies would treat Germany as an economic unit, the proposal called for each country to exact reparations from its own zone. The United States additionally provided for interzonal trading so the Russians could obtain from the West some of the industrial equipment they wanted so badly. Later in the conference the Americans and the British also compromised to enable the Soviets to secure a controlled amount of this equipment free if the USSR would supply the Poles with reparations from the eastern zone. The United States told the Soviets that the program would furnish them with 50 per cent of the total available reparations from all zones; * at the same time the Western powers would prevent Russia from depredating their zones.

* Actually, Clayton indicated that "the most reliable information" was that the eastern zone contained 40 per cent of the movable equipment and that little of it was of the "heavy industrial type" which

The other important aspect of the American scheme was that by February 1946 the military would construct a program—"the level of industry plan"—for a minimal German economy. At that time the USSR would receive from the western zones a percentage of the capital equipment the Control Council considered unnecessary for a peacetime German economy; the Russians would take part of this percentage in exchange for agricultural products from the east, part free of charge. The point for the Americans seems to have been that once the victors negotiated the plan, they would terminate unilateral reparations removals in all of Germany. Assent to the plan would halt removals in the east *and* the west except those that the Allies agreed upon in the determination of the economy. For the present the Russians would take reparations only in capital removals. After the military executed the plan and removals stopped, no nation would extract current production reparations until exports paid for approved imports. (This first-charge principle for the new German economy exempted the industrial removals that would serve as reparations: since these removals would come when the German economy was in a state of transition, they might technically be considered exports that had to be paid for, although they were actually the excess of an economy that would be balanced according to an agreed level of industry plan.)

In essence the new U.S. idea was a decision to delay attempts at implementing the first-charge principle for all of Germany in the hope that the Russians would support it later. As the first formal U.S. proposal stated: "This plan amounts in effect to an interim program and does not pre-

the Soviet needed. Pauley's estimate was 45 per cent. See *FR*, Potsdam, II, 900, 917.

clude a coordinated administration of Germany. It permits immediate removals, and at the same time is not inconsistent with such overall economic policies as the Zone Commanders, working through the Allied Control Council, may determine." [24]

Unfortunately the plan evolved throughout the conference, and no available single document unravels all of its aspects. The basis for the proposal was certainly the zonal program. To it the Americans added the restriction that the Allies waive reparations from current production until the Germans successfully exported in a world economy. The other elements resulted from attempts to meet Soviet demands that did not strike at the plan's basis and to paper over Soviet-American disagreements. It was the reasonable outcome of a situation in which the United States could not prevent Soviet zone removals and would not allow the violation of the first-charge principle in its own zone. The possibilities for the success of the plan may have been small, but, with its anti-Russian features most prominent, the new proposal was just the policy the State Department had advised so long. Reparations from capital removals and current production were circumscribed by a future German economy whose trade was to be "balanced." In conception it was an expedient that deferred final decisions. George Kennan felt it was "temporizing" with reparations; but it did prohibit the Russians from weakening the western zones and gave the appearance of Allied agreement to Russian dismantling. Later the Americans could piece together a unified Germany; they preserved the hope of four-power control.*

* The above "rational reconstruction" of the American plan is taken from the conversations and documents cited in this chapter. The

When the foreign ministers discussed the Economic Sub-committee's report on July 22, Byrnes successfully argued that they pass over areas of discord. On the twenty-third he informally approached Molotov with the new American strategy. Byrnes first commented that he did not see how the Soviet government could reconcile its positions with "the adoption of an overall reparation plan." The United States would not "pay out money to finance imports to Germany," and perhaps each country could take reparations from its own zone. Because about 50 per cent of existing German wealth was located in the Soviet zone, Byrnes continued, this zone would provide the reparations the Americans thought due the USSR; if the Soviets desired equipment from the western zones, trading could take place among the powers. In other matters, the Secretary concluded, the Allies would treat Germany as an "economic whole."

Molotov's reply was consistent with Soviet policy in this area: he tried to bargain. As Robert Murphy, the top State Department political adviser in Germany, had argued a week before, it was to the Soviet advantage to seek Allied unity in Germany: "The Russians were obviously under instruction to do that." Thus the Soviet Commissar said that Stalin "strongly favored an overall plan for reparations"; the Russians "would be quite prepared to consider reducing their reparations claims." [25]

Compromising on the amount of reparations was not

fullest one document statement is given in the July 25 proposal on reparations (*FR*, Potsdam, II, 867–869). See also the extract of the report on German reparations (pp. 943–945). For Kennan's view see his *Memoirs* (London, 1968), p. 260.

Molotov's only attempt to make concessions. When Eden joined Byrnes and the Soviet Commissar for the foreign ministers' meeting a few minutes later, Molotov presented two proposals negotiating the first-charge principle. The first stated that in the event of the inability of the German economy to meet export and reparations demands, the Control Council should reduce both proportionally. Before, the USSR claimed that reparations should have priority; now they would have only equal status. The second proposal was that the Control Council would agree on a minimal import program. In this program the first charge on exports would be imports; on imports for which there were no agreement, reparations would be the first charge. To be sure, this procedure would allow the USSR to veto any import program and thereafter claim that reparations took precedence over a Western-approved import program. But Molotov asserted later that there would be some minimal program.

Byrnes's reply is noteworthy. He said that the American position was clear. There would be no reparations until imports into the American zone were paid for. There would be, he claimed, "no discussion of this matter." He had stated his position that not a dollar would be paid on reparations until imports were paid for.[26]

Later that afternoon the foreign ministers met again, and Byrnes bluntly asked Molotov if the Soviets had already engaged in removals. The conversation that followed is instructive of the general nature of the Potsdam reparations diplomacy. Molotov confessed to USSR removals and went on to meet the American fear that they would preclude a joint reparations plan. If Soviet dismantling was "what was worrying the Secretary," the USSR would reduce its claim from $10 billion to $9.7 billion. Ten billion dollars may have been a basis for discussion, but Byrnes replied that it "was idle to discuss it on that basis." Molotov went to $9 billion. Byrnes stated that 50 per cent of German wealth lay in the Soviet zone and, after some bickering, turned down the $9 billion proposal and outlined the zonal plan. Molotov went to $8.5 billion and then to $8 but said that the Russians must have a fixed amount of about $2 billion in equipment from the Ruhr. Byrnes was afraid that quarrels might develop if the Allies accepted this plan. Molotov "repeated his willingness to reduce their figure. . . . He reiterated his belief that agreement could be reached." At this point the meeting ended.[27]

For the next few days exchanges remained at this level. The Soviet Union tried to negotiate both on the first-charge principle and on the amount of reparations to be collected. The United States refused to discuss either point; and Byrnes always returned to the zonal idea.[28]

On July 27, Molotov approached Byrnes again. The work done on reparations in the Economic Sub–committee was unsatisfactory, and Molotov asked if the Crimea decision was still in force. Byrnes explained the United States understanding of the Yalta Protocol to be that the powers would discuss $20 billion as an amount of reparations; this the Americans had done. They had not, he said, committed themselves to this figure, and now regarded it as impossible. Molotov "only wanted to know what remained of the Crimea decision as a basis for discussion." The Soviet Union would consider reducing the figure. Did the United States have a different basis to suggest? Yes, Byrnes replied: as he understood it, the United States had put forward a different plan. He thought it "very important that they adopt another plan." [29]

At this point even Molotov was ready to yield. Later that day he asked Byrnes what amount of removals from the Ruhr the United States would trade for Soviet zone products. Molotov would now negotiate on the zonal plan, although his main objective was still to name a specific dollar value of equipment to be taken from the Ruhr. The figure he mentioned again was $2 billion, and on the evening of July 27, Byrnes indicated to Sir Alexander Cadogan, the Permanent British Under Secretary of State, that the Western Allies might trade $1.5 billion from their zones. But Pauley advised the Secretary that the sum available to the Russians would probably amount to $214 million. He counseled that because this amount differed "so widely from the figure which the Russians have in mind," Byrnes should mention no sum at all. The Secretary took this advice. He answered Molotov's request by stating that "our experts felt that it was impossible to put any specific dollar value" on equipment available for dismantling; the U.S. proposal was to offer the USSR a percentage of what could be removed.[30]

Although the Soviets continued to press for a minimal value, they in effect acquiesced. Nonetheless, Molotov and Andrei Vyshinski, Assistant Commissar for Foreign Affairs, were seething about the turn discussion had taken. Joseph Davies told Truman that reparations had "poisoned" the conference.[31] Notwithstanding the show of gall, substantive bargaining now concerned the delineation of the percentage formula.

On July 29, after Molotov agreed "in principle" to the zonal proposal, he continued to argue for a fixed sum in reparations. But Byrnes suggested that Russia receive in trade 25 per cent of what was available from the Ruhr after the powers determined the peacetime German economy, or 12½ per cent from the combined western zones. But given the acceptance of a percentage formula, the United States showed itself willing to compromise. That day Clayton wrote to Byrnes that the United States was committed to dismantling much industry in the Ruhr: it was doubtful if other claimant nations for reparations would be able to use all the equipment which was to be removed from that area. "In other words," he went on, "to give a reasonable percentage of such equipment to the Russians will cost nothing." [32]

The next day Byrnes offered 25 per cent in trade from the Ruhr and 15 per cent free of charge. In addition the Russians were to satisfy Poland's reparation claims. Molotov responded that the 15 per cent figure be raised to 25 per cent and a specific sum named. "He repeated all his arguments on this point." Some hours later the British counterproposed that the USSR receive 10 per cent free from all the western zones. After again expressing his desire for a fixed figure, Molotov responded by asking for the American percentages, but requested that these be drawn from all of the western zones and not the Ruhr alone as Byrnes had wanted. The Secretary answered that the American figures would then be halved to 12½ per cent and 7½ per cent. Molotov next tried to secure 25 per cent in exchange and 25 per cent free, chiefly from the Ruhr, but quickly dropped the former figure to 20 per cent. After more quarreling like this, the foreign ministers shifted, without a consensus, to another question.[33]

When the Big Three (now Clement Attlee, Stalin, and

Truman) met the next day, Stalin said the Soviets "accepted the point of view of the Americans"—they "agreed not to mention" a fixed sum. The question the three would determine was percentages. He asked for 15 per cent in exchange and 10 per cent free from all the western zones. After more haggling, the Americans and British accepted these figures, and settled the issue.[34]

Far more important than the squabbling over percentages was the elusive debate over the status of the German economic system during the occupation. The accord reached by the three victors seems to have been left purposely ambiguous, but its outlines are clear. At least during the period of initial removals there would be no overall control. On July 27, when Molotov indicated that he might accept the American idea of zonal control of reparations, he quizzed Byrnes about it. "If we *fail* to reach an agreement," Molotov said, "the result will be the same." "Yes . . ." Byrnes replied. Two hours later Molotov brought up the question again: "would not the Secretary's suggestion mean that each country would have a free hand in their own zones and would act entirely independently of the others?" Byrnes replied that this "was true in substance." Later Molotov wanted to have the U.S. proposal clearly in mind: as he understood it, the Soviet Union would "look to its own zone for a fixed amount of reparations." Byrnes commented that that was not quite accurate "since . . . the Soviet Union would take what it wished from its own zone." [35]

The crucial question was what was to happen after the initial period of removals. Presumably the military occupation authorities, through the Control Council, would work out plans for an all-German economy. Even a Russian draft on reparations made this argument about the American plan: it stated that, subject to the zone commander's authority, the Control Council would determine the equipment unnecessary to the German peace economy and available for reparations.[36] But how would the determination take place for all of Germany if there were no limit to what the Russians could take from their zone? As Byrnes said to the Russians, the "advantage" to a percentage agreement was that "what was available in the Soviet zone would concern neither the British, French nor United States and they would not, therefore, be interfering in that determination." "If the Soviets agreed to this plan," Byrnes added later in the conversation, "they would have no interest in exports and imports from our zone. Any difficulty in regard to imports and exports would have to be settled between the British and ourselves. The Soviets would have no interest and they would get their percentages regardless of what happened to us." [37]

If the Russians were to receive a *carte blanche* in the east, the United States would refuse them influence in the west. As Harriman recalled his position, he was "interested most in preventing the Russians from having a hand in the western zones." [38] At last the State Department was committed to agree with the War Department on the issue of autonomy. Byrnes insisted that in all cases the zone commander have final discretion. When Molotov argued that negotiations on the German economy be carried out "on an allied basis in which the Soviets would participate," Byrnes answered that "that was a possibility and should be studied." The Control Council could determine "the general norms of living standards"; but "final authority" had to be left to the zonal commander-in-chief. Byrnes could consent to Control Council formulation of the general program only "so long as the commander had the right of veto." [39]

When the Americans developed the essentials of their zonal scheme at the start of the conference, they had little hope of quadrapartite accord in the immediate future. Because a four-power procurement and interim financing plan was not feasible, the only solution would be combined handling and financing for the western zones. An American official commented that the zonal decision was made "given a situation in which it was doubtful whether we could actually pull together in governing Germany." Later in the conference the United States continued to operate on the assumption that a zonal policy precluded "quadrilateral action on . . . programming, procuring, and financing of imports." [40]

When the Russians accepted the zonal idea, immediate Allied agreement on a united German economy was minimal. The Russians saw the plan's consequences, but Molotov was not able to get through to Byrnes, as the following exchange, one of their many fascinating dialogues, illustrates.

MR. MOLOTOV inquired whether we still intended to have some central German administration, not a government, but some central organization through which the Control Council could operate in matters affecting finance, transport, foreign trade, etc., on which it had been agreed to treat Germany as an economic whole. He pointed out that if reparations were not treated as a whole, what would happen to overall treatment of economic matters.

THE SECRETARY pointed out that under his scheme nothing was changed in regard to overall treatment of German finance, transport, foreign trade, etc. The Secretary subsequently repeated this statement in reply to a further observation of Mr. Molotov that the reparation proposal would affect the overall economic administration of Germany.[41]

The British were also incisive in deciphering the nature of the accord. During the first part of the Berlin meeting, before Attlee replaced him, Churchill commented on the "network of problems that lay at the heart of their difficulties." In the event of a "breakdown of the Conference," Churchill supposed that they might "have to fall back on the proposal of Secretary Byrnes." "Each would hold on to what was in their areas." [42] Sir David Waley, the senior Treasury representative on the British delegation and a member of the Reparation Commission and Economic Sub-committee, took a similar position. He felt that the most serious feature of Byrnes's plan was that the Americans "had now given up hope of collaborating with the Russians in the administration of Germany as a single economic unit." He believed that the United States had a "defeatist view" that the Russian zone "would be administered as a separate unit with lower standards of living and few facilities for the interchange of goods with the rest of Germany." During this British delegation meeting, Ernest Bevin, the new foreign minister, went on to say that the Americans "clearly wanted to make the best bargain they could and to end the discussion." [43]

At the end of the conference, the British took exception to an important aspect of the reparations understanding, again indicating their tendency to support a unified German economy. Byrnes had asked for the deletion of the paragraph stating the first-charge principle as it applied to exports and imports. He said that under the percentage proposal there was "no need for this paragraph." Stalin agreed, and the Allies apparently settled the issue without dissent, but a few minutes later Bevin came back to the question:

MR. BEVIN pointed out that he had raised the question of first charges at the Foreign Ministers meeting yesterday.

MR. STALIN pointed out that they had agreed to delete the whole paragraph.

THE PRESIDENT said that this was what he had understood.

MR. BEVIN said he did not agree.

MR. BYRNES asked why they did not handle this in their own way since they were in control in their zone.

MR. BEVIN replied because it cut across the agreement to treat Germany as a whole economy. It would divide Germany into three zones.

Why did the Americans allow the first-charge principle to go so easily by the boards? For two reasons it had become useless with the adoption of the interim zonal plan. First, the Western powers could control German exports and imports under a first-charge principle in their own zones but were in no position to exercise control in the eastern zone. Second, for the immediate future the USSR had forgone reparations from current production. The first-charge principle was designed primarily to protect the German economy from the effects of these reparations, and if they were prohibited, the principle became superfluous. Byrnes said that the conferees could excise the paragraph because "the Soviet [had] claim to equipment only." [44]

Actually the restriction on current production reparation was not final. Returning from the conference, Pauley stated that the Allies could make no decision on recurring reparation until they defined the future German economy. Admiral Leahy also made this point. The Russians had not for-

feited current output reparations forever, but only until the
export-import trade of the new Germany was "in balance." [45]

The British were unwilling to allow German unity to rest
on these tenuous grounds. Earlier in the conference they
had wanted the USSR to receive free a percentage of the
unneeded industrial equipment from the western zones, a
concession designed to get Soviet support for Anglo-American policies for all Germany. The British had additionally
wanted to ensure a basis for unity by having Germany's
interim economy supplied as it had been prior to defeat,
with the Poles sending food to the Germans.[46] The Americans paid little attention to this proposal. The Russians
would not accept it because it would have undermined
Soviet policy in Poland: under the proposal that portion of
the Reich which the Soviets had in effect annexed to Poland
would supply the western zones of Germany with food. The
plan would have contributed to the reintegration of Polish
Germany into the new Germany.[47]

When this attempt at securing a unified Germany failed,
at the last minute the British resorted again to the first-
charge principle, because in order to implement it, the zones
would have had to cooperate. But even before the clause
embodying it was deleted, the principle had been nullified
by the stress on the zone commander's autonomy. While this
autonomy protected the integrity of the western zones'
economy—and the principle in these zones—this autonomy
also assured the Russians a free hand in the east.

American officials in the United States at the time of the
Potsdam Conference shared the view of the British and the
Soviets. The American diplomats in Berlin did not clearly
see that they had gone a long way in dividing Germany;

they thought the Russians would eventually come around.
American diplomats at home were not so sanguine.[48] In the
Briefing Book Paper that State Department planners had
prepared and that Byrnes had carried to Potsdam, the
repercussions of what was to be the U.S. policy were spelled
out unambiguously. In regard to the treatment of Germany
as an economic whole, the Briefing Book read:

The continuation of present combined arrangements among the
Western Allies [to the exclusion of the Soviet Union] for supply
and other economic and financial matters after SHAEF [Su-
preme Headquarters, Allied Expeditionary Force] has been ter-
minated would involve serious dangers. It would greatly prejudice the chances of reaching agreement with the Russians on
economic matters, and it would tend toward the establishment
of an economic wall between Eastern and Western Germany,
and, probably between Eastern and Western Europe. The economy of Eastern Germany can be readily assimilated into an
Eastern economic sphere. In contrast, acceptance by the Western
powers of the task of finding a place for a Western German
economy would create extreme difficulties and would greatly in-
tensify the post-war economic problems of the United States,
Great Britain and Western Europe.[49]

In Washington on July 28, Clayton's deputy, Willard
Thorp, summarized the ongoing Potsdam negotiations for
other officials in the United States. Soviet policy had necessitated "a complete reversal of the U.S. approach." A new
plan—the ones Byrnes presented to Molotov on July 23—
"virtually abandoned the whole concept of joint economic
treatment of Germany in favor of splitting the country
sharply between the Russian and the three western zones."
Thorp predicted that if the United States was driven to
adopting this plan,

we shall have suffered a grave set-back in attaining our basic
objectives in Germany. . . . Acceptance of these [American]
recommendations would go very far toward a *de facto* division
of Germany into two halves and abandonment of the general
economic principles which we had tentatively agreed upon.
Under this scheme it would be extremely difficult in practice
to ensure uniform economic treatment in all zones of occupation.
The extent of removals on reparation account would probably
differ markedly as between Eastern Germany and Western Germany and the extent to which economic resources were left to
the Germans would also vary widely. In consequence, it would
be difficult, if not impossible, to reach agreement on the interzonal adjustment of surpluses and deficits and on an import
program for Germany as a whole, including the respective shares
of the occupying powers in the financing of such imports. It is
quite likely that the result would be to orient the economy of
Eastern Germany toward the Soviet Union and Eastern Europe
and that of Western Germany toward Western Europe.[50]

The Washington desk officers were equally pessimistic.
One of them wrote Isador Lubin in Berlin that the zonal
plan would "split Europe down the middle economically."
It was difficult to believe that disagreement could be so
fundamental, and the lower ranking men at home hoped
that the zonal plan represented "the nadir of the conference,
from which a long recovery will be made." [51] Clayton and
Emilio Collado, another U.S. official at Potsdam, tried to
answer these fears in a long cable to Washington in mid-
August. In a backhanded way they called attention to the
purport of the reparations decision:

There appears to be an unfortunate tendency to interpret the
reparations operating agreement as an indication of complete
abandonment of four power treatment of Germany. This is not

stated in the texts and should not be accepted as a necessary conclusion even though there may be many among the military forces in Germany who believe that a zonal treatment or a tripartite treatment of the western zones will be the only practicable method of operation.

They continued that the Control Council was directed to formulate "common policies" covering a variety of economic questions. Even within the reparations text itself the Control Council had "to reach decisions concerning the scale of demilitarization in the western zones. . . ." But they then concluded with the kernel of the American plan: "If as appears quite likely it becomes impossible to agree upon an approved import program in the Control Council the matter will revert to the zone commanders who will assess their own first charges on 'exports." At this level it would "undoubtedly be desirable to arrange tripartite programs," that is, those with the United States, Great Britain, and France.[52]

Pauley's official Report on German Reparations submitted to the President at the end of September also stated the consequences of American policy in an attempt to deny them. The report explained that Potsdam brought "an important shift in U.S. policy on reparations." The study concluded:

The U.S. has endeavored to maintain Germany as a *single economic unit,* in all operations including reparations. Consistent with this policy, all discussion, computations and formulas put forward by the U.S. mission were based on Germany as a whole, using the political boundaries of Dec. 31, 1937. While this situation was radically altered at the Berlin Tripartite Conference, as explained above, this in no way changed the policy of the U.S. to make every effort possible to hold Germany together as an economic unit.[53]

There is one issue related to reparations, that of dismemberment, which has been left undiscussed. If the United States pursued a zonal reparations policy, what stance did it now take in regard to an official division of the Reich?

In the months after the Yalta Conference the urge to create a formally partitioned Germany waned among all the Big Three. The Yalta committee established in connection with the EAC for the study of dismemberment held but two meetings, and none of the three powers pressed for more activity. On April 10, Winant received instructions from Roosevelt that the American position should be "one of study and postponement of final decision." The Soviet Union seemed to go along with this lead, and in May, Stalin went further in his "Proclamation to the People," stating that the Russians would not demand the division of Germany.[54] When Harry Hopkins queried him about this unilateral action, Stalin argued that he was supporting the Western powers and was willing to consider dismemberment. He felt that the British did not favor partition and that the Allies would not accomplish it by "lopping off parts of Germany." Again he evinced his belief that if the victors decided to fragment Germany, they should do it thoroughly. Hopkins responded positively and indicated that Truman was inclined toward dismemberment and approved the detachment and internationalization of the Saar, the Ruhr, and the west bank of the Rhine.[55]

Although the State Department advised the President against partition and internationalization, Truman did like both of these ideas.[56] One unofficial State Department paper prepared for the conference also proposed such a program, but on the way to Berlin, Clayton and Byrnes persuaded

Truman not to present this document, and Truman noted that the United States decided that the Ruhr and Rhineland "should remain in Germany[.]" [57]

Whatever the preconference maneuvering, U.S. diplomats agreed on their position throughout the Potsdam talks. No one even raised partition, and when the Soviets cautiously and informally brought up internationalization, there was an American consensus: there would be no Soviet influence in western Germany. Maisky introduced the issue on July 20, and the notes on the conversation indicate the prescient American response. Clayton said: "Which direction will the products flow?"; and Pauley: "If you could control coal—you could turn it on and off." The diplomats settled nothing at this meeting, and when Molotov took up the question with Byrnes and Eden, they stalled him. On July 30, Molotov submitted a formal proposal, and on its basis Stalin broached internationalization with Truman and Attlee at the end of the conference. Was the Ruhr, Stalin asked, to remain a part of Germany? "The Russian delegation would like to know if it were agreed that the Ruhr should not be detached." Truman said that there were no doubts in his mind that it was under the Control Council. Stalin could do nothing and did not object. [58]

At this point "Control Council" authority would mean "joint" Allied authority in only the weakest sense—the zone commander's authority was to be supreme: the Ruhr would be under British (Western) jurisdiction. Of course, the Department of State recognized this situation. The American reports indicate that the Allies originally decided to refer the Soviet paper on internationalization to the future conferences planned for the foreign ministers. But the Allies "dropped" this decision when they drafted the final version of the Potsdam Protocol.[59] Later in August, Truman and Byrnes informed Charles de Gaulle of this resolution to the problem; although the USSR had brought up internationalization on several occasions at Potsdam, the Americans had avoided discussing the matter. Byrnes also told French Foreign Secretary Georges Bidault that the United States was against "installing" four powers on the Rhine.[60]

The phraseology adopted at Berlin rejected dismemberment, but in fact the opposite was true. Ironically, when the Americans discarded partition in theory, they accomplished it in fact. With a strange dialectic, the drive to secure a global political and economic system was generating the division of Europe.

7 The Diplomacy of Omnipotence

Although the complexities of Potsdam diplomacy defy simple retelling, the American position there was unmistakable: the United States did everything in its power to cut off Soviet influence in the West and to deprive the Russians of reconstruction material. But even if some of the Americans did not entirely understand the consequences of this strategy, the policy would have a reciprocal effect, and the United States would have no influence in the East. Indeed, the reparations plan that the United States dictated to the other Allies was crucial in determining the future of the postwar world: the Americans all but ensured a partitioned Germany.

But why did they pursue a policy that could be expected to have such unfortunate results? The Americans were not happy about Soviet reparations demands, but the Russians were willing to compromise in order to reach accord in an inter-Allied economic program. The Soviet Union by no means *forced* the Americans into their zonal position, and they had many resources at their disposal to make a reasonable settlement. The severity of the U.S. proposal merits extended analysis. First, however, it is necessary to evaluate

the three reasons for their action that the Americans offered
to the USSR during various stages of the negotiations.

In discussing the zonal program with Molotov, Byrnes
mentioned that the wide Soviet definition of war booty precluded common policies; by stipulating that all equipment
and stocks of goods were war booty, the Russians could take
what they wished from their zone of occupation, not subject
to common reparations policies. This was true, but one must
realize that rather than contesting the Soviet definition of
war booty—and this the Americans had done before the
conference—the United States accepted the Soviet definition of July 21 on the following day. The Americans also
recognized that controversy over semantics was immaterial;
what was necessary for a settlement was agreement on the
total amount the victorious powers would extract—no matter what the Allies called the removals. As a U.S. official put
it, the diplomats needed "concrete applications" of the definitions, i.e., a calculation of how much went to whom.[1] But
the Americans were not prepared to seek agreement on a
calculation because they refused to name an amount. Definitions were a minor consideration in United States policy.

Related to the problems of definitions was American reasoning about the Polish border question *and* about Soviet
removals. In the first place the Americans argued that the
Russians had complicated the collection of reparations because they had given Poland a slice of Germany to ad-
minister. This meant *in fact* that the Poles would acquire
this area and that there would be less "Germany" from
which the powers could extract reparations. In the second
place, American argument went, because the Soviets had
begun extensive removals, computing reparations would be

difficult if not impossible. But we cannot consider these two problems of reckoning the amount of reparations to be fundamental. The Americans had extensive information concerning the effects on reparation payment that the cession of territory to Poland would have. Stalin agreed to "renounce" some reparations to make up for the Poles having taken a part of Germany. Molotov also told the foreign ministers that although the Allies could not include this German territory for the computation of reparations, Poland need receive no compensation in addition to the material in its new territory. Moreover, Molotov expressed willingness to reduce the Soviet share first to $9.7 billion, next to $9.0, then to $8.5, and finally to $8 billion to make up for Russian removals already made.[2] $2 billion represented an extraordinary sum in relation to what the Russians could already have taken. The Americans ignored all these concessions. Neither the question of definitions, nor that of Polish Germany, nor that of removals the Soviets had already made can be considered a prime determinant of U.S. policy.

If we admit that these three issues do little to explain American strategy, it is necessary to evaluate the more complex analysis that has become the standard explanation of U.S. aims. According to this interpretation, two conflicting goals pushed the Americans into a position permitting only moderate reparation. First, scholars have claimed, the Americans had no wish to subsidize the German economy as they had done after World War I. They were against industrial removals or recurring reparations that would bring economic chaos and force the United States to rescue German finances. Second, according to this standard explanation, the United States did not want Germany restored to first-rank industrial power. Hence, policy makers had another reason for limiting current production reparation that would entail that the Allies leave a great deal of German manufacturing plant standing. After the reparation period, Germany might become a major industrial source of supply with many nations dependent on it for goods. The Americans would be unable to achieve its "economic disarmament." The desire to prohibit Germany from becoming a financial burden but also from becoming an economic threat drove the United States to seek a moderate policy. Initial reparations would include that industrial equipment whose removal was consistent with a future stable economy, and subsequent current production reparations were to be minimal.[3]

Both these concerns were genuine, but they involved other issues and must be interpreted in a way different from that cited above. To comprehend their relevance we must put them in the context of wider American strategy. But here we face an immediate dilemma: despite the assemblage of evidence, there is no single document that sets forth a direct statement of overall American policy. We cannot explicate a framework in which U.S. decision making becomes intelligible by citing a "fact." Explication is an interpretive task, and we can measure its success only by seeing how well the evidence at our disposal sustains it. With this limitation in mind, we may draw several conclusions.

At Potsdam, American reparations policy was carried to its logical conclusion: at least for the time being the Soviets would get nothing from the western zones. During the same period—the spring and summer of 1945—the United States took no action on the USSR credit proposal. Truman did not discuss aid, a loan, or credits with the Russians in Berlin, and thereafter the two powers made little progress on these issues.[4]

One set of judgments makes these facts and many others intelligible. The Americans would use the Soviet need for economic assistance to their advantage. Meaningful aid to the USSR was a risky proposition for U.S. diplomats: it would be difficult to negotiate satisfactory terms for it and many policy makers doubted the benefits for the United States. They would not grant reconstruction credits until there were signs that the Russians would make concessions to multilateral ends. The price the Soviets would pay for economic assistance would be some compliance with American politico-economic aims. Without the aid, the USSR would be under severe pressure, and in exchange for a loan or credits, the United States might persuade the Russians to open up eastern Europe to American interests. The strategy was one of delay: temporizing on economic questions would give the Russians reason to think and make them adjust their policies in eastern Europe. Truman made the policy explicit when he informed Molotov in April that American assistance was dependent on Soviet action in eastern Europe.[5] Even if the Russians displayed hostility by their failure to yield, the United States would have cut its losses and slowed Soviet reconstruction: if the Soviets continued to oppose multilateralism, they would do so under economic handicaps. The zonal reparations program, which was little of a program at all, was part and parcel of this attempt to save multilateralism. For the present, the Americans denied the Soviet Union the heavy industrial equipment in the western zones, but they left a decision on these facilities open should the Russians come to terms. Capital removals and the possibility of current production reparations from a balanced economy remained as incentives.

We can also account for the diplomatic power of the

atomic bomb in this framework.[6] For whatever reasons it
was dropped, thereafter American diplomats used their control of the weapon as another lever in attempting to achieve
their global ends. There are two dimensions of this "atomic
diplomacy" that are significant for our discussion. First, un-
like most of the other levers at American disposal, the bomb
was a military threat and not a form of economic coercion.
Second, until August 1945 it was an untried weapon, unknown to many diplomats. I assume that it had less diplomatic importance at this time, than it subsequently had
when its existence and implications had been fully con-
ceptualized by U.S. policy makers. In all likelihood in 1945
and 1946 it was simply another trump card that the Americans might in some way play. The bomb fit into prior
American strategy: a further means to bring about a multilateral world. Diplomatic historian Herbert Feis was right
in his last appraisal: "the American Government did not
change its policies or expand its claims because it had
acquired the bomb; it faithfully followed the course defined
by officials who had known nothing about the bomb until
it was exploded on Hiroshima." [7]

With this structure in mind, we may return to what I
spoke of as the accepted rationale for the reparations program. It must be modified in order to provide an adequate
explanation of American policy in Germany.

Much in the customary analysis is correct. The U.S. reparations position was motivated by a desire to prevent economic chaos in Germany. It was surely credible for the
United States to want to maintain German stability on an
industrial basis; and there is little evidence to indicate that
the United States at this time desired to rebuild a strong
Germany as a "buffer" against the Soviets. But we must view

these facts in connection with the adoption of the zonal
idea. Byrnes's scheme prevented the Russians from gaining
equipment for reconstruction from the western zones. There
was a dialectic involved in slowing Russian reconstruction
and leaving western German industry inviolate: it had the
direct effect, if not the intention, of telling the Russians that
the United States preferred to rebuild a stable industrial
Germany than to help the Soviet allies recover from an ex-
hausting war. If subsidies would contribute to multilateralism, the Americans were willing to finance Germany; but
they would hold back on the USSR. The United States
favored German stability over Russian reconstruction to
such an extent that it would, in fact, virtually sacrifice the
eastern zone of Germany to achieve this end. To be sure,
this policy was not consonant with American fears of a
renascent Reich. Although the U.S. position was anti-Soviet,
it was not pro-German. Americans were not anxious in the
summer of 1945 to rebuild Germany as a major industrial
power, and here we must examine the second argument
advanced in the usual analysis.

Historians have maintained that U.S. diplomats opposed
reparations from current production because they would
lead to the creation of an industrial Germany with many
nations dependent on it. But it is also a mistake to view this
fact in isolation. The debate concerning imports and not
reparations being a "first charge" on exports involved the
status of the German international trade position in a subtle
way. What troubled the Americans was not simply that current production reparations might make Germany an industrial competitor of the United States. Rather, these
reparations would hinder the construction of the global system in which Germany was to play a role; in supplying free

goods when the world political economy was in a precarious state, Germany might get a head start in securing and retaining international markets, and might be led to autarchy. Equally dangerous was the possibility that current production reparations would create bilateral trade relations between the Soviets and the Germans. Germany might become the supplier of heavy industry to the Russians and be drawn into their economic orbit. These reparations imperilled multilateralism, the very heart of American policy, and in so doing presaged a threat to American security interests.

I have argued that in order to grasp the underlying nexus of American policy on reparations we must modify the usual interpretation. The United States did not want to support a depressed German economy, but this desire was a fragment of a program structured to coerce the Russians to yield to U.S. aims (or, if that failed, to oppose Russian reconstruction) and to secure a degree of German strength. Similarly, we must see the American desire to limit reparations from current production in terms of its larger implications: curtailing these reparations would enable the Americans to control and regulate German industrial growth when the Russians threatened its control and regulation. American policy was designed to force Russia to accede to multilateralism in the east and to secure it in the west.

But in a sense another aspect of this explanation holds the key to the reparations question. Herbert Feis writes that if the Russians succeeded in their demands, and the United States did not support the Germans, the Americans would be obliged "to witness prolonged misery and discontent in Germany; or to agree to the exercise of state controls of German economic life which would ease the way toward Communism." [8] Commenting on the Soviet renunciation of dismemberment in a more speculative passage, Feis theorizes: "Perhaps—who is to know?—Soviet aims reached even beyond this to the idea that if Germany was allowed to remain whole, and the awful destruction continued, it might be easier to bring it under communial domination later on."[9] In one sense it is exaggeration to argue that a fear of a Soviet takeover motivated American policy. The Russians had enormous reconstruction requirements and were not equipped to embark on expansion into western Europe. The United States occupied the position of strength, wielding overwhelming economic power in addition to controlling the secret of the atomic bomb. Finally, there is reason to believe that Stalin wanted to continue Allied unity: he feared German resurgence and needed American financial credits. At Yalta he had commented:

They all knew that as long as the three of them lived none of them would involve their countries in aggressive actions. . . . He said the main thing was to prevent quarrels in the future between the three Great Powers and that the task, therefore, was to secure their unity for the future. . . . He said the greatest danger was conflict between the three Great Powers represented here, but that if unity could be preserved there was little danger of the renewal of German aggression.[10]

It is worthwhile in this context to quote Stalin's statement to the Polish minister Stanislaw Mikolajczyk that "communism fitted Germany as a saddle fitted a cow." Remarking on this, Isaac Deutscher writes:

It harmonized so perfectly with the whole trend of his policy *vis-a-vis* Germany, it was so spontaneous, so organic, so much in line with what we know of this old disbelief in western European communism, and it accorded so much with all that he said and did in those days, that it could not have been sheer tactical bluff.[11]

It is difficult to believe that Stalin actually planned to take over Germany or that the United States felt he had this expansionist ambition. Indirectly, however, Feis has made an important point. Because the United States regarded the establishment of multilateralism as central to its foreign policy, it could hardly regard with equanimity the emergence of noncapitalist Russia as a great power, particularly when the prostrate economic, social, and political condition of Europe could only produce movement to the left. In a sense, we may construe U.S. diplomacy as a response to the danger it saw in the existence of the Soviet system and to the possibility that, favored by the Russians, systems like theirs would spread with postwar upheavals.

To this explanatory pattern we must add an historical dimension: the reparations experience of World War I influenced the attitudes of American diplomats in 1945. Of course, it would take another book to explore the way their vision of the past shaped their diplomacy. But this prior experience acted to sanction the moves Americans made in 1945. And this is not surprising if we consider the substance of U.S. policy from 1917 to 1919. As recent historians have pointed out, the desire to establish worldwide liberal capitalism propelled all of Wilson's diplomacy.[12] This ideal nurtured multilateralism in the twenties and thirties. After World War I, Wilsonians saw reparations as interfering with the ideal, destroying Wilson's plan for a contented, non-militaristic Germany and, in part, causing the collapse of the international economy in the early thirties. The economic misery to which payment of reparations contributed could have driven the Germans to Communism, and the fear of "Bolshevization" was a vital component in Wilson's views; instead, unwise reparations played a role in Ger-

many's turn toward the other extreme—Nazism. Diplomatic
memories might have moved U.S. decision makers at Potsdam, but they were simply one facet of the historical context that produced the multilateral persuasion.

What kind of reparations policy did the Americans pursue
elsewhere? In the early fall of 1944 the United States evolved
procedures in Rumania and Hungary that illuminate what
occurred in Germany.[13] The USSR controlled the Balkans,
and because there the United States only responded to Soviet maneuvers, issues were clear cut. The Americans quickly
grasped the principles fundamental to understanding the
reparations question in eastern Europe, and these principles
are consonant with those ignored in explanations of the German situation.

In taking the predominant role in the Rumanian negotiations, the Russians repeatedly cited the precedent in Italy,
where the Americans and the British, doing the fighting, excluded the Soviets from participation in the surrender. The
Americans admitted the justifiability of the Russian procedure, and the USSR assumed control of the Allied Control
Commission. Two weeks before the armistice was signed in
Moscow on September 13, 1944, the Soviets asked for $300
million in reparations from Rumania. Although the Americans, under Harriman's leadership, were against setting a
sum because Allied policy was "undetermined," they nevertheless acquiesced. But Secretary of State Hull's cable to
Harriman indicated the wary American attitude: the United
States did not feel its agreement established "a precedent in
any way for the reparations settlement with Germany or
any other satellite countries." [14]

A month later the USSR demanded $400 million from

Hungary, also attempting to bow out of the war, and Hull again informed Harriman of the State Department's concern for reparations.[15] This time the United States was not willing to give in so easily.

Although America had interests in Rumanian oil, they were minimal. But Standard Oil of New Jersey controlled the oil industry in Hungary. These oil fields were in the developmental stage before the war, but by this time they had "become significant." [16] Standard wrote the State Department concerning its interests on October 20, and three weeks later a representative of the company put pressure on the Department. He asked what measures the United States had devised to govern the use of the oil products that the USSR would receive from Hungary as reparations. He feared that the Soviet demands might have "an adverse effect upon American oil interests in Hungary." The departmental official who saw the Standard representative was noncommittal,[17] but the Americans had already decided what to do.

Stettinius was now Secretary, and Harriman urged Washington to remain adamant that the Russians name no specific sum; the United States should "refuse to yield even at the risk of a breakdown of negotiations." Stettinius was not willing to go so far as Harriman, but he did advise the Ambassador to sign the armistice with a reservation concerning the power the United States would have on the Russian-dominated Allied Control Commission. The Americans would allow the USSR to exact a sum in reparations if they could have an equal voice with the Soviets in determining how it was exacted. The Russians refused to concede this point; they would run the Control Commission, and its economic section handling reparations, as they pleased. The

United States then reserved the right to reopen the question of how the Control Commission would carry out its policies.[18]

There was much room for a discussion of boundary disputes and definitions in the Rumanian and Hungarian negotiations. But Washington did not bring up these secondary matters, as it did later in the German situation. In Germany, where the Americans had more control, they argued that the Allies could justify a jointly administered reparations program only if there were agreement on these irrelevant questions. When the USSR was in control, the Americans claimed a joint program was necessary to protect American interest in the restoration of liberal trade on an international basis and in Hungary's investment and trade.[19] Harriman emphasized the crucial point: "Whoever controls reparations deliveries could practically control the Hungarian economy and exercise an important economic influence in other directions." He was so impressed by the relevance of reparations to control of economic matters that he suggested economic coercion to obtain U.S. aims. The Americans should explain to the Russians that lack of cooperation could not help but "affect the final Lend-Lease settlement adversely to the Soviet interest." But, as we have noted, the State Department declined to raise the issue of Lend Lease in connection with this discussion.[20]

Another aspect of these negotiations illuminates the mainsprings of American policy in Germany. Regarding both Rumania and Hungary, Hull and his associates reasoned that the central issue was "the economic relationships of the reparations paying and receiving countries." Therefore, the Big Three should jointly decide on settlements with enemy countries. They should not treat reparations "unilaterally" but rather approach them "as related parts of a broad problem." More than once Hull implied that this should be the procedure in Germany.[21] The eastern European developments underscored "the need for early tripartite agreement" on reparations.[22] The Department argued that "genuinely tripartite administration of the reparations program" was the "crux" of the problems in Rumania and Hungary.[23] Stettinius reaffirmed this view when he informed the President that the United States might sign the Hungarian armistice terms with reservations. The United States would present to the Russians "the American position" that reparations be treated "generally on a tripartite basis." [24] Only this procedure would enable the British and the Americans to have an "equal interest" in the "economic stability" of the eastern European countries.[25]

The striking contrast between this conception and the zonal reparation plan calling specifically *for* unilateral action points to one conclusion: where the United States was in control, it was determined to retain control; where another exercised control, the United States demanded equal representation. In this respect we may analyze U.S. policy in terms of what William A. Williams has argued is an enduring component of its diplomacy: the American desire to maintain its dominance in those areas where it exercises influence and to obtain an "open door" in those areas where influence is exercised by others.[26]

In dealing with Germany, the Americans refused to operate on what we may call the realities of the Russian position—the need to rebuild, the fear of a resurgent Reich, and the desire to form an entente with the West. Instead, United States policy makers emphasized the Russian attempt to establish a sphere of influence in the east and what they felt was the ideological evil of this sphere of influence. They did not comprehend that for those who did not share their cultural outlook, their demand for multilateralism was equivalent to United States hegemony throughout the world. Although reparations is only one strand in a complicated fabric of policy made by the United States at the end of the war, because the issue was bound up with the place of Germany in the postwar order and the relation of the West to Russia, the issue epitomizes the dynamics of American strategy.

What emerges clearly from a study of U.S. reparations policy is American responsibility for the division of Germany (a condition I do not regard as an evil) and perhaps for a rigid and hostile division of Europe. Did the United States *cause* the division? I am unwilling to use the word "cause" unless we can assert that in other possible situations the victors would not have divided Germany. Since we can only speculate on what would have happened if the Americans had not pursued the policies they did, our ability to talk about causation is limited. I think great-power cooperation could have occurred in different circumstances. Judicious compromises might have eased great-power tensions, and the Allies might have neutralized Germany, or at least divided it in a cooperative fashion. While the Russians were concerned with securing a sphere of influence east of Germany, U.S. intransigence on Germany and pressure for multilateralism in eastern Europe possibly moved the USSR to more unyielding policies in some of these countries: the policy of economic coercion may have forced the Soviets to tighten up their control. As William Hardy McNeil has written, "the termination of Lend-Lease and Mutual Aid meant an abrupt return to an almost completely autarkic economic system . . . and the Russian Government did not hesitate to plunder . . . in order to relieve somewhat the terrible poverty which afflicted the Russian people themselves." [27] The concomitant future emphasis on heavy industry and armament in Russia may have made the Soviet more independent than it otherwise would have been. If these conjectures have any basis, I think we can at least state that the United States did cause the *kind* of division that occurred; that is, the Americans shaped the pattern of the early Cold War in Europe. They may not have *caused* the division of Germany—if they had behaved differently, partition of some sort or another might still have occurred— but they did cause Germany to be partitioned in the hostile way that it was; and perhaps they also caused the rigid division of Europe.

The Americans may have thought that if *they* yielded in eastern Europe, *they* would have surrendered to the Soviet; but subsequent events have shown that the United States can thrive even if half of Germany and all of eastern Europe are Communist. It is much more doubtful that the USSR could have survived if the United States had had its way in eastern Germany and eastern Europe. The Americans confronted the Soviet with a real threat; the Soviet threat in east-central Europe was real only in a multilateral world.

It is peculiar that some decision makers at the highest level did not comprehend or could not admit that the policies they devised for Germany would have the opposite consequences from those they envisaged. While men at the "expert" level analyzed the situation correctly, many higher ranking figures continued to operate on multilateral premises. The full meaning of Potsdam diplomacy influenced their outlook slowly. Certainly they were unwilling to permit Russian control over the eastern zone.[28] On the contrary, with their enormous economic resources and the diplomatic power of the atomic bomb, many still thought they could control all of Europe. They grasped some of the consequences of zonal reparations and hedged their policy so that the eventual treatment of Germany as a unit was not precluded. If the USSR had capitulated, as the Americans appear to have expected and hoped, they could unite Germany on terms satisfactory to them. As Truman told a member of the military in June, the United States "held all the cards and . . . the Russians had to come to us." Truman made it very clear that "he proposed to play them as American cards."[29]

In this respect we must view U.S. strategy as an enormous error—not a tactical mistake, but rather a basic intellectual failing. From an historical perspective, it is clear that the Americans were in no position to force Russian submission in eastern Germany or substantial compromises in eastern Europe. After the Americans had defined the issues as they had, only Soviet surrender could have prevented a dismembered Germany.

I have found it impossible to measure this lack of realism with any precision or to specify for just how long American diplomats believed the Russians would come around. The problem is complicated by the fact that the attempt to coerce an ally into accepting multilateralism was imperceptively transformed into a policy of slowing the reconstruction of a hostile power. Nonetheless, during 1945, Truman, Byrnes, Harriman, and Clayton—to name some of the most important—believed a multilateral world possible.

A more reasonable appraisal was made later, but even through 1946, as we shall see, many officials thought a policy of economic coercion would work.

The Americans did not recognize the limitations of their power and, therefore, the larger significance their policy would have. The sophistication with which they approached the Soviet attempt at reconstruction was matched by blindness about their ability to force concessions from the USSR after the war ended and the armies drew international boundaries.

William Appleman Williams has called this misapprehension of the power realities "the vision of omnipotence." [30] In 1944, Harriman stated an appraisal that he long retained. "I am satisfied," he said, "that in the last analysis Stalin will back down." [31] Although a few diplomats initially expressed doubt about this opinion, it gradually became the consensus. Albert Z. Carr, an associate of Donald Nelson, War Production Board chairman, made the point when he asserted that many in the State Department believed that "Russia could not survive economically without our aid." [32] Joseph Davies, however, appraised the situation correctly. He said that if the United States got tough with the Soviets and did not give them aid, they would survive without it; the USSR, he declared, had already gotten along without the Americans for twenty-eight years. [33]

The various coercive devices the Americans were willing to use were not sufficient to realize their goals. In clinging to their idea of a world politico-economic system dominated by the United States, the Americans negated the possibility of any sort of cooperative regional arrangement with the USSR. In the last analysis, Harriman was wrong.

8 Patterns of the Early Occupation Period

General Lucius Clay, appointed the deputy military governor for the U.S. zone, took command in Germany in April 1945; he had not previously seen any version of the Treasury-inspired occupation directive, JCS 1067, nor had he conferred with State Department officials about it. When he examined one version of the document in late April, he was shocked by its "failure to grasp the realities of the financial and economic conditions." The provisions of JCS 1067, Clay recalled, "contemplated the Carthaginian peace which dominated our operations in Germany during the early months of occupation."[1] At Clay's request his financial adviser, Lewis Douglas, returned to Washington in July to secure modification of the directive. When he failed, Douglas resigned.[2] In October, Clay himself returned to Washington to discuss what he recalled in his memoirs as a revision of JCS 1067, and what was at least a discussion of his German policy, a policy aimed at rebuilding the German economy. Although Clay may have been mistaken about revision, he recollected that the policy makers in Washington with whom he discussed the issue held views on Germany similar to his own and that they commented favorably on his suggestions. The general also remembered that the head of the drafting committee was confident that the U.S. government

would have a new directive in a few weeks. The new document, however, did not materialize, and American diplomats did not make formal policy modifications until July
1947, nearly two years later.*

Although we lack an explanation for the delay in Washington, it is clear that no matter what Clay recalled about a
"Carthaginian peace," no one in Washington was thinking
in terms of the Treasury intent of JCS 1067, and few in Germany were executing it.

Those governing the defeated nation argued almost without exception that their program of military government
should reactivate a German peace economy as quickly as
possible. Even before the defeat in May, an important State
Department adviser considered Clay's views extreme in
their advocacy of reconstructing Germany. If the military
took this position "without any immediate reference to long-
range security and other objectives," it might precipitate
"a revival of the opposite doctrine," i.e., the Treasury policy.[3] In June 1945, Clay impressed an official on the Reparation Commission with the idea that JCS 1067 would be "laid
on ice for a considerable period of months."[4]

On a practical level, the general made his own decisions

* See Clay, pp. 72–73; U.S. Department of State, *Bulletin* (2
December 1945), p. 855; and U.S. Congress, Senate, Sub-Committee
of the Committee on Military Affairs, *Elimination of German Resources for War, Hearings* (Washington, 1945), pp. 1057–1058, for
evidence that the government was thinking about revision; the State
Department records for Clay's October visit apparently no longer exist.
John Gimbel, who has had access to the military records, argues that
Clay's memory was faulty and that no one was contemplating revision at the time. See Gimbel's *The American Occupation of Germany, Politics and the Military, 1945–1949* (Stanford, 1968), pp. 18–
34. I discuss below why the Americans may have kept JCS 1067 in
nominal effect so long.

in Germany but observed formalities and accepted JCS 1067 as a broad guide. In effect, as one scholar-observer has pointed out, he followed the middle of the road policy of the German Country Unit, whose manual FDR had censored, and of Washington, that is, the State Department.[5] Clay himself wrote that some of the provisions of JCS 1067 were general in nature and that others were changed in favor of moderation at Potsdam; they allowed his "discretion." The Potsdam modifications, Clay reported, charged the United States with the development of a balanced economy, placing Germany on a self-sustaining basis.[6]

General William Draper, an associate of Clay's in Germany and head of the Economics Directorate, was as uncompromising as his chief. At an American Military Government staff meeting in May he emphasized that his directorate would be concerned with the conversion and not destruction of wartime industries suitable for peacetime production. The destruction of large cities and armament plants by the war, he went on, had achieved "a considerable part of the program for industrial disarmament." The present plan was to get enough production going to avoid chaos and to devise long-range controls to prevent the revival of war production.[7]

Clay's assistant, James Pollock, summed up the strategy in the middle of 1947:

Actually we did have a policy—the ill-fated 1067, but it was the wrong policy. Military Government cannot be blamed for this. Military Government did however in the day to day battle with the actual situation evolve practices which Mr. Byrnes finally in his Stuttgart speech [of September 1946] elevated to a new policy. What we found in practice to be sound, finally became the policy. . . .[8]

In the daily routine, lower echelon authorities seem to have operated on the military expedient of making a viable economy function again. Lamenting the limitations of the denazification program, Elmer Plishke, an official American historian, has testified to this fact. JCS 1067 was not declassified until October 1945. The U.S. government kept the document in the top-secret classification for so long, he said, "that it never did obtain very wide circulation" at lower military levels. It was at these levels that officers would have required a thorough familiarity with general policy "in order to institute an effective occupation," that is, one in conformity with JCS 1067. Military officials, he claimed, were indoctrinated with the principle that they should contribute to the army's efficiency and were prompted into "getting things going again." [9] But we do not have enough information to get a statistically accurate account of what the lower ranks were doing in occupied areas. The available information suggests that Treasury policy was far from the minds of personnel. An official in Bavaria was quoted as saying, "What's our policy in Germany? . . . Brother, I don't know . . . they snow me under with all sorts of papers. How'm I going to read them when I'm doing forty-eleven different things to get this burg running again." [10]

As William Harlan Hale, a ranking military government authority, put it, the Americans were "specialists at making things go."

The Civil Affairs field detachments contain many veterans of American city administration—ex-mayors, fire chiefs, social service workers, sanitary engineers. . . . They seemed to see their job . . . as one . . . of quickly restoring some sort of civil order out of chaos. As one watched their teams go into city after city, attempting above all to bring back normal life to a devastated area, one got the impression of a large number of welfare workers whose approach to the Germans resembled that which they might have made to the victims of a great flood in the Mississippi.[11]

Wolfgang Friedmann, a high-level British official, described policy succinctly. All three Western powers, he said, "preserved in its essentials, the social and economic system which they found. They have eliminated many of its most objectionable features, but hardly touched the foundations." [12]

In Washington, Clay's superiors backed his program. By the time Truman dismissed Morgenthau in July 1945, policy was securely in the hands of the War and State Departments, whose only disagreement was over the zone commander's authority. At Potsdam the State Department resolved this dispute by supporting zonal autonomy to prohibit Soviet influence in the western zones. This entente enabled Washington to agree on policies and to support military practice on a diplomatic level.

James W. Riddleberger, the top State Department expert on Germany, accurately summed up American policy at the end of 1945 and showed its congruence with what the army was doing. "For the most part," he said, "the industrial reconversion of Germany is still in the survey state and will take time." "Meanwhile the terrific devastation wrought by the war upon the German economy is adequate insurance against any immediate threat of revived war power." "The great need," Riddleberger argued, was "not for imposing further curbs but for rebuilding to meet the most urgent needs if disaster not only for Germany but for Europe is to be averted." [13]

John McCloy of the War Department praised Clay's program. He recalled that whenever the general came to an unworkable clause of JCS 1067, he whittled away at it "empirically and piecemeal," and worked out something like a recovery program using the standard military formula of preventing "disease and unrest." [14] After his trip to Europe in November 1945, McCloy reiterated that the United States had to take constructive measures in Germany.[15] Early in 1946 he declared that "it will be a struggle to get *some* economic life going." The danger did not lie in the tendency toward loose controls or even ultimate revival, but in *"immediate* prostration and a state of *permanent* desolation." Although the Americans had to do considerable work on "basic reconstruction," they had already fulfilled the short-range objectives of JCS 1067, prevention of German resurgence.[16] As long-range goals always concerned the State Department, they now concerned McCloy.

If diplomats were committed to the implementation of the War-State program, and if army officers executed positive policies, why did the early postwar years look so weird and chaotic to so many critics? Why, as one scholar has asserted, was recovery nonexistent and the occupation a major scandal of the period? [17] The answer lies in the unrealistic optimism of State Department planning. The policies aimed at achieving German participation in multilateralism were ineffective, and American decision makers did not come to grips with the magnitude of the reconstruction problem until work on the Marshall Plan was under way. In retrospect, Roosevelt's desire not to make commitments until the Allies got into Germany appears to have been wiser than the simplistic aim of many who surrounded him. Some of the Americans were so fixated on their utopia that they were oblivious to the chaos of 1945 and 1946.

The situation in Germany was part of the economic and social disruption that the war had brought to Europe. Conditions were anarchic, and the measures the Americans took to restore stability, no matter how great they thought them, were of little help. A few statistics make this clear. In March 1946 the Allies set the limit of German steel production at a maximum of 5.8 million tons, a figure regarded by most observers as much too low. But at the end of 1946 steel production for the year was slightly over 3 million tons, two-thirds of this from the Ruhr.[18] By July 1947, when there was no hint of Morgenthauist policies, the Ruhr steel industries, providing the great bulk of German output, had an annual production rate of only 2.5 million tons.[19] Coal output per man-shift in the Ruhr was 1.547 tons in 1938; in 1946 it had dropped to 0.860 and had not increased materially by the end of 1947.[20] The state of the German economy was more catastrophic than the Treasury Department hoped, and remained in that condition long after the Americans began reconstruction and long after they dropped any pretence at securing a "peace of vengeance."

Germany's status as the principal enemy created additional problems for the defeated nation. Although calling for its reconstruction and integration into a world system, State policy subordinated the Reich's reconstruction to that of the rest of western Europe. The Americans would suppress German consumption in the initial postwar period and export its coal to northwest Europe and the Mediterranean. This program "during the period of critical coal shortage" would "delay the resumption of economic activity in Germany"; German needs had priority only to ensure the safety and health of the occupying forces.[21] Washington carried out this plan; until the latter part of 1946, when they used more coal in Germany itself, Britain and the United States diverted to export coal that normally went for internal consumption.[22] As originally conceived, this strategy would play a part in the restoration of the European economy. The policy would retard the rehabilitation of Germany but would not compromise its ultimate return to industrial strength; indeed, the policy would assure it. Nevertheless, the war's effect on Europe was so disastrous that the diversion of coal complicated German problems and did not help the liberated areas.

The State Department had also called for the immediate rehabilitation of those aspects of German industry necessary to the increase of coal export. Again, the Americans overestimated the rapidity with which they could achieve their aims. Allied bombing strategy had three principal objectives: demolishing selected industrial targets, wrecking the transportation system, and destroying civilian morale. Thirteen and one-half per cent of the total bombing tonnage was directed against German industry, 32 per cent against transportation, and 24 per cent against large cities. As the United States Strategic Bombing Survey argued, the Allies did not attempt to destroy the German economy, or even the war economy, as a whole. The bombing offensive sought rather to stop it from operating by damaging key points, and destroying selected industries accomplished this goal. More significant was the obliteration of the transportation system—"the most important single cause of Germany's ultimate economic collapse."

The Western Allies designed the attacks on German cities to undermine morale, particularly that of the industrial worker. "In sheer destructiveness," the U.S. Strategic Bombing Survey reported, "these raids far outstripped all other forms of attack." They demolished or heavily damaged 20 per cent of Germany's total residential units, and left 7.5 million Germans homeless.[23] Under these conditions the Americans had a limited ability to restore conditions enabling Germany to export coal. Transportation remained disrupted, and homeless and war-torn people made poor workers. The State Department Intelligence Service reported that at the end of 1945 the primary problem of the Ruhr coal industry was labor and transportation; the mines were in good condition and there was enough electricity.[24]

A last obstacle to U.S. policies was the stress on zonal autonomy. Four military sectors were not one unitary state, and the dis-integration of the German economy was bound to take place in air-tight zones. These circumstances would have prohibited the interzonal trade necessary to the functioning of a *single* Germany even if industry were active and transport functioning.[25]

The economy was in a state of suspended animation. The best German summary of the situation at the end of 1944 indicated that collapse had become evident "only in the field of transportation." [26] After the war overall damage to industrial equipment and plant, in comparison to 1936, does not appear to have exceeded 10 per cent.[27] In 1947, Eugene V. Rostow estimated that except for the areas lost to Poland, the German economy had a *greater* capacity in all the crucial categories—machine tools, locomotives, steel, and engineering—than in 1939. "Wartime increases in capacity," he wrote, "were greater than bombing losses." [28] The State Department reported that the Allies could make the industrial repairs quickly and that Germany would be ready to wage full-scale war.[29] Henry Fowler, director of the Enemy Branch of the FEA, asserted in June 1945 that "the most important single fact about Germany today is the size and range of the existing German industrial plant. . . . It had been geared for total war and can be geared again; the bone, muscle, and sinew of the economic industrial war-power that nearly conquered the world is still in existence." [30] At the same time, Reparation Ambassador Pauley toured Germany before going to Moscow. Despite the arguments he made to the Russians, Pauley left Germany with the impression that "a large part of German industry is either intact or can readily be repaired within a few months." [31] But without an operating transportation system and a supply of efficient labor, Germany remained in a state of paralysis.

However the state of the German economy might affect U.S. plans, at the beginning of the occupation the American military was more eager than the State Department to compromise with the Russians in solving common problems. The United States had put off discussion of reparations, the basic question, and Soviet-American negotiations during 1945 concerned many matters on which the powers agreed in the glow of conquest. Immediate difficulties lay in the refusal of the French, under the unanimity rule, to allow the Control Council to establish the central administrative agencies essential for a unified Germany. The Russians supported the United States against France, and the public reports of the American Military Governor singled them out for praise. [32] The French position on unification was the greatest problem for four-power harmony until the early spring of 1946. [33] As late as April, Major General Oliver Echols, the new head of the War Department's Civil Affairs Division, testified that French intransigence thwarted all policies for a centralized Germany. [34] The obvious question to ask is why Britain and the United States allowed France to obstruct unification. The French government had little prestige and attained its status as an occupying power only late in the war at Anglo-American sufferance. Its zone of occupation consisted of two triangular pieces cut from the British and American zones, and the French economy depended on the coal that it obtained from the British-controlled Ruhr. Either the other Western Allies could have forced France into line or they could have unified Germany without the French. Eventually Britain and the United States did amalgamate their zones without France, and still later they compelled it to join them.[35]

Clay believed that the United States had to exert pressure on France, but he did not have the leverage: the State Department wielded diplomatic weapons. But repeated War Department attempts to have State use what the Secretary of War termed "all requisite pressures" on France had little effect.[36] After some urging by Clay, the State Department authorized him to negotiate with Britain and Russia on creating central administrative agencies. At that time, however, neither power would contravene the Potsdam Protocol, which demanded unanimous policy by the four nations.[37] In late November and December, Secretary Byrnes formally suggested to the French that unification might proceed without them, but subsequent War Department protests into the spring of 1946 indicate that the State Department was not willing to go further.[38]

Why did State take this position? Why did Washington treat the French so gently while it did bring "all requisite pressures" to bear on the Soviets? Even if we cannot give conclusive answers to these questions, some explanation is possible.

Although the weakness of the French might suggest that

they were an easy target for American diplomacy, this was not the case at all. France was *so* weak that the United States feared pressure might result in the collapse of the moderate French political regime and triumph of the Left. The French government needed aid to relieve a desperate economic situation and to demonstrate to the French electorate the government's effectiveness, that is, its ability to get money from the United States. By February 1946, Jefferson Caffrey, the American ambassador in France, urged that Washington weigh a proposed loan to the French in terms of its "political importance." To refuse it would be to pull away "one of the last props of substance" from those who wanted "to see France remain an independent and democratic country." By April, Caffrey believed that the French Communists would benefit in the June elections if the United States did not grant a loan.[39] And Byrnes linked the issues directly with Bidault.[40] The Americans were again using economic means to achieve political ends. But in choosing to influence French domestic politics, they were less able to shape her diplomacy.

If the threat of the Left was one reason for the United States to support France without extracting a *quid pro quo*, another issue also explains American reluctance to pressure France. The crucial problem for the future of Allied diplomacy in Germany was reparations, and the Allies had deferred determining them under the Potsdam accord: within six months of August 1, 1945, the Control Council was to arrive at a "level of industry" plan and to agree on the structure of the peacetime German economy and the "amount and character" of industry that the military would remove from the western zones. A satisfactory solution to the question of economic unity was dependent on the

Russian attitude, and until this attitude became clear, French intransigence was not critical. It may be true that the French view allowed the Russians temporarily to consolidate their position in the eastern zone, and in fact U.S. diplomats believed this was so.[41] But this belief did not lead them to coerce France. The State Department seems to have felt that French policies were a minor consideration in its German strategy. The position of France would not prevent a settlement if the Soviets capitulated to U.S. goals; if the Russians would not yield—and the Americans would not learn this until late March 1946—French obstructiveness would matter little to the fate of Germany.

To bring the Russians to the negotiating table, the State Department, as in the earlier part of 1945, appears to have been committed to a policy of economic coercion, effected by what I have called the strategy of delay. Pressure on the Soviets would hopefully force them to reach a détente with the Americans. Thus, although the USSR wanted to discuss reparations at the first session of the September foreign ministers' meeting, Byrnes stated that he would not take up the issue. He did argue that the military should expedite the determination of the amount and character of removals, and instructed Clay to "proceed urgently" on the problem.[42] A month later the American general was told that the U.S. government had used no leverage on the French. When he said France would frustrate American policy, State Department officials advised him that "it was not clear that the Soviets intended to carry out the political and economic principles of the Berlin protocol." [43]

Multilateralism was a global policy. The U.S. commitment to subsidizing the French government so that it could participate in this system prevented the Americans from using aid as a tool to coerce the French to help secure multilateral goals in Germany. But the basic problem in Germany was not France but Russia. The Americans could defer dealing with the French until the USSR clarified its position.*

Creating a level of industry plan was one of the central tasks the Potsdam conferees had given to the Control Council. It was to come up with an inter-Allied plan for the defeated country by February 1946. As matters turned out, the military was nearly two months late in producing a plan, although from August 1945 through March 1946 ranking occupation officials spent much time discussing the future German economy. The essential idea was that the military authorities would define the economic structure of the new Germany: there would be a balance of industry and agriculture, and of exports and imports. German heavy industry would be reduced and the light industry increased. The excess heavy industry would be distributed among the victors as reparations, and the first-charge principle would finally go into effect for all Germany. Thus, those working out the level of industry plan were dealing with the two critical problems—export-import balance and reparations—that had stymied diplomats at Potsdam. From the U.S. point of view

* It may be that the Americans formally kept JCS 1067 in effect for reasons of this sort. If they reached accord with the Soviet on economic matters, the powers would carry out a strictly controlled program for a "demilitarized" Germany; by not discarding JCS 1067, the U.S. government may have been indicating that it had not ruled out a "severe" policy toward Germany. But if the Allies reached no settlement, the western zones would need a concentrated industrial structure, and on a practical level the Americans did nothing to make a concentrated structure impossible. They replaced JCS 1067 ten days after the Russians had walked out of the Marshall Plan discussions and Allied disharmony became public.

the (original) six-month delay might make the Soviets more amenable to negotiating on American terms; and the delay would at least preserve the industrial integrity of the western zones. In retrospect, all the negotiating that led up to the plan seems foolish. By stressing the zone commander's authority the way they did, the Americans at Potsdam had —although not in their own eyes—almost precluded interzonal cooperation thereafter; by emphasizing their ideal of the way the German economy should function, the Americans almost guaranteed that the USSR would not agree to any plan; and by taking an unrealistic view of Europe's political and economic situation, the Americans—as well as the other powers—pressed for a plan that, as we shall see, appears unrealistic even on paper, although cooperation broke down before the powers tried to implement it.

By August 12, 1945, ten days after the end of the Potsdam Conference, Pauley was in Moscow in what Truman described as "another—futile—attempt" to reach agreement on reparations with the Soviets. Pauley had already concluded, Clay recalled, that a satisfactory solution was impossible.[44] When Pauley and his staff departed for the United States, they left only a few documents in Berlin. The Americans in Germany responsible for reparations received no further instructions for months. The U.S. government did not appoint Pauley's successor until late October 1945. Although it granted the new ambassador broad powers, he did not arrive until January 1946, when the U.S. version of the level of industry plan was nearly in final form.[45]

If the Allies could work out an overall plan for Germany, they could dismantle more industry for reparations than if each power ran a separate economy. In the latter case each zone would leave a substantial amount of industry standing. The memorandum that Pauley did write for the Americans recognized these alternatives. Washington should submit its own program for removals from Germany *as a whole* to the Allied Control Council on the February 2 deadline, even though he thought that the Allies *would not* agree to the program the Americans would call for: Pauley said that this program should be based on the needs of the U.S. zone, and therefore removals should not be extensive. If the powers did not assent to the plan immediately, the Americans should introduce safety measures for running their zone independently. When the Allies later reached accord, the United States could revise its unilateral plan in favor of greater removals and a quadripartite treatment.[46]

The military was more committed to working out a joint reparations scheme with the Soviets. The American Economics Directorate attempted a judicious appraisal of the kind and amount of industrial equipment necessary to maintain a minimal standard of living in a hypothetical economy. Any industry not needed for this economy would be dismantled and distributed among the various nations. In devising their program, the Americans tried to collaborate with the Russians; [47] this attempt apparently reflected Clay's attitude that the French and not the Soviets were troublesome in Germany. The military policy was a retreat from Potsdam, where the Americans insisted on zonal primacy, and came closer to Molotov's desire that the Allies work out reparations on a compromise basis.[48]

When the State Department issued a general policy statement on Germany in December 1945, the document indicated no disagreement with the military line. But there was also no retreat from the American goals. After the exaction of reparations, the State Department hoped that the German economy would exist without external assistance, that is, it should have no balance of payments problem. No provisions were made, however, for an export-import balance in the immediate future; the Americans would attempt to preserve only the potential for this balance, and they might not establish a minimum standard of living until all of Europe was in a normal condition. Until then Germany would receive U.S. support, and in effect the Americans once more stated their willingness to subsidize the Germans *if* this would promote multilateralism. As the State Department pointed out, "it is our desire to see Germany's economy geared to a world system and not an autarchical system."

In a statement made to accompany the departmental declaration, Byrnes outlined how this would occur. Through the spring of 1946, Germany would make its maximum contribution to European recovery, meaning that it would export coal. After the Allies had decided on the reparations program, Germany's recovery would take place within its new balanced economy while removals occurred. When the Allies finished dismantling two years later, any limitations they imposed on industrial production would be connected with the prevention of rearmament and "not to restrict or reduce the German standard of living." [49]

In opposition to U.S. aims, the Soviet government ordered its representatives on the Control Council to achieve the lowest industrial levels obtainable. The lower the level of the postwar German economy, the more industry the Western powers would dismantle for the USSR. And the Russians were apparently instructed to demand a level of industry that would generate a pre-1933 German standard of living. They chose the depression year of 1930, and from the industry needed to maintain that standard the Russians additionally subtracted all industry that produced for export.[50] Thus the USSR advocated programs that differed widely from those of the other three powers. The Americans based their calculations on the need to eliminate certain strategic industries, to maintain a standard of living which did not exceed that of the central European countries, and to establish minimal import requirements;[51] from the American perspective this strategy represented a genuine effort to come to terms with Russia. If the Allies were to regard a level of industry plan as an actual basis for a German economy, there was little room for compromise on the interrelated industrial capacities. But the Americans were not interested in, and from their point of view could not contemplate, giving the Russians dismantled equipment of the magnitude the Soviet desired. The Russians, on their side, had no desire to promote multilateralism.

The outcome of these conflicting aims was a series of trades on various levels of industry. The "swaps" reflected no serious economic thought and little attempt to view the German economy as an integral totality. Within the limits imposed by their vision, the Americans honestly tried to negotiate, and more than once sided with the Soviet to achieve agreement that would foster German unification.

The dispute involving capacities for steel production was symbolic of the manner in which the military formulated the whole plan. The British, who most desired a "soft" peace, wanted a production capacity higher than that wanted by the Russians. After much bargaining, Clay persuaded the English to come from their original figure of 11.0 million tons to a 7.5 million ton limit. At this point the Soviets were willing to come up to a figure of 5.8 million. Under Clay's guidance the four powers acceded to the Soviet figure.[52] This was a considerable compromise for the British, but Clay was adamant in supporting a figure close to the 3.0 million originally proposed by the USSR. His position was motivated by a desire to reach accord with the Russians, and the State Department shared this desire. In a document that went to Clay at the time, the Department suggested a figure of 3.2 million tons, and Clay recalled that this viewpoint influenced him considerably.[53]

During the debate Clay declared to the British that the United States regarded a balanced export-import program as "definitely secondary" to the destruction of war potential. The United States had "no obligation to guarantee a certain standard of living to Germany." When the British representative said that Clay's remarks had a corollary, a "wilderness" in Germany, the American retreated, and argued that this had never been U.S. policy—at home or abroad.[54]

Some authorities have argued that this series of events was the last vestige of a "Morgenthau orientation," [55] but this is an inappropriate way to describe the dynamics of American behavior. U.S. military officials were sometimes as unrealistic about the German economy as the State Department, and they also attempted to reach what they thought was a reasonable agreement with the USSR. Although this lack of realism eventually produced what we might regard as an unsound level of industry plan, the Americans negotiated on the basis of a "balanced export-import program," that is, from a multilateral standpoint.[56] Indeed, within a week of the British remark of a "wilderness" in Germany, Clay and his ranking political assistant, Robert Murphy, reassured the English. And whatever the American rhetoric, the Americans were never willing to *act* in a way that would compromise German industrial strength. Through optimism, the military spokesmen were often conciliatory to the Russians, but a more hardheaded approach intruded when the Americans had to do something concrete. Finally, in all these discussions, we must understand the limited nature of the U.S. compromises. As we shall see, the level of industry plan was never implemented, but even had the dismantling in it occurred, it is doubtful that the Russians would ultimately have consented to the plan. The United States never thought of granting the Russians reparations of the magnitude they wanted.*

All these concerns became important when the four powers concurred on the plan at the end of March 1946, nearly two months after the time limit set at Potsdam. Immediately thereafter, when the Allies tried to execute the plan, hopes for unification collapsed. What made execution of Allied policy impossible was the Potsdam reparations accord.

* For reasons I shall indicate in the next chapter, it is impossible to tell how much the United States would offer the Soviet. If we can use Pauley's July figures as a basis for computation, the USSR would at best get $250 million free of charge. If the Russians were starting from $10 billion and if even Grew had once suggested that the Americans could pay $6 or $7 billion, one gets a feeling for the kind of "compromise" the Americans were now offering. See *FR*, Potsdam, I (1960), 519, and Potsdam, II, 892.

9 Economic Consequences of the Peace, February–May 1946

The Potsdam Protocol implied that after the Allies had decided on the level of industry for Germany, they would determine which industries would remain in the defeated nation and which would be dismantled in the western zones. In implementing the plan, the four powers would evaluate the capital plant in Germany; teams would ascertain the amount and nature of industry left in the eastern zone after Soviet removals and that existing in the western zones. Knowing the total amount of industry in Germany and the total contemplated under the plan, military authorities would remove the difference between the two from the western zones. What was taken would constitute reparations, part of which would go to Russia; what remained would constitute the new German economy. In fact, while the Allies were preparing the plan, the Americans did what they called "token" advance dismantling in accord with the Potsdam Protocol.[1] But the greater the amount the Soviets took from the eastern zone, the greater the amount that would have to remain standing in the western zones. The total German economy would be maintained at a low but agreed level. As the American Economic Directorate argued in January:

In order to determine the amount of reparations available for this purpose, it is necessary to consider, for Germany as a whole, the amount of existing industrial capital equipment, taking into account war damage and removals, and then to compare that amount with the amount necessary to meet the minimum needs of the German peace economy. The excess of existing over required equipment is the amount available for reparations.[2]

The Potsdam Protocol was not so explicit, but if its intent were carried out, the victors would execute some such program for the entire, and not just the western, German economy.[3] The Americans claimed that this kind of plan was the purpose of their negotiations at Berlin, and in early September they informed the Soviet of their viewpoint. The Russians appeared to agree with this interpretation that the Allies would undertake "a common policy." The USSR indicated that it would supply information about equipment in the eastern zone and would give mixed commissions of specialists "the opportunity to become familiar with this equipment on the spot."

Precisely why the Soviets responded in this way is unclear. In the same memorandum they proposed that the Control Council send the mixed commission only to the *western* zones.[4]

The Russians would evidently study the level of industry plan to see if it would give them needed reconstruction goods, but they would not relinquish the rights the United States granted them at Potsdam. Byrnes had again and again told Molotov in Berlin that the Russians could take what they wished from the eastern zone. He had repeatedly made it plain that there were to be no limits imposed on the removals the Soviets could make. But if the occupying powers were to execute a plan for the whole German econ-

omy, the Russians would have to give up their claim to unlimited removals in their zone. In exchange they would receive a percentage of the unneeded industrial equipment
from the western sectors. But the more they had removed
from their own zone, the less there would be available
from those of the others. It was even possible that if the
Russians had removed enough, they would receive nothing
from unification and lose their rights in the east. To give a
simplified example, suppose that the level of industry plan
called for a reduction of the German economy from fourteen
to ten industrial units, and that eight units existed in the
Western-controlled areas. Suppose also that of six units that
originally existed in the eastern area, the Soviets had removed four. The ten remaining units, eight from the west and
the two now in the east, would only be equal to the new
proposed German economy of ten units. The Russians would
gain nothing by accepting the plan and would give up their
right to the remaining units in the Soviet zone.

The situation was probably not so extreme, and had the
Russians acquiesced, they would have gained some of the
industrial equipment from the Ruhr they wanted so badly.
But acquiescence would have entailed the surrender of their
zone to the United States and made the move unlikely, to
say the least.

There were two other complicated aspects of the level of
industry plan that need explanation. First, a plan would produce a minimal German economy where exports balanced
imports. A level of industry plan and a plan for German
foreign trade were one and the same, or at the very least,
had to be considered simultaneously. When the Americans
raised this question, the Russians cited "Section II, Clause
19" of the Potsdam Protocol.[5]

The part of "Section II, Clause 19" relevant here exempted the reparations equipment going to the Russians under a level of industry plan from the first-charge principle that would govern the exports and imports of the new Germany; this principle would apply only to current production reparations in a future German economy under the plan. The United States was responsible for this clause, and it was consistent with the overall American position on Germany that had been arrived at in Berlin. U.S. diplomats had considered that this exemption from the first-charge principle which would govern the new German state was necessary to reach an accord with the USSR. If the principle applied to reparations equipment, the Russians might get nothing from the western zones free of charge: the removals would occur before the German economy was functioning properly, and the principle would technically require payment for them. There would have been no incentive for the Russians to have agreed to the U.S. zonal formula. The reparations accord at Potsdam was barely an accord at all, but if the Allies were to maintain even the façade of unity at Potsdam, the Western powers had to give the Russians something. "In view of the present form of the reparations agreement," an American official wrote at Potsdam, "it would be unwise, although perhaps not absolutely fatal" to leave the clause out—the United States could not otherwise obtain Soviet assent. According to Clayton, this aspect of the reparations pact "superceded" the concern for an immediate export-import balance.

But the proposal did not jeopardize U.S. aims. Under any circumstances the Americans thought that Germany would run at a deficit in the near future, and for the present they were protecting the potential for a multilateral Germany.

Plant dismantling in the western zones was a way of compromising with the Russians, but if the Russians accepted,
they would guarantee realization of the American goal: the
USSR would get free factories, but these would be the excess of an economy the Americans were reconstructing on
multilateral lines. As Clayton commented, to give the Soviets these factories would cost the Americans nothing.*
Byrnes, at Potsdam, had assured the USSR of its rights in
Germany; he told Molotov that once the Russians agreed to
the American zonal plan, they would have "no interest in
exports and imports from our zone." "Any difficulty in regard to imports and exports," Byrnes declared, "would have
to be settled between the British and ourselves." *"The Soviets would have no interest and they would get their percentage [of unneeded equipment] regardless of what happened to us."* [6]

Of course, Clay and the Americans in Germany were not
privy to the many Byrnes-Molotov discussions; except in
simple terms Byrnes himself had no clear idea of the policies
that he was pursuing. In the confusing reparations accord,
the military had before it only the final product of the involuted and tortuous negotiation. We could not expect the
U.S. military authorities to take the Soviet side, and in late
August 1945, Clay expressed a view inconsistent with "Section II, Clause 19." He said the first-charge principle applied
both *after* removals were made and *before* they were made.[7]

* See *FR*, Potsdam, II, 520–521, 823, 826–827, 829, 1485–1486,
and the other citations mentioned therein. "Section II, Clause 19" is
a baffling section of the Protocol, and I make no final claims for the
soundness of my interpretation. Although it is consistent with most
of the evidence, my analysis can only weakly account for the Soviet
hesitation in accepting the principle. I assume the Russians had their
own problems in deciphering the clause.

The Russians would not get their reparations until the Americans were sure the plan would succeed, and Clay's statement was congruent with that part of the Protocol that stressed that the military construct a balanced economy.

As work progressed on the level of industry plan, the significance of the conflicting Russian and American interpretations became more plain. It was the intent of the Protocol that the Soviets would get their capital removals as soon as the Allies concurred on the plan; only thereafter would the four nations see if the German economy functioned in a viable way. The point may have been of only technical importance if the level of industry plan that the powers were developing were realistic; but because the Western Allies understood the way the four powers were concocting it, they were unwilling first to dismantle and then to see if German exports and imports would balance. On their side, the Russians agreed that determining the level of industry plan and establishing an export-import plan were coordinate problems.[8] But after the victors had worked out a solution, the Soviet stood on the Potsdam legality that they must execute the two plans independently. In this way the USSR might get some removals under an impractical plan while the problem of paying for exports remained unsolved.

U.S. diplomats were placed in a peculiar dilemma. They were not committed to achieving an export-import balance in the immediate future, but only the potential for one. The Americans did not expect Germany to have a viable economy until all of Europe was in a more normal condition. Under any level of industry plan, the new Germany would first run at a deficit; as the world political economy was realized, the German economy would also become stable. One way to learn if this would occur—a way stipulated at Potsdam—was to dismantle, and wait and see. But Clay would take no such chance with the plan the Allies were working out, and the Americans were therefore unrealistic in their desire to reach agreement with the USSR on low levels of industry: in practice their commitment was contingent upon the unlikely possibility that these levels would ensure a minimum economy. When he had to choose between dismantling plants and guaranteeing German industrial potential, Clay chose the latter. The military first wanted to know if the new German economy would work; when it knew this, it would dismantle.

The second additional aspect of the level of industry accord which merits attention is the issue of balanced exports and imports as it applied to each zone. Although the areas governed by the West were highly industrialized, they needed food and some raw materials. Operating at a deficit, they required large imports. The eastern zone, on the other hand, was not highly industrialized, but did have an agricultural economy with a net surplus. The United States in particular was interested in an *interzonal* export-import plan in which the Allies would pool the zonal economies to make up for western deficits.[9] The Russians argued for "zonal programs" in which each sector would maintain its own net economic balance.[10] The U.S. Legal Directorate considered the latter procedure in accord with the Potsdam Protocol, but the legalities were insignificant. The Legal Directorate recognized that the answers were not "wholly clear."[11]

Moreover, the USSR was not opposed to pooling resources to relieve the western imbalance. The Russians would agree to this policy if there were also a common pool in the *production* of resources. In short, they were willing to trade food from the eastern zone for goods from the western zones. In March 1946 the British asked the Russians for food, and the Soviets assented on the condition that they receive steel from the Ruhr in return. When the British replied that there was not enough steel, the Russian representative answered that "there were not sufficient food reserves in the Soviet zone." [12] Clay's description of the situation in *Decision in Germany* neglects to note this aspect of interzonal problems. He said that the Soviets would not "place the resources of east Germany into a common pool unless they were assured of a large payment of the productive output of all Germany without payment." He did not mention that it was the Americans and British who were asking for goods from eastern Germany without charge, and that the Russians were willing to trade. But in October 1945, Clay was clearer on the issue and initially opposed the State Department. A refusal to reciprocate with the Soviets on these matters, he warned, would "make progress in Quadripartite negotiations more difficult and perhaps impossible." [13]

The USSR got no bargains at Potsdam, but in attempting to secure Germany for multilateralism, the Americans were in effect repudiating their minimal Berlin concessions. If we consider the three questions on which disagreement was crucial—the extent of removals from the eastern zone, the export-import balance, and the interzonal plan—the weight of legalities is heavily on the Soviet side. The legalities, however, counted little. The crunch came in early April 1946, just ten days after the four powers formulated the level of industry plan.

On April 8, Clay said that he heard it rumored that exports and imports were a "zonal" problem, not to be resolved until the powers consummated a reparations program. This was not, Clay stated, the American position. The Allies based the level of industry plan on balanced exports and imports in all of Germany, and if the powers did not establish the balance, "the reparations plan had no validity." Were they not to agree on a common export-import plan, then "at a suitable time in the not too distant future, the U.S. delegation would invoke . . . the basic assumption of the level of industry plan." This "basic assumption" was the economic unity of Germany, and if the victors did not act on it, the Americans would require "revision of the reparations plan." [14]

In his threat Clay brought together all the critical disputes. Unless the Soviets sent food to alleviate western deficits, he would not execute the reparations plan in the U.S. zone. Even were the Russians to yield, Clay would not undertake any substantial dismantling until economists ascertained that the new German economy functioned, and what the Russians would eventually get from the west would decrease in proportion to what they had removed on their own. In return for the eastern zone of Germany, the Soviets would receive an undetermined amount of industrial equipment—at the most well below what they wanted—and they would get it at an unspecified time in the future. "Negotiations" came to a halt.

On April 27, Clay brought up the problems once more when he stated that "reparations, export-import policy, and the establishment of central machinery in Germany" were interdependent questions. They necessitated "integrated decision at government level." Citing Potsdam II, 19, the Soviets responded that the export-import stipulation was not applicable to items for reparations deliveries. To make the connection between an export-import balance *and* capital equipment designated for removal was a breach of the Potsdam accord. Again Clay argued that there was no "separate solution." The ability of the German economy to meet its balance of payments was "tied up" with reparations. He would have to report to his government that there must be a decision "as to whether Potsdam would be carried out as a whole or not." The U.S. delegation would "definitely stop the work" of the men dismantling factories for reparations.[15]

On May 3, the Allies took up the problem of interzonal exports and imports, and the Soviets indicated that they did not concur on a common plan that would require them to subsidize the western zones. Immediately afterward Clay announced that the Americans would discontinue dismantling. Yet the exact intent of Clay's move is unclear. At least for a time he was more concerned with French intransigence than with Russian, and the penalties to the USSR in Clay's action were minimal. John Gimbel, an authority on the occupation who has dealt with this problem, writes that "the dismantling stop was an attempt to force a government level agreement on the general economic features of the Potsdam decisions." Clay was motivated, Gimbel argues, by a desire "to force economic unity and central administrations." This is true; but Gimbel adds the decision was thus not "a basically anti-Soviet measure." [16] But "economic unity and central administrations" on Clay's terms *were precisely* "anti-Soviet" positions: unless Germany were reunited on multilateral lines, the Soviets would not get even the minimal reparations the Americans were willing to grant. In the context of American decision making, Clay's wish to clarify policy had one clear implication: further attempts to temporize in Germany would be minimal. The United States general had taken a large step in terminating the State Department's strategy of delay.[17]

Although Clay's action has a symbolic value for historians, there are other indications that the strategy of delay was about to end. The flurry of diplomatic activity at the time suggests that the Americans were attempting a last series of maneuvers to reach accord with the Russians.

In late April at the Foreign Ministers Conference meeting in Paris, Byrnes publicly offered the Soviets a twenty-five-year demilitarization treaty. Senator Arthur Vandenberg had made a similar suggestion in Congress over a year earlier, and in June 1945, Truman had conceived the original proposal for the version Byrnes took to Paris. The treaty theoretically would enable the Soviets to liberalize their policies in eastern Europe and would eliminate the necessity for spheres of influence in Europe as a whole. The victorious nations would police Germany for twenty-five years, and there would be no need for the British, and more particularly the Russians, to seek an area of hegemony.[18] In September 1945, Byrnes had asked Molotov to study the offer with the eastern European problem in mind. Although Molotov treated the idea casually, Byrnes apparently got a more positive reply from Stalin in December. On April 28, 1946, he brought up the issue again with Molotov, but both then and the next day, when the Secretary officially introduced the treaty into Big Four discussion, Molotov would not consider it, and continued to stall on the issue.[19]

In May, after Byrnes's failure to reach a détente, Clay went to Paris to report to the Secretary. Byrnes agreed with the general that suspension of reparations deliveries had

been wise in view of difficulties with the Soviets.[20] Then, at
the Foreign Ministers Conference, Byrnes announced the
new U.S. policy in anti-Soviet terms: the Americans would
not send plants to the eastern zone if Germany were not administered as an economic unit.[21] As Clay recalled the
events, "we were faced with a major decision which was
certain to have lasting effects on our relationship with Russia." [22] On May 20, Harriman claimed that the German
problem was "hopeless." [23]

In July, Byrnes asked Molotov what the Russians "*really*
wanted in Germany." "The Soviet Union," Molotov replied,
"wants what it asked for at Yalta . . . and it also wants to
participate with the United States, the United Kingdom,
and France in a four-power control of the industries of the
Ruhr." [24] These demands had caused the Soviets to reject
the twenty-five-year American treaty. Byrnes believed that
if the USSR agreed to the treaty, Molotov would ask for the
"two things he wants," $10 billion in reparations and a part
in the control of the Ruhr." [25]

In its essentials, the dilemma was the same one that confronted Washington in the early summer of 1945: how could
the United States convince the Russians to support multilateral plans for Germany and prohibit them from taking
reparations that compromised these plans? The USSR would
not assent to economic fusion if it did not receive substantial
reconstruction goods either in dismantled equipment or in
trade of heavy industrial products.[26] Although the diplomatic and economic issues are complex, the basic point is
simple. If we estimate what the Americans were offering
and what value eastern Germany had for the USSR, it
is clear that the Americans were demanding capitulation

from the Soviets. For the United States to compromise
would be for it to jeopardize its goal of a reconstructed
German political economy in an international system. For
the Russians to yield would be for them to surrender their
portion of Germany for almost nothing.

Under the level of industry plan as originally conceived
at Potsdam, reparations would come from the dismantling of
heavy industry. But the Soviets' demand for industrial products under any agreed interzonal program again raised the
question of reparations from current production. This kind of
compensation was not discussed but not excluded by the
Potsdam accord, and during the level of industry negotiations, the USSR and France made it plain that they would
consider recurring reparations. Although the United States
was against these reparations and gave them a low priority,
it never made its commitment explicit. But when the Allies
reached accord on the plan, the Americans expounded their
position at length.

The United States and Great Britain agreed that the limitations on the capacity of light industry set by the plan
would not be permanent. They regarded these restrictions
as "estimates" of the light industry Germany would need to
function with whatever heavy industries the Allies would
not dismantle.[27] They would remove some excess heavy industries as reparations; those that remained would function
with light industries operating at a certain capacity. When
conditions changed, the victors might remove the strictures
on light manufactures, and the United States held out the
prospect for the "unlimited development of the productive
capacity of light industry." [28] In May 1946, Clay argued that

the reparation plan should require no reparations from current output until the German economy was balanced.[29] By implication these reparations could come only from the possibly "unlimited" capacity of the light industries. The U.S. Legal Directorate argued that when the German economy no longer operated at a deficit, current production payments would be "proper subjects" of reparations. No factories, however, were to be left in Germany specifically for manufacturing these items.[30]

On May 3, when Clay announced the dismantling halt at the Control Council meeting, the Soviets responded by raising the current production issue. Their zonal economy was in balance; even were it not, if no deliveries were forthcoming from the western zones, they could obtain material by taking current production from the east. After an evasive discussion, Clay learned that "the Soviet delegation does not undertake that it would not exact reparations from current production and stocks." [31]

Despite its serious implications, this move came after much hesitation and grew out of the cautious Russian attitude torn between weakening Germany for security purposes and maintaining heavy industry for current output reparations. Toward the end of the war the USSR stressed dismantling. Not until the summer and fall of 1945 did the "sovietization" of the eastern zone and current production compensation from it become a real possibility to the Russians. Until then they thought that a "Western peace" would preclude this outcome. Although there is little direct evidence, the chronology suggests that the Potsdam reparations program was responsible for this new Soviet hope. But only in the spring of 1946 did those favoring current production reparations gain control of Russian policy. The Russians stopped dismantling and initiated recurring shipments from the east.*

Soviet intentions became plainer at the July Foreign Ministers meeting when Molotov renewed his demand for current reparations from all of Germany. The American response came quickly. Under the Potsdam agreement there was good reason for thinking that the Russians could extract these reparations only from a united Germany whose economy was balanced; that is, there was a basis for the United States to object to their exaction until the Allies unified Germany. Instead, the Americans argued that the Potsdam accord and the level of industry agreement ruled out recurring reparations altogether.[32]

By this time, dispute over subtleties had become meaningless. The Allies were thrown back to the positions they had occupied at Potsdam except that the veneer of unity imposed by the United States had worn off. The Americans insisted that German problems be treated in conformity with their plan for a multilateral order. The Soviets refused to turn over their zone for this purpose unless the United States compensated them with substantial reconstruction goods. The U.S. diplomats could not compromise because the extraction of reparations, either in removals or current

* See *Soviet Economic Policy in Postwar Germany: A Collection of Papers by Former Soviet Officials*, ed. Robert Slusser (New York, 1953), pp. 19, 36, 40, 46–47; Gregory Klimov, *The Terror Machine*, trans. H. C. Stevens (New York, 1953), p. 197; and Manuel Gottlieb, *The German Peace Settlement and the Berlin Crisis* (New York, 1960), pp. 48–49; *FR*, 1946, V (1969), 602–603. The parallels between Russian and American policy have their significance. The Treasury dismantling plan represented a belief that the United States would not be able to "Americanize" Germany, but the more confident Americans had rejected this conception earlier.

production, was inconsistent with multilateral aims for Germany. Behind the complex fabric of legalities, the tortuous and complicated negotiations, and the evasions of diplomatic language, the crux of the German problem remained the same: the desire of the United States to integrate a peaceful industrial Germany into an international order. But unless the Americans were, in effect, willing to "buy off" the Russians, the Soviets would not relinquish the eastern zone.

Although the Americans had agreed to a level of industry plan that all the powers appeared to think would be unworkable, the Americans were never willing to act on it in a way that would compromise the existing German economy. Moreover, *in conception* the plan was consonant with multilateralism. Like the first-charge principle, it encapsulated the American concern over Germany's place in a utopian global system. It was not based on the single assumption that Germany would have enough industrial capacity to maintain itself without external assistance: it was based on the assumption that "exports from Germany will be accepted in the international market." [33] This assumption would have made the plan difficult to execute under optimal conditions, and this assumption governed American action.

As finally set forth, the plan contemplated a reduction in exports of German heavy industry to about two-thirds of their prewar level. This reduction meant a loss of $0.8 billion in heavy exports, and an expansion of the exports of light industry by about $0.08 billion. The German export total under the plan was to be $1.2 billion, $0.4 billion from the reduced heavy industry and $0.8 billion from the increased light industry.[34] This rearranging of exports meant that the

Allies would radically alter the structure of the German economy. No longer would it export great quantities of heavy industry: on the contrary, it would be required to sell more light industry on the world market. In Berlin during 1946 there was, indeed, "great doubt" over the ability of foreign markets to absorb these light industrial exports.[35]

The Russians got at the problem in the level of industry discussions when the British argued that the basic question was subsidizing the German economy. The Russian general, Vassily Sokolovsky, replied that the problem was rather the wish of certain delegations to finance imports by heavy industrial exports. These goods, Sokolovsky went on, should be kept at a minimum. The financing of imports should take place by exports from the *light* industries and mining. When Clay urged that production from heavy industry could provide for a minimal standard of living and payment for imports, Sokolovsky focused on the dilemma a second time: there was no reason to pay for imports by heavy and not light industry.[36] Clay himself delineated the American position in a conversation with Naval Secretary Forrestal. He said that the Allies had reached a consensus on the necessity of denying heavy industry to Germany, but were also unwilling to provide export markets for German light industry. For example, Clay stated, Eastman-Kodak would oppose imports from the German camera industry into the United States.[37]

Reparations from current production would further complicate the American goal of a healthy German political economy with an export-import balance. If reparations came from the unrestricted production of light industry, they might undermine the level of industry plan entirely. Germany would have difficulties in finding customers for its increased light industrial exports, particularly when prospective customers received the same goods free as reparations. Reparations from light industries might exhaust the limited demand for similar German exports, and Germany would remain in a deficit status. Products from the mining industries—mainly coal—were also unavailable in large quantities for reparations or export. In line with U.S. plans, by the end of 1946 the Western Allies were using more coal production than they had previously used for Germany's internal reconstruction.[38]

The most important problem was current production reparations from heavy industry. The renewed Russian request of July 1946 for $10 billion would mean such reparations, and the powers could have revised the level of industry plan to yield them. Under a new program, world trade would not suffer in the immediate future because there was a great need for heavy industrial goods. The international demand was sufficient to ensure their purchase even while they were supplied in reparations. But the Americans felt that in the long run only Russia could continue as Germany's customer for these products. Either the industries would be persistently underemployed, or the Soviet Union would establish close economic ties with Germany.[39] Heavy industry reparations to the Russians threatened multilateralism and the military security of the United States.

The Americans could achieve their goals in Germany only if they would "bribe" the Russians in one way or another. A policy of this kind at least would make a *modus vivendi* possible. But any agreement on reparations was undercut because it would mean a modification of U.S. plans and partial Russian control over all of Germany. The other alternative was for the Americans to finance Russian recovery as they had begun to do for the economies of western Europe. But the United States could not or would not seriously contemplate a solution of this sort.

In this respect the Americans still linked reparations and financial aid with Soviet policy in eastern Europe. Although the Russians might have made some settlement in Germany, they were not willing to give way in eastern Europe. The USSR considered quadripartite control in Germany highly desirable, but would not consent to this kind of great power "cooperation" in eastern Europe. The Americans would make a settlement only if the Allies reunited Germany in conformity with the United States program and pursued joint policies in the countries east of Germany.[40] Because the Soviets did not agree to U.S. terms, they received no assistance. But the Americans also believed that the lack of economic help might force the Russians to the bargaining table. Harriman still emphasized this approach in 1946, and State Department officers, Secretary Byrnes, and Under Secretary Dean Acheson joined him.[41]

As 1946 wore on, very likely it became apparent that this tool would not do the job; at the same time domestic pressure in the United States was building up against the Soviet because of its eastern European political practices. Aid negotiations dragged on but the State Department came to believe that perhaps the USSR would not make the necessary concessions, or congressional approval for aid would be impossible, or both.[42] For the United States, however, Soviet refusal to yield was almost synonymous with Soviet hostility. Consequently, when the Americans saw that the lack of reparations, as well as lack of aid, was ineffectual in shaping Russian diplomacy, they also saw the lack of reparations as protecting U.S. interests against a belligerent power. Strictures on reparations might not pressure the USSR, but they would help preserve the West's strategic, economic, and political position in Germany.

Multilateralism could not succeed once the Russians decided to resist United States global policy. The only alternative that might have prevented great-power friction was American acceptance of a Soviet sphere of influence and joint Allied agreements in Germany itself. The USSR was eager for compromise on this basis, and even had it proved impossible, the victors might have cooperated in dividing the Reich. But the Americans were unwilling to concede in Germany; their demand to extend liberal capitalism led them to consider "negotiations" as relevant only to eastern Europe, where they overestimated their power. Herbert Feis has recognized the dynamic at work. Both powers, he writes, were concealing their real intentions by 1947: the Soviets denied they wanted all Germany under Communist control; the Americans denied they wanted to "shake Communist control of Eastern Germany *and the Soviet satellites.*"[43] Perhaps the one consequence of the U.S. drive was to lead the Russians to tighten up control in the areas under their sway; when the drive failed, intense Soviet-American hostility accompanied the partition of Germany.

In October 1946, Clayton wrote Forrestal that "it would be unwise to release any advantage which we might have in the present administration of Germany." The control of the Ruhr dictated Russian recovery to a considerable extent.[44] Other American leaders went further. At the end of 1946, Secretary of War Robert Patterson, who had replaced Stimson the previous year, argued that the United States should use its assets "to force unity" with the Russians. Eisenhower agreed with this appraisal: economic leverage "would be a great political weapon" in bringing about German unification "since the Russians have need for Ruhr steel." [45] The economic power of the United States, General John R. Deane also wrote about this time, was one medium for combatting the Soviet program. "It may be the means," he said, "by which we can convince Soviet leaders that it is possible for our respective ideologies to live peacefully." [46]

In retrospect the Americans gravely miscalculated the Russian need for Western assistance. When it became plain that the Soviets would neither meet American terms in Germany nor allow American interests in eastern Europe, the Cold War became public and the division of Europe a fact.

Conclusion: The
End of Ideology

American plans for Germany during the war and their realization in the peace were subject to many complex forces. At various times the U.S. government developed and carried out policies not because of any rational assessment or consensus but because of institutional rivalries, personal animosities, individual idiosyncrasies, and administrative inefficiency. At times ignorance on factual matters, avoidable misunderstandings with the other powers, and a lack of knowledge concerning past commitments make U.S. decision making appear totally disordered.

Nevertheless, this has not been a history of chaos or human frailty. The essential tool for comprehending American foreign affairs from 1939 to 1946 is the multilateral conception of an international politico-economic system. This ideal generated a series of responses to world affairs which had become second nature to many U.S. diplomats by the late thirties; its basic assumptions were at the core of their view of the collapse of international order in 1939 and governed the commitment to internationalism and interventionism until Pearl Harbor; the Americans had long planned for its execution, and victory in 1945 made execution seem possible. Multilateralism decisively shaped American diplo-

226

macy toward Germany and was at the center of the serious American disputes with the Russians. State Department foreign policy is the single most important thread for leading one through the tangled maze of great-power strategies.

To be sure, only a single agency espoused multilateralism in a pure form. But Stimson and McCloy, those members of the War Department who had the greatest interest in policy matters, also acted on State Department assumptions. And the belief in the necessity for trade expansionism so fundamental to multilateralism was a deep and pervasive commitment among the American governmental elite. Even the Treasury, whose programs were felt to be so much at odds with those of the State Department, believed that only greater foreign markets could achieve American domestic prosperity. Increased exports to the Soviet were to compensate for the loss in exports that the "deindustrialization" of Germany entailed. Roosevelt, who at no time grasped economic subtleties, often saw the German problem in terms of the possibilities of greater British and American trade after the Axis defeat; moreover, from the late thirties onward the President advocated at least a mild form of political "internationalism." The State Department viewpoint provides a convenient framework from which to elaborate the strategies basic to U.S. diplomacy.

Many of the Americans—Clay, Forrestal, Harriman, and Stimson, most importantly—explicitly saw the conflict with Russia as a clash of world views.[1] But they were men of affairs and not philosophers, and assumed unquestionably that their vision of global order and harmony was the sole legitimate one; they considered their ideas those that all men of right reason must accept. The State Department took this line most directly. Within the department it was agreed that the vital interests of the United States lay in the "diplomacy of principle"—"of moral disinterestedness instead of power politics." [2] When Soviet intentions in eastern Europe began to clarify in late 1944, Stettinius made the same point to FDR. In relation to Europe and the Near East, the Americans should "assert the independent interest of the United States"; this was "believed to be in the general interest." [3] During the same period Secretary Hull recalled he had explained this repeatedly to the Soviets. Washington had concluded that small nations had parity, equality, and security with the larger countries. This assumption guided American diplomacy in Latin America, where "we had given up the thought of intervention." "By our own actions," Hull argued, the Americans must give Russia "a concrete example of how we thought she should act." [4]

State was not alone. In 1943, Stimson reflected that there was one way to combat "isolationism": "everything must be centered in Washington so that the Yankee thinks he is not being taken in by foreigners." [5] Assistant Secretary of War McCloy felt this procedure would result "in a greater objectivity of decision." "European deliberations," he told Harry Hopkins, "must be made in the light of the concepts of the new continent." [6]

When Truman became president, these notions received less sophisticated but equally forceful expression. He asserted that no nation in history had taken the American position upon complete victory; no nation with American military power had been so generous to enemies and so helpful to friends; perhaps, he thought, the United States could effectuate the teachings of the Sermon on the Mount.[7] And, consequently, Truman indicated an idea of parity in diplomatic affairs that expressed his belief that no one could disagree with the U.S. view: in April 1945, when Harriman explained to him that "in any international negotiations there is give-and-take, and both sides make concessions," Truman assented; he would not expect to get 100 per cent approval of American plans; the United States should expect to get only 85 per cent.[8]

Although in many cases economics had operative primacy within the American world view, economic ideas did not exist in isolation. They functioned as means for bringing about a world in which war was nonexistent and the economic frictions leading to war were canalized in peaceful directions. Although the increase in trade and the access by all countries to all national markets would supremely benefit the United States, these commercial practices would raise living standards everywhere. Most importantly, this economic climate was essential to the existence of societies that preserved values the Americans believed applicable all over the world. In this respect United States conduct presents a curious phenomenon to the historian. As the Americans acted on their world view in day-to-day decisions, we can understand their orientation as one whose aims were political but whose methods were economic.

This relationship between economics and politics is here best reflected in the American conflict with the Soviets. The development of four-power agreement for Germany would have been difficult under optimal conditions. But if the Allies were to agree, some Soviet influence, no matter how minimal, would have to extend throughout Germany, that is, up to the Franco-German border. It was just this influence that the Americans assumed could not, under any circumstances, be allowed to occur.

In Berlin, where there was quadripartite control, it would be a delicate job "to democratize and lead the Berlin population back to concepts of government and living" as American democracy exemplified them.[9] Stimson argued in 1945 that the United States must rehabilitate a "contented" Germany and find a way of making the Soviet play ball; Washington had to prevent communistic influence in western Europe.[10] Naval Secretary Forrestal feared that Germany might turn to the USSR.[11] A memo the State Department prepared for Byrnes at Potsdam made this point in an over-dramatic way:

We must assume, although we have no explicit knowledge, that the Russians are clear as to their intentions. . . . Presumably they propose to substitute for Nazi Germany a Germany at least sympathetic to Communism. We presumably believe that a Germany converted to respect for the worth and dignity of human beings and a belief in the basic principles of justice and in the right of men to govern themselves would be a Germany which we could trust. If this, however, is our purpose, we must recognize it and pursue it consciously. We must play again the role we played at the beginning of our history. We must be ready and willing to propagate ideas of liberty and justice and human dignity.[12]

Carrying out policy in Germany, General Clay maintained that the Americans could not attempt political unification on terms involving compromise with the Soviets. The Russians, he said, interpreted the Potsdam agreement differently from the other powers. They "wanted to create conditions that would provide opportunity for communist penetration and domination of German political life and economic resources." He told Secretary of State Byrnes in May 1946 that the economic chaos was favorable "to the *development of communism in Germany and a deterrent to its democratization"*; in July 1946 he reiterated that the United States had to nullify the Communist appeal.[13] In November 1946 he recommended to Byrnes that the Americans approach the Soviets again on reparations. Although nothing came of the recommendation, Clay declared that one of the benefits of its acceptance would be "the full political unification of Germany, thus extending Western liberalism to the borders of countries now under Communist influence." [14]

The Americans defined the political situation in such a way as to leave the USSR with the options of conversion to the ways of democracy or surrender. If they had succeeded, it is doubtful whether the Soviet state would now exist. The Russians made no such demands on the United States; they were intransigent and ruthless in eastern Europe, but this did not *in fact* entail the destruction of the American way of life. The Americans might have felt that a red east-central Europe was something with which they could not live, but this was a fear that time would not justify; it was a justifiable fear only for those who could see no other world than a multilateral one.

In Germany the Americans accepted the axiom that political programs had to proceed on their lines; and this outlook was the concomitant of an identical perspective in U.S. foreign economic policy. By mid-1945 the success of American policy in Germany turned on a solution to the reparations problem, an economic issue. When the Soviet refused to yield on this problem, there was no alternative within the American framework that would make a unified Germany possible.

The Potsdam reparations pact is so decisive that we could

justify concluding this book with an analysis of the Berlin agreements. In retrospect the decisions the Americans made at Potsdam, just ten weeks after the successful conclusion of the war, made impossible the multilateral globe that had been envisioned for so long. In this regard the Berlin Conference was the principal turning point in the history of the postwar world: it fixed the fate of Germany.

Whatever the historical judgment, many American policy makers did not perceive the Potsdam accords in this light; for them the Berlin agreements were interim in nature and postponed some ultimate confrontation. In Germany, Robert Murphy, the United States Political Adviser, elucidated the State Department's perspective in a telegram of October 1945:

Some of us here wonder whether it is fully comprehended by the Dept that when the decisions were made . . . determining the zones of occupation, that power to implement American wishes in respect of coal production and export as well as removal of industrial equipment on reparations account passed from direct American control. . . . Yet much of the American approach to this subject, both on the governmental level and in the press would lead to the impression that the determination of these questions rests exclusively in the power of the American representatives. As you know, General Eisenhower and General Clay can and do present our views as forcibly as may be desirable but the physical control of these properties rests with somebody else.[15]

The State Department's view was that the Russians might be amenable to unifying Germany along American lines when the four powers negotiated the level of industry plan six months after Potsdam. For this reason the narrative has followed the details of occupation policy until Clay stopped dismantling in the wake of difficulties in implementing the plan. The Americans recognized soon afterward that the reparations halt had a serious symbolic effect on relations with the Soviets. One must assume that from this point on the Americans also knew that cooperation on their terms was impossible.

Even this may be something of an overstatement of the clarity with which some U.S. diplomats saw the contours of postwar events. As late as October 1946, Murphy himself sensed a final triumphant battle. Emphasizing the "dynamic aspects of our position," he cabled Byrnes:

At some time [the] test will come for all Germany and thus we are forced to gamble on [the] whole rather than to fall back to [a] defensive position in [the] western zones alone. Accordingly, we believe that we must attempt to exploit any and all possibilities of opening up [the] Soviet zones.[16]

For the next two years negotiations continued their complicated course. Diplomacy and evasion veiled the issues although argument wandered further and further from the legalities of Potsdam. The Soviets insisted on reparations, the Americans on unification; the more vociferously the Russians demanded compensation, the more unwilling were the Western powers, led by the United States, to dismantle German industry or to put it to use for the USSR. The response of the Soviets was to hold on more tightly to what they had in eastern Europe.

Very little dismantling occurred in western Germany. By October 1946 the Allies had removed only five of the 1850 plants scheduled for dismantling in the west under the level of industry plan.[17] The total monetary value of this variety of reparation to the Russians was probably no more than

$25 million and could not have exceeded $50 million.[18] George Kennan has estimated their worth at "several million" dollars.[19] In July 1945, Pauley argued that if reparations were taken on a zonal basis and unification impeded, the Western powers should remove only "direct war potentials" from their zones; the Soviet share of these removals he appraised at $214 million.[20]

Even had Pauley's minimal dismantling taken place, the effect on the German economy at that time would appear to have been negligible. In May 1946, Clay declared that under the level of industry plan *the removal of plants for reparations purposes has no major bearing on the extent of economic recovery during this period.*[21] The State Department shared this belief. German economic revival was contingent "primarily on improvements in coal and raw material supply, transport, on expansion of inter-regional and inter-zonal trade, and in general on efficient reorganization."[22]

Despite the potential for economic restoration in western Germany, no improvement took place. As Dean Acheson repeatedly argued, it took two years for the United States to comprehend the seriousness of the European situation.[23] The dislocations caused by the war were so great and the measures to promote stability so inadequate that Germany and Europe remained in a chaotic state. Theoretically, Russo-American cooperation was still possible. As long as western German productive might was inoperative, Britain and the United States would not necessarily appear unfriendly to the Russians. On the other side, the United States could only feel that the prolonged misery in western Europe might lead to its domination by the Left, more or less under Soviet influence.

Great-power hostility became public in mid-1947 with the American offer of massive economic aid to Europe under the Marshall Plan. At last the United States planned to revive the western European economies on a reasonable basis. But the terms of the program were similar to those the Soviet Union previously found unacceptable. When Molotov left the Paris conference on the Marshall Plan, those who stayed behind made plans to reactivate western German industrial strength.

Given the perspectives of U.S. decision makers, this clarification of Soviet-American relations left one alternative: that new series of policies connected to multilateralism and conveniently labeled "containment"—Washington would realistically implement its policies in those parts of the world it controlled. This idea, Acheson wrote, differed from Hull's views "by relegating to the future the attempt at universality . . . and achieving . . . more limited and, it was hoped, transitory ends." [24] Within the framework generated by this new *credo* and its accompanying economic commitments, Europe was formally divided and the Cold War inconclusively fought.

Appendix: Multilateralism and Revisionist Historiography

I have written a monograph that attempts to illuminate one aspect of wartime diplomacy. I am very much aware of how parasitic my study is on the work of contemporary revisionist historians, most importantly William Appleman Williams' *Tragedy of American Diplomacy*. Nonetheless, in devising a strategy for the writing of this book, I encountered distinctive problems whose resolution seems to me to be worth discussing.

The concept of the "Open Door" is central to Williams' famous analysis of twentieth-century American foreign relations. He claims that successive generations of U.S. decision makers have advocated and carried out a policy committed to the expansion of trade and the exportation of American cultural influence. The U.S. economic machine produces much more than Americans can consume domestically; and implicit in the Washington world view is the belief that if the United States is to avoid an anticapitalist redistribution of wealth, businessmen must sell abroad. Since the economy also efficiently manufactures an incredibly varied array of goods, a commitment to lower tariffs or at least nondiscriminatory tariffs has usually accompanied the commitment to commercial expansion. For Williams the idea of an "Open Door" embodies all of these notions: the most important strand of past U.S. diplomacy has been its attempt to maintain and extend American trade advantages where they exist and to secure them where they do not. Critics have sometimes complained that the Williams thesis is one of mere

economic determinism; but more carefully considered, it concerns the functioning of an entire political economy. In short,
Williams details the *Weltanschauung* of the policy-making
community.

Two aspects of Williams' study—his use of the world view
idea and the manner of its use—are of particular theoretical interest. In the first place Williams makes an implicit attack on the
analysis of motivation that is conventional in orthodox history.
Many scholars—most notably George Kennan, Hans Morgenthau, and Robert Osgood—have interpreted the history of American foreign relations in terms of the alternation and conflict of
"ideals" and "self-interest," between legalistic moralism and
political realism.[1] It is ungenerous to write off this motivational
account entirely: it has the virtue of bringing much disparate
data together under one rubric, of organizing material into a
single framework. But there is a serious conceptual confusion in
the analysis. One must believe that diplomats are a breed of
schizophrenic robots who have two alternative centers of motivation, one quasi-Machiavellian (in a favorable sense), the other
starry-eyed and impractical. In its extreme form this is a feeble
version of the old "faculty theory of mind" which postulated different "powers" to explain human action. These forms of analysis
neglect an elementary psychological and philosophical insight—
that human beings normally see the world as a coherent whole
and that ideology and interest are inseparable. Although behavior may be self-serving, it will always be justified in moral
terms and may possess a moral dimension.

Williams' use of the idea of world view in diplomatic history is
a great advance over the Kennan approach, but the manner in
which Williams writes about the "Open Door" presents difficulties. I have obliquely taken up this second theoretically interest-
ing aspect of his work in my introduction. He writes as if the
"Open Door" concept exists in some timeless platonic heaven
and that U.S. diplomats grasp it upon accession to power. In

this sense his treatment of some dimensions of American conduct is deeply ahistoric. Of course, he might reply that the "Open Door" notion is simply an analytic construct useful for organizing his material. But this reply only points to the weakness of constructs that have no historic dimension.

In my study I used the concept of *Weltanschauung* but anchored it in a specific historical period. To be sure, I applied the concept of multilateralism in only one area—that of policy for Germany—but its possible usefulness in interpreting wider areas of U.S. international affairs during the war is worth noting, as are the ways in which it sheds light on the analyses of the realist-idealist school.

The major aims of my essay are to account for the motives of U.S. policy makers, to study the organization of their diplomatic community and the structure of a world view in action. To interpret policy at this time in terms of the conflict and congruence of moral and prudential behavior is pointless. Fundamentally, the Americans acted on the multilateral principles exemplified by the famous Atlantic Charter that Franklin Roosevelt signed in 1941. The declaration celebrated national self-determination, free elections, liberal trading arrangements, international political and economic cooperation, and disarmament. This set of goals, Roosevelt maintained, "was worth while for our type of civilization to seek." [2] But these economic and political ideals do not have absolute value; they flourish in and are nourished by a specific cultural environment and gain their credibility from the social relations existent in that environment. To contrast a U.S. "legalistic-moralistic" mentality with *Realpolitik* implies that American standards of conduct have an undeniable worth even if they are sometimes foolishly applied. Even a slight acquaintance with cultural relativism makes this view impossible to accept.

Nonetheless, this conventional categorization of motives does focus on an aspect of U.S. diplomatic behavior that must be correctly understood. We are able to reinterpret in the context of multilateralism that facet of diplomacy that the Kennan school has made central—the set of precepts and activities labeled "unrealistic" and "moralistic." The goal of multilateralism—international morality and U.S. politico-economic supremacy—was unrealistic. Lack of realism led the Americans to overestimate their strength and to misconceive the goals of the other powers. Most dramatically it caused the Americans to take a grossly optimistic view of the shape of the postwar world and led them to believe, initially, that the USSR would support the U.S. view and, later, that it could be forced to do so. The lack of realism was apparently rooted in an analysis of the recent diplomatic past. The optimism with which the Americans faced the aftermath of war seems to have been derived from what they thought were U.S. postwar reconstruction successes during Wilson's presidency. Similarly, their belief in Russian weakness may have derived from their knowledge of Soviet weakness after World War I. Finally, their overestimation of the British challenge to American power at the end of World War II may have reflected their respect for Great Britain's past leadership of the world economy.

The multilateral goal was moralistic in that it stressed the absolute righteousness of the American cause, and this moralism reinforced the lack of realism: the drive for global supremacy was conceived as the struggle for an ultimate good. (It is also true that we can largely explain some aspects of policy making by stating that someone believed that what he was doing was right. A good example of this is Truman's decision of April 1945 to withdraw American troops to western zones from their position in the Soviet zone. The President was implementing a prior agreement the three powers had made.) Perhaps even more significant than the unrealistic conception that the Americans could easily shape the postwar world was the moralistic conception that no men of good will would challenge them. For many who took this belief seriously, it made sense to argue that devils and traitors must exist when the Russians proved recalcitrant and American plans went unfulfilled. And the most extreme historians who shared this moralistic view could argue, among other things, that Roosevelt "sold us down the river at Yalta." The historical dimension to multilateral beliefs was also important here. When the American design was thwarted, *Communist* Russia easily took the place of Nazi Germany as the embodiment of that system of government that stood in the way of the establishment of multilateralism: the USSR was not only held responsible for the problems the United States faced all over the world, but also was conceived of as a totalitarian foe with whom there was no common ground.

Notes

Most substantive notes appear as footnotes on appropriate pages, designated with an asterisk. I have made all references to *Foreign Relations of the United States* using the abbreviation *FR* followed by a brief identification of the particular volume and its date of publication in parentheses. I have specified documents found in the State Department files by SDF, followed by number or lot designation.

Introduction

1. Quoted from William Appleman Williams, ed., *The Shaping of American Diplomacy* (Chicago, 1956), II, 633.

2. Cordell Hull, *Memoirs*, 2 vols. (New York, 1948), pp. 69, 81–85, 133–134.

3. Hull, p. 107.

4. Hull, p. 175.

5. John Foster Dulles Papers, Princeton University, Box 220, Dulles to Hull, 24 November 1952.

6. Theodore Wilson, *The First Summit* (Boston, 1969), p. 247.

7. Robert A. Divine, *The Illusion of Neutrality* (Chicago, 1962), p. 42.

8. Fred L. Israel, ed., *The War Diary of Breckinridge Long* (Lincoln, 1966), pp. 332–333, 392.

9. George Messersmith Papers, University of Delaware, Box III, Correspondence 1944, Folder C, Messersmith to Hull, 27

November 1944; and Messersmith to William L. Clayton, 26 December 1944.

10. *FR*, 1935, II (1952), 444–445.

11. Quoted in C. C. Tansill, *Back Door to War* (Chicago, 1952), pp. 341–342.

12. Robert A. Divine, *Second Chance* (New York, 1967), p. 42.

13. Henry L. Stimson and McGeorge Bundy, *On Active Service in War and Peace* (New York, 1947), pp. 298, 300.

14. Cordell Hull Papers, Library of Congress, Oct.–Nov. 1944, Stimson to Hull, 28 November 1944.

15. Willard Range, *Franklin D. Roosevelt's World Order* (Athens, Georgia, 1959), p. 137.

16. Wilson, p. 175; see also p. 173. For another cautious appraisal of Roosevelt's views, see Robert A. Divine, *Franklin Roosevelt and World War II* (Baltimore, 1969).

1. Planning for the Peace, 1939–1944

1. Hull, *Memoirs*, pp. 732, 746.

2. SDF, Lot 60D-224, Box 2, Chron File, "Chronology of War and Peace, 1939–1946."

3. *FR*, 1941, I (1958), 361–369, 373; Hull, pp. 975–976 (italics mine, BK). See Wilson, *The First Summit*, pp. 122, 173–202, for a complete discussion.

4. SDF, Lot 60D-224, Box 2, Chron File, "Chronology."

5. U.S. Department of State, *Postwar Foreign Policy Preparation, 1939–1945*, ed. Harley Notter (Washington, 1949), p. 133.

6. SDF, Lot 60D-224, Box 24, Political Subcommittee Min. (chron), nos. 1–20, p. 7, 8 April 1942.

7. *Ibid.*, nos. 32–49, m-32, 7 November 1942.

8. *Ibid.*, Box 22, Policy Summaries, H-24, Germany Partition, 27 July 1943.

9. See, for example, John L. Snell, *Wartime Origins of the*

East-West Dilemma over Germany (New Orleans, 1959), pp. 10, 27–28, and Paul Y. Hammond, "Directives for the Occupation of Germany: The Washington Controversy," in *American Civil-Military Decisions*, ed. Harold Stein (Birmingham, 1963), pp. 317–318. William M. Franklin in "Zonal Boundaries and Access to Berlin," *World Politics*, 16 (1963–1964), 3, associates Welles with Henry Morgenthau, Jr. This identification, as will be seen, is mistaken.

10. Sumner Welles, *Time for Decision* (New York, 1944), pp. 349, 351, 353, 360.

11. Sumner Welles, "Blueprint for Peace," in *Prefaces to Peace: A Symposium* (New York, 1943), pp. 429, 433.

12. *FR*, 1943, III (1963), 15; Anthony Eden, *The Memoirs of Anthony Eden, The Reckoning* (Boston, 1965), p. 432.

13. SDF, Lot 60D-224, Box 2, Chron File, "Chronology"; Hull, pp. 1284–1285, 1638–1639.

14. U.S. Department of State, *Postwar Foreign Policy Preparation*, pp. 559–560.

15. SDF, Lot 60D-224, Box 17, CAC Docs. 1–50, CAC 14, 23 September 1943.

16. *Ibid.*, Box 28, S-Germany (Swope and Welles), Division of Political Studies to Secretary of State, 22 January 1943; U.S. Department of State, *Postwar Foreign Policy Preparation*, p. 560.

17. Welles, "Blueprint for Peace," p. 431; Welles, *Time for Decision*, pp. 402, 408.

18. Hull Papers, Box 52, 1 September 1943.

19. *FR*, 1943, I (1963), 542; Hull, p. 1265.

20. *FR*, 1943, I, 723 (italics mine, BK).

21. *Ibid.*, 631–632.

22. *FR*, Cairo and Tehran (1961), p. 253; Franklin, 10–12; for the map see Maurice Matloff, *Strategic Planning for Coalition Warfare, 1943–1944* (Washington, 1959), facing p. 341.

23. *FR*, Cairo and Tehran, pp. 510–514, 554–555, 568–571.

24. *Ibid.*, pp. 600–604.

25. U.S. Department of State, *Postwar Foreign Policy Preparation*, p. 200.

26. Franklin, pp. 13–18.

27. SDF, Lot 60D-224, Box 22, S. Documents 21–49, S. Document 46, 11 November 1942; Box 29, WS Docs. 1–45, WS 15-a, 27 January 1944; *FR*, 1944, I (1966), 249–250.

28. For details see Hammond's definitive treatment, pp. 329–340; and Bruce Kuklick, "The Genesis of the European Advisory Commission," *Journal of Contemporary History*, 4 (1969), 189–201.

29. Walter Dorn, "The Debate over American Occupation Policy in Germany in 1944–1945," *Political Science Quarterly*, 72 (1957), 487.

30. Hammond, pp. 327–328; and John L. Chase's analysis of early directives in "The Development of United States Policy towards Germany during World War Two" (Ph.D. dissertation, Princeton University, 1952), pp. 184–190.

31. SDF, Lot 60D-224, Box 29, WS Docs. 46–58a, WS 54 and 55, 3 February 1944; WS 55a, 22 February 1944; and WS Docs. 200–210, WS 202, 20 July 1944.

32. Hammond, p. 336.

33. SDF, 740.00119 Control (Germany)/12–1643, "Draft Instructions with Respect to Germany . . . ," 15 December 1943; Lot 60D-224, Box 8, PWC Committee, Minutes 1–66, Minutes PWC, 5 April 1944.

34. *Ibid.*, Box 33, E. Docs., 216–234, Rep. 2, 22 November 1943.

35. *Ibid.*, Box 29, WS Min. 26—, WS Minutes, 15 February 1944.

36. See, for example *FR*, 1943, III, 22; and Sherwood, *Roosevelt and Hopkins*, p. 388.

37. SDF, 740.00119 EW/2037, Hamilton to Hull, transmitting translation of E. Varga, "The Reparation of Damage by Hitlerite

Germany and her Accomplices," Received Division of European Affairs, 27 December 1943.

38. SDF, Lot 60D-224, Box 20, Germany, Policy Questions, Reparation 12a, 14 December 1943; Box 38, Reparation Min., 30 November 1943; Reparations Memos 1–15, Reparation 1a, 7 January 1944.

39. Ibid., Box 31, ECEFP (44) Minutes, Minutes 14, 5 July 1944.

40. Hull Papers, Box 89A, Weekly Report of the Office of Economic Affairs, 1 April 1944–8 April 1944; SDF, Lot 60D-224, Box 8; PWC Committee Minutes 1–66, Minutes, 20 June 1944; Box 38, Reparations Memos 1–15, Memo 12 (Rev), The Amount of Reparations.

41. SDF, 740.00119 EW/2581, Memo: Hiss to Stinebower and Hawkins, 25 April 1944.

42. SDF, Lot 60D-224, Box 8, PWC Committee Minutes 1–66, PWC Minutes, 20 June 1944.

43. FR, 1944, I, 276–299, 302–325.

2. Morgenthau, Roosevelt, and the Russians

1. SDF, 740.00119 EW/8–144, Memo by Under Secretary of Conversation with Stimson and McCloy, for the Secretary, 1 August 1944.

2. Hammond, "Directives for the Occupation of Germany," pp. 340–341.

3. Forest C. Pogue, The European Theater of Operations: The Supreme Command (Washington, 1954), pp. 353–354, 357–358; U.S. Congress, Senate, Subcommittee to Investigate the Administration of the Internal Security Act and Other Internal Security Laws of the Committee on the Judiciary, Committee Print, Morgenthau Diary (Germany), 2 vols. (Washington, 1967), I, 424, 657.

4. In addition to the work of Dorn and Hammond, accounts of

the development of Treasury ideas include: Fred Smith, "The Rise and Fall of the Morgenthau Plan," *United Nations World*, 1 (March 1947), 32–37; *FR*, Cairo and Tehran, pp. 881–882; E. F. Penrose, *Economic Planning for the Peace* (Princeton, 1953), pp. 245–250; Frederick H. Gareau, "Morgenthau's Plan for Industrial Disarmament in Germany," *Western Political Quarterly*, 14 (1961), 517–534; John L. Chase, "The Development of the Morgenthau Plan through the Quebec Conference," *Journal of Politics*, 16 (1954), 324–359; Sven Ulric Palme, "Politics and Economic Theory in Allied Planning for Peace, 1944–1945," *Scandinavian Economic History Review*, 7 (1959), 67–78; and John Morton Blum's two narratives in *From the Morgenthau Diaries: Years of War, 1941–1945* (Boston, 1967), pp. 327–414; and *Roosevelt and Morgenthau* (Boston, 1970), pp. 559–649.

5. *FR*, 44, I, 290–292.

6. Smith, "Rise and Fall," p. 35; *Morgenthau Diary*, I, 422, 424, 462; *New York Post*, 24 November 1947; Hammond, p. 350.

7. Henry Morgenthau, "Our Policy Toward Germany," *New York Post*, 29 November 1947. Although this plan was more severe, it had some things in common with that of Sumner Welles. See the *Morgenthau Diary* (*Germany*), I, 453–460.

8. Penrose, p. 246; *New York Post*, 28 November 1947; Dorn, "American Occupation Policy in Germany in 1944–1945," 494.

9. *New York Post*, 25 November 1947; Hammond, p. 341.

10. *Morgenthau Diary*, I, 526, 528.

11. Hull, *Memoirs*, pp. 1601–1610.

12. *Morgenthau Diary*, I, 536–537, 608–609; *New York Post*, 28 November 1947.

13. Henry Stimson Papers, Yale University Diary, 6 September 1944; Correspondence, 8 September 1944; Stimson and Bundy, *On Active Service in War and Peace*, pp. 572–574.

14. See *Roosevelt and Morgenthau*, pp. 598–599.

15. SDF, 711.61/9-1344, Morgenthau Conversation with FDR, 13 September 1944; *Morgenthau Diary*, I, 717-718; *New York Post*, 29 November 1944.

16. Hull, pp. 1610-1614.

17. *Morgenthau Diary*, I, 426; Hammond, pp. 372-377; Dorn, pp. 488-495.

18. James Forrestal, *The Forrestal Diaries*, ed. Walter Millis (New York, 1951), p. 12. See also *Morgenthau Diary*, I, 567-568.

19. SDF, 740.00119 Control (Germany)/9-1544, Developments in the Formulation of American Policy for the Post War Treatment of Germany (no date).

20. Hammond, pp. 384-397, 400-404; *FR*, Yalta (1955), pp. 142-154.

21. *FR*, Yalta, p. 142; Hull, pp. 1616-1617, 1621.

22. *FR*, Yalta, p. 155.

23. *New York Post*, 28 November 1947.

24. *Morgenthau Diary*, I, 487, 498; Dorn, p. 494.

25. Stimson Papers, Diary, 27 September 1944; Correspondence, 3 October 1944.

26. *FR*, Yalta, pp. 156-158.

27. *Ibid.*, pp. 158-159.

28. Richard L. Walker, *E. R. Stettinius, Jnr.*, pt. I of vol. XIV of *The American Secretaries of State and Their Diplomacy*, ed. Robert H. Ferrell (New York, 1965), 28.

29. *FR*, Yalta, pp. 165-171.

30. *Ibid.*, pp. 171-172.

31. *Morgenthau Diary*, I, 757-758, 783-795 (a large typographical error has been made on pp. 791-793); Blum, *Years of War*, pp. 387-388; and *Roosevelt and Morgenthau*, p. 608; Franklin Roosevelt Papers, Hyde Park, Memos to John Boettiger of 20 October 1944, in Germany Folder, 1944, PSF 132; and 16 January 1945, in File: Germany, 1945; Morgenthau Diaries, Hyde Park, vol. 804, pp. 13-21, 19 December 1944.

32. *FR*, Yalta, pp. 172-173.

33. *Ibid.*, p. 174; Roosevelt Papers, PSF, Edward R. Stettinius, Memo: Department of State to Roosevelt, 17 November 1944; Memo: Stettinius to Roosevelt, 21 November 1944; Memo: Department of State to Roosevelt, 8 December 1944; PSF, Germany, Telegram No. 10115, Winant to Secretary of State, 18 November 1944.

34. *FR*, Yalta, p. 172; Roosevelt Papers, Germany, 1945, Roosevelt to Stettinius, 6 March 1945.

35. Harry Dexter White Papers, Princeton University, Folder 22, Germany, Chapter IX; *Morgenthau Diary*, I, 464.

36. *Morganthau Diary*, I, 609; SDF, 711.61/9–1344, Morgenthau Conversation with Roosevelt, 13 September 1944.

37. *FR*, Yalta, p. 174.

38. *Morgenthau Diary*, I, 786.

39. *FR*, 1944, I, 424.

40. Snell, *Wartime Origins*, p. 71. Others were making a similar point. In August 1944, Secretary of the Navy James Forrestal claimed that there were "widespread fears" in America that a Russian menace would replace a German one (James Forrestal Papers, Princeton University, Box 100, Memo: De-Gaulle-Forrestal Conversation, 18 August 1944). In September, when Stimson discussed his plan to internationalize the Ruhr with McCloy, the Assistant Secretary displayed alarm that the USSR would then have a part in the management of the industrial heart of Germany (Stimson Papers, Diary, 7 September 1944).

41. Morgenthau could make overmuch of the State Department's anti-Soviet bias in attempting to have his views accepted. At one point, he dredged up an old statement by Stimson that Europe needed a strong Germany as an enemy of the USSR. Stimson had made the statement, however, when he was Secretary of State in 1931. See the White Papers, Folder 22, Germany, Chapter II; *FR*, Yalta, p. 175; and *Morgenthau Diary*, I, 859; II, 882.

42. White Papers, Folder 22, Germany, Chapter IX; Memo: Is European Prosperity Dependent on Germany?, 7 September 1944.

43. Warren Leroy Hickman, *Genesis of the European Recovery Program* (Gen'eve, 1949), p. 162.

44. Stimson Papers, Correspondence, "Treasury Program for the Treatment of Germany," 8 September 1944.

45. *Morgenthau Diary*, I, 492, 499.

46. *FR*, Yalta, pp. 309–310, 315. See also William Leahy Diary, Library of Congress, 10 January 1945; Sherwood, *Roosevelt and Hopkins*, p. 777; and *FR*, 1944, I, 973–974.

47. White Papers, Folder 23, White to Morgenthau, 7 March 1944.

48. *FR*, Yalta, p. 315.

49. Stimson Papers, Correspondence, "Treasury Program for the Treatment of Germany," 8 September 1944; Hull, *Memoirs*, p. 1606; *FR*, Yalta, p. 176.

50. *Morgenthau Diary*, I, 612.

51. Morgenthau Diaries, vol. 810, p. 157, 17 January 1945.

52. See, for example, Snell, *Wartime Origins*, pp. 78, 94, 106.

53. *FR*, Yalta, pp. 168–169.

54. *FR*, 1943, III, 17; *FR*, 1944, IV (1966), 995; see also William Hardy McNeil, *America, Britain, and Russia* (London, 1953), p. 406; and Edward J. Rozek, *Allied Wartime Diplomacy* (New York, 1958), p. 247.

55. *FR*, 1943, III, 16; *FR*, 1944, III (1965), 11; SDF, Lot 60D-224, Box 6, Policy Com. Min. 32–49, Policy Com. Min., 10 May 1944.

56. *FR*, 1944, I, 404.

57. *FR*, Cairo and Tehran, p. 154; SDF, Lot 60D-224, Box 6, Policy Com. Min. 32–49, Policy Com. Min., 10 May 1944.

58. *FR*, 1944, I, 332.

59. Hull Papers, Box 61, Memo of Conversation: Pasvolsky and Sobolev, 28 September 1944.

60. *Morgenthau Diary*, I, 700. See Blum, *Roosevelt and Morgenthau*, p. 617, for a similar view Maisky expressed to Morgenthau in March 1945.

61. *FR*, Yalta, pp. 133, 176. For other instances of conflicting Soviet views see Blum, *Years of War*, pp. 398, 404.

62. Stimson and Bundy, p. 563.

3. *Yalta and Its Aftermath*

1. *FR*, Yalta, pp. 611–612, 614–615, 626, 628.

2. *Ibid.*, pp. 656–657, 660, 700.

3. SDF, 740.00119 Control (Germany)/3–2445 Memo: Eric Biddle to Harold Smith. See also *FR*, 1945, III (1968), 318.

4. Diane Clemens' analysis of these points in *Yalta* (New York, 1970) is unclear; she has the Soviets pressing hard on dismemberment (140–150), yet trading agreement on it for a share in German industry (138); and then not really caring about it (272).

5. James F. Byrnes, *Speaking Frankly* (New York, 1947), p. 26.

6. *FR*, Yalta, pp. 619–623, 630–632. Churchill also indulged this kind of thought. A few days later he told Stalin and Molotov that although their reparations demands were too great for the Allies to collect, the Soviets would do the British a service by a policy of removals. These removals would put an end to German exports that British exports would replace (Llewellyn Woodward, *British Foreign Policy in the Second World War* [London, 1962], p. 493).

7. *FR*, Yalta, pp. 702–717.

8. *Ibid.*, p. 874.

9. *Ibid.*, p. 631.

10. *Ibid.*, pp. 702–703.

11. *Ibid.*, pp. 809, 812, 874–875.

12. Edward R. Stettinius, Jr., *Roosevelt and the Russians*, ed. Walter Johnson (Garden City, 1949), p. 230.

13. *FR*, Yalta, pp. 807–809.

14. Stettinius, p. 230.

15. *FR*, Yalta, p. 875.

16. Stettinius, pp. 255, 299.

17. The only other relevant statements that I have been able to find about this ambiguous accord may be found in *FR*, 1945, III, 453, and 1945, IV (1968), 712.

18. Edward Stettinius Papers, University of Virginia Library, Box 372. Stimson-Forrestal Meetings, 13 March 1945. While preparing *Roosevelt and the Russians* in November 1948, Stettinius recalled the situation differently; he remembered then that FDR wanted only to set up a commission (Box 227, German Reparations in Kind).

19. *FR*, Yalta, pp. 909, 914–915.

20. Stettinius, pp. 265–266, 272; *FR*, Yalta, pp. 915, 921, 979.

21. Herbert Feis, *Churchill, Roosevelt and Stalin* (Princeton, 1957), p. 536; Gabriel Kolko, *The Politics of War* (New York, 1968), p. 355.

22. Isador Lubin Papers, Hyde Park, Box 13, German Reparations, James Dunn to Postmaster General Frank Walker, 18 April 1945.

23. Walker, *E. R. Stettinius, Jnr.*, 11; author's memorandum of conversation with Averell Harriman, 19 May 1969.

24. *FR*, Yalta, p. 920 (italics mine, BK).

25. *Ibid.*, p. 903.

26. *Ibid.*, p. 903.

27. *Ibid.*, pp. 875, 926, 929–930, 970–971.

28. *Ibid.*, p. 192.

29. Snell, *Illusion and Necessity* (Boston, 1963), p. 180.

30. Snell, *Wartime Origins*, pp. 149, 154.

31. U.S. Congress, *Morgenthau Diary*, II, 952. For details on interdepartmental bickering see Hammond, "Directives for the Occupation of Germany," pp. 414–427.

32. Hammond, p. 414; Chase, "Development of United States Policy Towards Germany," pp. 386–400.

33. Stimson Papers, Correspondence, 2 March 1945; Diary, 3 March 1945.

34. *Morgenthau Diary,* II, 952–956.

35. Morgenthau Diaries, vol. 830, "Memorandum of Treasury-War Conference on Germany," pp. 1–3, 28 March 1945.

36. *Morgenthau Diary,* II, 970–971, 976, 1044; *FR,* 1945, III, 457.

37. *Morgenthau Diary,* II, 972–975, 1002; *FR,* 1945, III, 377, 462–463, 467, 1181.

38. *Morgenthau Diary,* II, 1075–1076, 1116–1117.

39. *Ibid.,* p. 1045; Blum, *Roosevelt and Morgenthau,* p. 620; Morgenthau Diaries, vols. 829–831.

40. *Morgenthau Diary,* II, 787–788.

41. Joseph Grew Papers, Harvard University, Conversations, 22 March 1945.

42. Hammond, pp. 418–420.

43. Hammond, p. 421. Roosevelt was still playing Treasury off against State. On March 22, FDR was sent a memorandum described as "the most extreme statement" of the Treasury position. The President sent the document to Stettinius, asking "Do you think it is all right for me to sign this?" See *FR,* 1945, III, 1179–1181; and SDF, 740.00119 EW/3–2445, attachment to Memo: Clayton to Despres, 24 March 1945.

44. Grew Papers, Conversations, 23 March 1945.

45. Stimson Papers, Diary, 29 March 1945.

4. Contours of Soviet-American Relations, 1943–1945

1. For a recent example see Geoffrey Warner, "The United States and the Origins of the Cold War," *International Affairs,* 46 (1970), 543–544.

2. Schlesinger, "The Origins of the Cold War," *Foreign Affairs,* 46 (1967), 36, 40.

3. Warner, 531–535.

4. Arthur Ageton and William H. Standley, *Admiral Ambassador to Russia* (Chicago, 1955), p. 95.

5. Joseph E. Davies Papers, Library of Congress, Washington, D.C., Box 18, 17 July 1945.

6. Kennan, *Memoirs* (London, 1968), p. 232.

7. John R. Deane, *The Strange Alliance* (New York, 1947), p. 143.

8. Ageton and Standley, p. 195.

9. U.S. Congress, Senate, Committee on Armed Services and Committee on Foreign Relations, Hearing, *Military Situation in the Far East* (Washington, 1951), p. 3328.

10. Quoted in Matloff, *Strategic Planning*, p. 497.

11. *FR*, 1943, III, 722–723.

12. Hull Papers, Box 89A, Weekly Report, Division of Commercial Policy and Agreements, 8 April 1944; see also the Weekly Report for 23 December 1943.

13. *FR*, 1944, IV, 958, 960.

14. *FR*, 1943, III, 591; 1944, IV, 958.

15. *FR*, 1944, IV, 968.

16. Philip E. Mosely, "The Occupation of Germany: New Light on How the Zones Were Drawn," in his *The Kremlin and World Politics* (New York, 1960), pp. 176–177.

17. *FR*, Yalta, p. 155.

18. *FR*, 1943, III, 782; 1944, IV, 1054, 1064.

19. *FR*, 1944, IV, 1115, 1125.

20. *FR*, 1943, III, 714, 788–789; 1944, IV, 1043.

21. *FR*, 1944, IV, 1035, 1037.

22. *Ibid.*, 815–817, 824–825.

23. *Ibid.*, 951.

24. SDF, 740.00119/EW10–2044, Kirk to Secretary of State, 20 October 1944.

25. See the discussion in Martin F. Herz, *Beginnings of the Cold War* (Bloomington, 1966), *passim.*

26. U.S. Congress, *Military Situation in the Far East*, pp. 3341–3342.

27. See the discussion of this point in Chapter 7.

28. *FR*, 1944, IV, 992.

29. Roosevelt Papers, Department of State Dispatches, 1944, Telegram No. 3572, Harriman to Hull, 19 September 1944.

30. *FR*, 1944, IV, 991, 994–997.

31. *Ibid.*, 1053.

32. *FR*, 1944, III, 910–911.

33. SDF, Lot 60D-224, Box 16, Pol. Com. Min. 81–, Min. 25 October 1944.

34. *Ibid.*

35. For later arguments see *FR*, 1945, V (1967), 843–844, 846, 995.

36. *FR*, 1944, IV, 989–990.

37. *FR*, 1944, III, 952.

38. *FR*, 1944, III, 955.

39. Herz, pp. 153–169; McNeil, *America, Britain, and Russsia,* pp. 448–449, 514–515; Albert Z. Carr, *Truman, Stalin, and Peace* (Garden City, 1950), pp. 14–26; and most authoritatively Thomas G. Paterson, "The Abortive American Loan to Russia and the Origins of the Cold War, 1943–1946," and George C. Herring, Jr., "Lend-Lease to Russia and the Origins of the Cold War, 1944–1945," *Journal of American History,* 56 (1969), 70–92; and 93–114.

40. U.S. Congress, *Morgenthau Diary,* II, 867; *FR,* Yalta, pp. 310–313.

41. *FR,* Yalta, pp. 319, 322–324; *FR,* 1945, V, 845.

42. Blum, *Years of War,* pp. 305–306.

43. James F. Byrnes Papers, Clemson University, *Speaking Frankly,* Manuscript.

44. Grew Papers, Conversations, 24 January 1945.

45. Quoted from Blum, *Roosevelt and Morgenthau,* p. 593.

46. *FR,* 1945, V, 819.

47. Roosevelt Papers, PSF, Crimea Conf., Currie to FDR, 19 January 1945.

48. *FR,* Yalta, p. 610.

49. *FR*, Yalta, p. 610; *FR*, 1945, V, 989.

50. Stimson Papers, Diary, 16 March, 3 April 1945.

51. SDF, Lot 60D-224, Box 100, Edward R. Stettinius Diary, 3, 4, 6 April 1945; *The Forrestal Diaries*, ed. Walter Millis, pp. 39–41; James V. Forrestal Papers, Princeton University, Box 24, Harriman to Stettinius, 11 April 1945; *FR*, 1945, V, 995.

5. American Consensus, April–July, 1945

1. U.S. Congress, *Morgenthau Diary*, II, 1144.

2. *FR*, Potsdam, I (1960), 524.

3. *Ibid.*, p. 501 (italics in original). Assistant Secretary Archibald MacLeish authored this memo, and in a reply to it economic expert Willard Thorp took a more pessimistic position. Nevertheless, the top-level Staff Committee of the State Department approved and passed on to the Secretary of State a somewhat revised paper embodying MacLeish's central ideas. See pp. 503–505, and *FR*, Potsdam, II (1960), 780–784.

4. Harry S Truman, *Memoirs*, I (New York, 1955), 235, 327, 332; Blum, *Years of War*, pp. 465–476.

5. Robert Murphy, *Diplomat among Warriors* (London, 1964), p. 332.

6. Morgenthau Diaries, vol. 783, p. 232, 19 October 1944.

7. See, for example, *Morgenthau Diary*, II, 1184–1185.

8. *FR*, Potsdam, I, 612–614, 623, 629; *FR*, Potsdam, II, 1028–1030.

9. F. S. V. Donnison, *Civil Affairs and Military Government, North-West Europe, 1944–1946* (London, 1961), pp. 405–409 (italics mine, BK).

10. *FR*, Potsdam, I, 468–471, 477–482, 491–493, 524–526; *FR*, Potsdam, II, 780, 801, 820–823.

11. Hammond, "Directives for the Occupation of Germany," p. 425.

12. Grew Papers, Conversations, 10 May 1945.

13. Stimson Papers, Correspondence, 3 July 1945; Diary, 3, 4 July 1945.

14. Stimson and Bundy, *On Active Service in War and Peace*, pp. 582–583, 591–592; Truman, *Memoirs*, I, 236–237.

15. *FR*, 1945, V, 841.

16. SDF, Lot 122, SC Minutes, Secretary's Staff Committee, 20 and 21 April 1945.

17. Truman, *Memoirs*, I, 70–71. Harriman was fond of the phrase "barbarian invasion of Europe" as applied to Russian advances. For another striking instance of its use see *FR*, 1945, V, 831.

18. *FR*, 1945, I, 389–390. In the text this material appears in indirect discourse.

19. See Gar Alperovitz, *Atomic Diplomacy: Hiroshima and Potsdam* (New York, 1965), pp. 35–39; Robert Coakley and Richard M. Leighton, *The War Department: Global Logistics and Strategy, 1943–1945* (Washington, 1968), pp. 694–699; and for a view opposed to the one expressed here, the Herring article, "Lend-Lease to Russia."

20. SDF, Lot 122, SC Minutes, Secretary's Staff Committee, 11 May 1945.

21. Stettinius Papers, Box 732, Stimson-Forrestal Meetings, 5 June 1945.

22. *FR*, Potsdam, I, 520; *Morgenthau Diary*, II, 1341.

23. *FR*, Potsdam, I, 521.

24. Penrose, *Economic Planning for the Peace*, pp. 281–282. There is a typographical error in this passage, but the context makes the author's meaning clear. See also *Morgenthau Diary*, II, 1112–1114, 1140–1144.

25. *Morgenthau Diary*, II, 1223–1224.

26. *FR*, 1945, III, 1186, 1195. Originally Harriman, Molotov, and Clark Kerr, British ambassador to the USSR, were to discuss reparations in Moscow, but nothing seems to have come of this Yalta agreement. See *FR*, Yalta, p. 947.

27. SDF, 740.00119 EW/4–345, Telegram 812, Stettinius to American Embassy, Moscow, 7 April 1945.

28. Lubin Papers, Box 9, Reparations Cables to London, Secretary of State to Winant, 12 April 1945.

29. See note 20.

30. *FR*, 1945, III, 1197. Apparently Harriman had not read this telegram immediately and repeated his warning the next day: he asked if the Secretary had seen his previous cable in which he "strongly recommended" that Lubin defer his departure, SDF, 740.00119 EW/4–1445, Telegram 1166, Harriman to Secretary of State, 14 April 1945.

31. SDF, 740.00119 EW/4–2045, Memo for the President from the Secretary, 18 April 1945.

32. *United States News*, 18 (11 May 1945), 62.

33. Jonathan Daniels, *The Man of Independence* (New York, 1950), pp. 305–306.

34. Waldo H. Heinrichs, Jr., *American Ambassador: Joseph C. Grew and the Development of the United States Diplomatic Tradition* (Boston, 1966), p. 385.

35. Joseph Grew, *Turbulent Era*, ed. Walter Johnson, II (Cambridge, Mass., 1952), 1446.

36. Grew Papers, Correspondence, 5, 7, and 15 May; 20 June 1945; *Morgenthau Diary*, II, 1441.

37. Truman, *Memoirs*, I, 308

38. *FR*, 1945, III, 1177–1202, 1213, 1221.

39. For the delays, see *ibid.*, pp. 1211–1215, 1217–1218, 1227–1229.

40. *FR*, Potsdam, I, 36; Llewellyn Woodward summarizes these negotiations in *British Foreign Policy*, p. 527.

41. *FR*, Potsdam, I, 521, 526–527, 530–531.

42. *Ibid.*, pp. 513, 523; *FR*, Potsdam, II, 840, 846.

43. Leahy, *I Was There* (New York, 1950), p. 355; Leahy Diary, 28 April 1945.

44. *FR*, Potsdam, I, 519.

45. Richard Scandrett Papers, Cornell University Library, Box

19A, "Summary of Procedures of Allied Commission on Reparations, August, 1945," pp. 3, 7, 8; Assignment of Staff, 8 June 1945. Scandrett sometimes assumed that "junketing" was the only aim of the trip.

46. *FR*, Potsdam, I, 522–523.

47. *FR*, Potsdam, I, 510, 511, 538; *FR*, Potsdam, II, 834.

48. Truman, *Memoirs*, I, 310; *FR*, Potsdam, I, 522; David Ginsburg, *The Future of German Reparations* (Washington, 1947), p. 7.

49. *FR*, Potsdam, I, 527–528, 537.

50. *FR*, Yalta, p. 193; *FR*, Potsdam, I, 520.

51. *Ibid.*, pp. 537, 549.

52. *Ibid.*, p. 547.

53. *FR*, Yalta, p. 195; *FR*, Potsdam, I, 448 (italics mine, BK). The relation is also hinted at in the State Department memorandum of March 10 (*FR*, 1945, III, 438) and Pauley's May instructions (*FR*, 1945, III, 1225).

54. Manuel Gottlieb, "The Reparations Problem Again," *Canadian Journal of Economic and Political Science*, 16 (1950), 34–37.

55. *Ibid.*

56. See Chapter 3, note 20.

57. *FR*, Potsdam, I, 530–531; and Manuel Gottlieb, "The German Economic Potential," *Social Research*, 17 (1950), 65–89.

58. Lubin Papers, Box 10, Reps.-Misc., Letter, Crowley to Pauley, 4 May 1945. Harriman also recalled that Pauley's and Crowley's policies "complemented" each other (author's memorandum of conversation with Averell Harriman, 19 May 1969). See also *Morgenthau Diary*, II, 1360–1361.

59. SDF, Pauley File, Box 27, Work Reports, July 1945, Pauley to the Boys, undated.

6. The Economics of the Potsdam Conference

1. *FR*, Potsdam, II, 942.

2. Quoted in Ross Pritchard, "Will Clayton, A Study of

business-statesmanship in the formulation of U.S. economic foreign policy" (Ph.D. dissertation, Fletcher School of Law and Diplomacy, Tufts University, 1956), p. 186.

3. Quoted in Richard Gardner, *Sterling-Dollar Diplomacy* (Oxford, 1956), p. 196.

4. Quoted in Pritchard, p. 192.

5. For more evidence of Harriman's influence see the Paterson and Herring articles, "The Abortive American Loan" and Lend-Lease to Russia"; and Coakley and Leighton, *The War Department*, pp. 694–699.

6. *FR*, Potsdam, I, 511; Davies Papers, Box 18, *passim*.

7. Roosevelt Papers, PSF, Box 48, Byrnes to Roosevelt, 1 January 1945.

8. Gaddis Smith, *American Diplomacy during the Second World War, 1941–1945* (New York, 1965), p. 167.

9. Welles, *Seven Decisions that Shaped History* (New York, 1950), pp. 206–208.

10. Penrose, *Economic Planning for the Peace*, p. 327.

11. Davies Papers, Box 18, 16, 19, 21 July 1945.

12. Leahy Diary, 12 April 1945.

13. George Curry, *James F. Byrnes*, pt. II of vol. XIV of *The American Secretaries of State and Their Diplomacy*, ed. Robert Ferrell (New York, 1967), p. 313.

14. Llewellyn Woodward, "Some Reflections on British Policy, 1939–1945," *International Affairs*, 31 (1955), 281.

15. For the best example of the theory I am disputing see Alperovitz, *Atomic Diplomacy*, *passim*.

16. James Byrnes, *All in One Lifetime* (New York, 1958), p. 290; author's memorandum of conversation with Averell Harriman, 19 May 1969.

17. Truman, *Memoirs*, I, 357.

18. When the factories reached the Soviet Union, there were also difficulties in reassembling them. See Vladimir Alexandrov, "The Dismantling of German Industry," and Vassily Yershov,

"Confiscation and Plunder by the Army of Occupation," in *Soviet Economic Policy in Postwar Germany: A Collection of Papers by Former Soviet Officials,* ed. Robert Slusser (New York, 1953), pp. 1, 14–15, 17; also *FR,* Potsdam, II, 873–876, 888–889, 902–903. The Soviets responded with a report of their own on American removals (pp. 903–911).

19. *FR,* Potsdam, II, 52, 70–71, 76, 110–111, 141–142, 832–835.

20. *Ibid.,* pp. 813, 853–854, 856–859 (italics mine, BK).

21. *Ibid.,* pp. 799, 808–809.

22. *Ibid.,* pp. 861–862; Davies Papers, Box 18, 22 July 1945.

23. Lubin Papers, Box 12, German Reparations, Pauley Report on Reparations, third draft, 19 September 1945.

24. *FR,* Potsdam, II, 868.

25. *Ibid.,* pp. 232–234, 237, 274–275; Davies Papers, Box 17, 13 July 1945.

26. *FR,* Potsdam, II, 279–281, 810. The March 10 directive of the State Department had considered a compromise on the first-charge principle. See *FR,* 1945, III, 438.

27. *FR,* Potsdam, II, 295–298.

28. *Ibid.,* pp. 323, 866.

29. *Ibid.,* pp. 428–430.

30. *Ibid.,* pp. 473, 892; Woodward, *British Foreign Policy,* p. 561.

31. Davies Papers, Box 19, 28, 30 July 1945.

32. *FR,* Potsdam, II, 473–476, 901. On this issue Byrnes had overruled Harriman and Pauley, who wanted to give the Soviet no material free (author's memorandum of conversation with Averell Harriman, 19 May 1969).

33. *FR,* Potsdam, II, 481, 921. Molotov also presented a proposal calling for current production reparation on an overall basis (pp. 913–914). Byrnes's offers were tied up with aspects of the Polish and Italian questions (484–492).

34. *Ibid.,* pp. 514–518, 529–533.

35. *Ibid.,* pp. 439–440, 450, 475 (italics mine, BK).

36. *Ibid.*, p. 923; see also pp. 488, 922–923, 1593–1594.

37. *Ibid.*, pp. 487, 491.

38. Author's memorandum of conversation with Averell Harriman, 19 May 1969.

39. *FR*, Potsdam, II, 481, 488.

40. *Ibid.*, pp. 812, 823, 871.

41. *Ibid.*, p. 474.

42. *Ibid.*, p. 385.

43. Woodward, *British Foreign Policy*, p. 566.

44. *FR*, Potsdam, II, 520–521, 535.

45. U.S. Department of State, *Bulletin*, 2 September 1945, p. 309; Leahy, *I Was There*, p. 427.

46. Woodward, *British Foreign Policy*, pp. 565–567; *FR*, Potsdam, II, 486–487, 1033–1034. This had been Churchill's idea in April. See *FR*, 1945, III, 232.

47. See, for example, *FR*, Potsdam, II, 233–234.

48. In addition to the citations below students ought to read Richard Scandrett's vivid recollections of his service on the Reparation Commission in 1945 in the Scandrett Papers, O H interview, vol. 1, esp. pp. 84–85.

49. *FR*, Potsdam, I, 440–441. See also *FR*, 1945, IV, 98, and SDF, Research and Analysis Report 2673A, "The Economic Character and Interdependence of the Possible Zones of Occupation in Germany," pp. 9–10.

50. SDF, Lot 122, No. 6, SC Minutes, Secretary's Staff Committee Minutes, 28 July 1945, Memorandum by Mr. Thorp for the Committee.

51. Lubin Papers, Reparations, Box 10, Kindleberger to Lubin, 28 July 1945.

52. *FR*, Potsdam, II, 829, 938–939.

53. Lubin Papers, Box 12, German Reparations, Pauley Report on Reparations, second draft, 11 September 1945; and third draft, 19 September 1945 (italics in original, BK).

54. Feis, *Churchill, Roosevelt, and Stalin*, p. 620; *FR*, 1945, III, 221, 318, 368; Snell, *Wartime Origins*, p. 45.

55. *FR*, Potsdam, I, 50–51.

56. *FR*, Potsdam, I, 205. For other opinions see pp. 461, 595–596, 754–757, 990–991; Leahy, p. 390; Davies Papers, Box 18, 16, 18 July 1945.

57. *FR*, Potsdam, I, 754, 989; SDF, 740.00119 (Potsdam)/7-2145, Dunn to Leverich and Harris, 21 July 1945 (brackets in original).

58. *FR*, Potsdam, II, 184, 298, 482, 496–497, 521–522, 535–536, 1000–1001.

59. *Ibid.*, pp. 602–603.

60. Byrnes Papers, Private Conferences and Documents, 22, 23 August 1945. Leahy has made what is simply an egregious error in his narration of the Potsdam proceedings. He wrote that Truman's greatest success was the incorporation into the Berlin Protocol of the major parts of the United States political and economic plan for Germany. The Russians, he said, finally receded from their stubborn insistence on a dollar-value in reparations. Then, he continued, "on the liability side, our proposals for dismemberment of Germany and internationalization of the industry-rich Rhineland failed of acceptance" (Leahy, pp. 427–428).

7. The Diplomacy of Omnipotence

1. *FR*, Potsdam, II, 274, 846–847, 850–854, 895, 943, 1557.

2. *Ibid.*, pp. 209, 296–298, 841–842, 854–856, 877–887.

3. Snell, *Wartime Origins*, pp. 210–211, 214–216; Herbert Feis, *Between War and Peace* (Princeton, 1960), p. 256.

4. See Paterson, "The Abortive American Loan," especially 81–88.

5. Truman, *Memoirs*, I, 74–82.

6. For a discussion see Alperovitz, *Atomic Diplomacy, passim*.

7. Feis, *From Trust to Terror* (New York, 1970), p. 94.

8. Feis, *Between War and Peace*, p. 255.

9. Feis, *Churchill, Roosevelt, and Stalin*, pp. 619–620.

10. *FR*, Yalta, pp. 665–666.

11. Deutscher, *Stalin: A Political Biography*, 1st ed. (New York, 1949), p. 537.

12. See Gordon Levin, *Woodrow Wilson and World Politics* (New York, 1968), and Arno J. Mayer, *The Politics and Diplomacy of Peacemaking* (New York, 1967) and *Wilson vs. Lenin: Political Origins of the New Diplomacy, 1917–1918* (New York, 1964).

13. I am indebted to Gabriel Kolko for this suggestion.

14. *FR*, 1944, IV, 161, 222, 228.

15. *FR*, 1944, III, 906–907.

16. SDF, 740.00119 EW/10-2644, Memo by Luthringer, 20 October 1944.

17. SDF, 800.6363/11-1444, Memo of Conversation, Standard Oil Public Relations Representative and John Loftus, 14 November 1944.

18. *FR*, 1944, III, 461, 473, 963–968, 979.

19. *Ibid.*, pp. 917–918.

20. *Ibid.*, pp. 952, 955.

21. *Ibid.*, p. 908; *FR*, 1944, IV, 228.

22. SDF, 740.00113 EW/9-1644, Telegram, Hull to Winant, 12 October 1944.

23. Lubin Papers, Box 12, Reparations-Satellite Countries, "Reparation Policy with reference to the Satellite Countries: Rumania, Hungary, and Bulgaria," 5 January 1945.

24. Roosevelt Papers, PSF, Edward R. Stettinius, Memo: Stettinius to Roosevelt, 3 November 1944.

25. *FR*, 1944, III, 952.

26. See William A. Williams, *The Tragedy of American Diplomacy*, rev. ed. (New York, 1962), *passim*.

27. McNeil, *America, Britain, and Russia*, p. 670; see also Paterson's comments, especially pp. 89–92; and Clemens, *Yalta*, pp. 31, 269–270, 290.

28. See Feis' comment in *Between War and Peace*, p. 258.

29. U.S. Congress, *Morgenthau Diary*, II, 1555.

30. Williams, *Tragedy*, pp. 202ff.

31. *FR*, 1944, IV, 997.

32. Carr, *Truman, Stalin, and Peace*, p. 26.

33. Davies Papers, Box 16, 30 April 1945.

8. Patterns of the Early Occupation Period

1. Lucius Clay, *Decision in Germany* (Garden City, 1950), pp. 7, 18–19.

2. Manuel Gottlieb, *The German Peace Settlement and the Berlin Crisis* (New York, 1960), p. iii; Dorn, "American Occupation Policy in Germany in 1944–1945," 481–482.

3. 740.00119 Control (Germany)/5–845, Matthews to Clayton and Despres, 8 May 1945.

4. Lubin Papers, Box 14, German Reparations, Notes and Personal Correspondence, Memo: Richard Scandrett Conversation with General Clay, 15 and 16 June 1945.

5. Harold Zink, *The United States in Germany, 1944–1945* (Princeton, 1957), pp. 70, 95.

6. Clay, pp. 18, 41.

7. Charles Fahy Papers, Roosevelt Library, Box 31, Staff Meeting, USGCC, 26 May 1945.

8. James K. Pollock Papers, University of Michigan Historical Collections, Box 16-11, Pollock to Harold Zink, 8 August 1947. Pollock added that the credit for this policy went to Clay and not the Department of State, neglecting to note that the Department was quite happy to retain in command someone who had contempt for JCS 1067.

9. Elmer Plishke, "Denazifying the Reich," *Review of Politics*, 9 (1947), 167–168.

10. Quoted in Drew Middleton, *The Struggle for Germany* (Indianapolis, 1949), pp. 33–34.

11. William Harlan Hale, "Our Failure in Germany," *Harper's Magazine*, January, 1946, p. 517.

12. Wolfgang Friedmann, *The Allied Military Government of Germany* (London, 1947), p. 113. See also p. 202.

13. James W. Riddleberger, "United States Policy on the

Treatment of Germany," U.S. Department of State, *Bulletin*, 25 November 1945, pp. 846–847. For an analysis similar to this one see John Gimbel, *The American Occupation of Germany, Politics and the Military, 1945–1949* (Stanford, 1968), pp. 1–18.

14. Dorn, p. 501.

15. Robert V. Patterson Papers, Library of Congress, Box 23, War Council Meeting, 7 November 1945.

16. John J. McCloy, "American Occupation Policies in Germany," *Proceedings of the Academy of Political Science*, 21 (1946), 548–550 (italics in original).

17. Gottlieb, *German Peace Settlement*, pp. 79–80.

18. Joachim Joesten, *Germany—What Now?* (Chicago, 1948), p. 173.

19. James Stuart Martin, *All Honorable Men* (Boston, 1950), p. 184.

20. Lewis Brown, *A Report on Germany* (New York, 1947), p. 208. For an analysis similar to the one presented here see Gimbel, p. 58.

21. *FR*, Potsdam, I, 623.

22. Brown, pp. 207–208; Manuel Gottlieb Collection, Harvard University, Box B, Coal, 1945–48, Part II; *FR*, 1946, V (1969), 772ff.; for statistics see Nicholas Balabkins, *Germany under Direct Controls: Economic Aspects of Industrial Disarmament, 1945–1948* (New Brunswick, 1964), pp. 121–127.

23. U.S. Strategic Bombing Survey, *Overall Report (European War)* (Washington, 1945), pp. 36–37, 71, 72. *The Effects of Strategic Bombing on the German War Economy* (Washington, 1945), pp. 7–13. The remaining 30.5 per cent of the total tonnage was dropped on all purely military targets, naval and water transportation targets, and all other miscellaneous targets. For a similar analysis see Alan Milward, *The German Economy at War* (London, 1965), pp. 162–189.

24. SDF, U.S. Department of State, Interim Research and

Intelligence Service, Research and Analysis Branch, No. 3370, *Observations on the Ruhr Coal Situation in the Summer and Fall of 1945*. Electrical power plants had not been priority bombing targets.

25. B. V. Ratchford and W. D. Ross, *Berlin Reparations Assignment* (Chapel Hill, 1947), p. 64.

26. Gottlieb Collection, Box B, Mimeo Pamphlets on the German War Economy.

27. Gottlieb, "The German Economic Potential," p. 78.

28. Eugene V. Rostow, "The Partition of Germany and the Unity of Europe," *The Virginia Quarterly Review*, 23 (Winter, 1947), pp. 24–25.

29. U.S. Department of State, *Occupation of Germany, Policy and Progress, 1945–1946* (Washington, 1947), p. 30.

30. U.S. Congress, Senate, Sub-Committee of the Committee on Military Affairs, Hearings, *Elimination of German Resources for War* (Washington, 1945), p. 147.

31. U.S. Congress, *Morgenthau Diary*, II, 1583.

32. See, for example, Office of the Military Governor (US), *Monthly Report of Military Governor, U.S. Zone*, Nos. 2, 4, and 5, 20 September, 20 November, and 20 December 1945, respectively.

33. See, for example, *ibid.*, Nos. 6 and 7, 20 January and 20 February 1946, respectively; and Frank Howley Papers, New York University, "Personal Diary of Colonel Frank Howley," 1 March 1946.

34. U.S. Congress, Senate, Special Committee Investigating the National Defense Program, Hearings, Part 42, *Military Government in Germany* (Washington, 1946), pp. 25797–25798.

35. Gottlieb, *German Peace Settlement*, pp. 97ff.

36. *FR*, 1945, III, 909, 922–925; Gimbel, pp. 27–28, 58.

37. *FR*, 1945, III, 879, 884, 886, 888, 911, 921.

38. *FR*, 1945, III, 907, 914, 916–917, 919–921, 923–925; *FR*, 1946, V, 498, 501–503, 507, 539–540; Gimbel, pp. 27–28, 58;

Curry, *Byrnes*, pp. 70–71; and the Pollock Papers, Box 58-11, Diary Book I, 11 and 13 October 1945.

39. *FR*, 1946, V, 413–422; for further documentation, pp. 432, 434, 441–446, 511.

40. *FR*, 1946, II (1970), 205–206.

41. See, for example, *FR*, 1946, V, 506.

42. *FR*, 1945, III, 1309. But see also 1946, V, 532–533.

43. Gimbel, p. 28.

44. Truman, *Memoirs*, I, 433; Clay, p. 49.

45. Rachford and Ross, pp. 35–36, 47, 69–70, 101, 133.

46. *Ibid.*, p. 45.

47. *Ibid.*, p. 83. For a different appraisal see Gottlieb, *German Peace Settlement*, p. 159.

48. Byrnes Papers, London CFM 9/45, 25 September 1945.

49. U.S. Department of State, *Bulletin*, 16 December 1945, pp. 960–962, 965.

50. Gregory Klimov, *The Terror Machine*, trans. H. C. Stevens (New York, 1953), p. 199.

51. For early versions of the U.S. plan see the Gottlieb Collection, Box D, Berlin Quad 1945/46, LOIC/P (45/3), 17 September 1945.

52. *Ibid.*, Coordinating Committee Minutes, 31 December 1945; 12, 17 January 1946.

53. Clay, p. 108.

54. Gottlieb Collection, Box D, Berlin Quad 1945/46, Coordinating Committee Minutes, 15 January 1946.

55. See Gottlieb, *German Peace Settlement*, p. 159, and Penrose, *Economic Planning for the Peace*, pp. 295–296.

56. *FR*, 1946, V, 491ff.

9. *Economic Consequences of the Peace, February–May, 1946*

1. *FR*, 1945, III, 1350–1351, 1388–1389.

2. Gottlieb Collection, Box D, Berlin Quad 1945/46, Direc-

torate of Economics, The Future Level of German Industry, 28 January 1946.

3. *FR*, Potsdam, II, 488, 922–923, 1593–1594.

4. *FR*, 1945, III, 1054, 1284–1286, 1295–1296.

5. *Ibid.*, p. 1254; Gottlieb Collection, Box D, Report to the CFM, Appendix A, Section 5, Part 1, 24 February 1947.

6. *FR*, Potsdam, II, 491 (italics mine, BK).

7. Fahy Papers, Box 32, Coordinating Committee Minutes, 21 August 1945.

8. Gottlieb Collection, Box A, "The Basic Source," Coordinating Committee Minutes, 4 May 1946.

9. Gottlieb Collection, Box A, Germany, Economics Directorate Minutes, 22 February 1946.

10. *Ibid.*, Box B, Germany, French Zone, Economic Directorate (Note by the Secretariat), Export-Import Plan, 22 February 1946.

11. Fahy Papers, Box 67, OMGUS Legal Division, Selected Opinions, 1 January 1946–28 February 1946.

12. Fahy Papers, Box 32, Coordinating Committee Minutes, 4 March 1946.

13. Clay, *Decision in Germany*, p. 123; *FR*, 1945, III, 1530–1531, 1533–1534.

14. Fahy Papers, Box 32, Coordinating Committee Minutes, 8 April 1946.

15. *Ibid.*, 27 April 1946.

16. Gimbel, *American Occupation*, pp. 60–61. See also Robert Murphy's explanation of the halt in *FR*, 1946, V, 623.

17. See Kennan's comments in his *Memoirs*, pp. 259–260.

18. *FR*, Potsdam, I, 191, 204, 450.

19. U.S. Department of State, *Bulletin*, 2 June 1946, p. 953; Byrnes Papers, Private Conferences and Documents, Byrnes-Molotov, 20 September 1945; Curry, *Byrnes*, p. 181; Byrnes, *All in One Lifetime*, p. 337; and *FR*, 1946, II, 146–147, 166–173, 842–851, 881–899.

20. Curry, *Byrnes*, p. 235.

21. U.S. Department of State, *Making the Peace Treaties, 1941–1947* (Washington, 1947), pp. 24–25.

22. Clay, pp. 120, 125.

23. Leahy Diary, 20 May 1946.

24. Byrnes, *All in One Lifetime*, pp. 378–379; Curry, *Byrnes* (italics in original).

25. Byrnes, *Speaking Frankly*, pp. 175–176.

26. See Gottlieb's discussion in *German Peace Settlement*, pp. 92–94, 124–127.

27. Ratchford and Ross, *Berlin Reparations Assignment*, pp. 93, 178; and, for example, *FR*, 1945, III, 1386, 1389.

28. Fahy Papers, Box 31, Control Council Minutes, 8 March 1946.

29. Clay, pp. 74–75.

30. Gottlieb Collection, Box C, OMGUS Legal Division Selected Opinions, 15 July 1945–31 December 1945; Fahy Papers, Box 67, Selected Opinions, 1 January 1946–28 February 1946.

31. Gottlieb Collection, Box A, "The Basic Source," Coordinating Committee Minutes, 4 May 1946.

32. Byrnes, *Speaking Frankly*, pp. 86–87; Byrnes Papers, Paris Papers, 10 July 1946; Pollock Papers, Box 64–9, Clay to Byrnes, "The German Problem," November 1946.

33. Pollock Papers, Box 62-23, Economic Directorate, ANNEX A to Deco/M (46)20.

34. Ginsburg, *German Reparations*, pp. 16, 18–19, 38. This book contains a wealth of information on German economic questions. Its author was a high level American official in the Economics Directorate of the military government. Before the war, export figures were $1.2 billion in heavy, and $0.72 billion in light, industry. Heavy industry includes metals, machinery, and chemicals; light, textiles, ceramics, mining, and lumber. I have computed the figures on the value of the mark to the dollar in 1936.

35. Ginsburg, p. 38.

36. Fahy Papers, Box 32, Coordinating Committee Minutes, 21 December 1945.

37. *Forrestal Diaries*, p. 182.

38. See Ginsburg, p. 38; and the citations in note 23, Chapter 8.

39. Ginsburg, pp. 38–39; *FR*, 1946, V, 603.

40. See Paterson's analysis, in "The Abortive American Loan," especially 89–92. The "Open Door" thesis of Williams is also of value here.

41. *FR*, 1946, VI (1970), 820–822, 828–830.

42. *Ibid.*, pp. 834, 836, 841–845, 853.

43. Feis, *From Trust to Terror*, p. 273 (italics mine, BK).

44. Forrestal Papers, Box 69, Clayton to Forrestal, 11 October 1946.

45. Patterson Papers, Box 23, War Council Meetings, 5 December 1946.

46. Deane, *The Strange Alliance*, p. 332.

Conclusion: The End of Ideology

1. For Clay see *Decision in Germany*, pp. x, 77–78; for Forrestal, *Forrestal Diaries*, ed. Walter Millis, p. 144, and the Forrestal Papers, Box 70, Forrestal to Lippmann, 7 January 1946; for Harriman, the citations in Chapter 4; for Stimson, *On Active Service in War and Peace*, p. 611, and his Diary, 21 July 1945. See also the Arthur Bliss Lane Papers, Yale University, 6 September 1945, Correspondence *From*, Lane to Matthews; and W. B. Smith's comments in the Forrestal Papers, Box 101, 5 April 1946.

2. U.S. Department of State, *Postwar Foreign Policy Preparation*, p. 123.

3. *FR*, 1944, IV, 1025.

4. Hull, *Memoirs*, p. 1460.

5. Stimson Papers, Diary, 28 and 29 October 1943.

6. *FR*, Cairo and Tehran, pp. 417–418.

7. Truman, *Memoirs*, I, 437, 537.

8. *Ibid.*, 71.

9. Howley Papers, Book 1, vol. 1, Administration of AMGBD, Allied Commandatura, p. 11.

10. Stimson Papers, Correspondence, 16 May 1945; *FR*, Potsdam, II, 808–809.

11. *Forrestal Diaries*, p. 57.

12. *FR*, Potsdam, II, 783.

13. Clay, *Decision in Germany*, pp. x, 77–78 (italics in original).

14. Pollock Papers, Box 64–9, Clay to Byrnes, "The German Problem," November 1946.

15. *FR*, 1945, III, 1536. Murphy argued also that the original decisions on occupation zones made before Potsdam were responsible for this situation.

16. *FR*, 1946, V, 632–633.

17. *Ibid.*, p. 630.

18. Gottlieb, *German Peace Settlement*, p. 138.

19. Kennan, *Memoirs*, p. 270.

20. *FR*, Potsdam, II, 892.

21. Clay, *Decision in Germany*, pp. 74–75 (italics in original).

22. *FR*, 1945, III, 1342. See also p. 1369 and Pauley's statement in "The Potsdam Program Means Security," *Prevent World War III*, 21 (June–September 1947; Summer ed.), 40.

23. Acheson, *Present at the Creation* (New York, 1969), p. 122; see also pp. 725–726.

24. *Ibid.*, p. 727.

Appendix. Multilateralism and Revisionist Historiography

1. See Kennan, *American Diplomacy 1900–1950* (Chicago, 1951); Morgenthau, *In Defense of the National Interest* (New York, 1951); and Osgood, *Ideals and Self-Interest in America's Foreign Relations* (Chicago, 1953).

2. Quoted from Williams, ed., *Shaping of American Diplomacy*, II, 914–915.

Bibliographical Note

The literature of wartime diplomacy is vast, and I have made no attempt to survey it below; rather, I have tried to cite the sources that are directly related to this study and that are little known, or that were of particular interest to me.

There are some general works invaluable for any monograph on German-American relations; among them: Robert Divine, *Second Chance* (New York, 1967); Herbert Feis's *Between War and Peace* (Princeton, 1960), *Churchill, Roosevelt, and Stalin* (Princeton, 1957), and *From Trust to Terror* (New York, 1970); Lloyd Gardner's *Architects of Illusion* (Chicago, 1970) and *Economic Aspects of New Deal Diplomacy* (Wisconsin, 1964); Richard Gardner, *Sterling-Dollar Diplomacy* (London, 1956); Gabriel Kolko's, *The Politics of War* (New York, 1968) and *The Limits of Power* (New York, 1972) Walter LaFeber, *America, Russia, and the Cold War, 1945–1966* (New York, 1967); William Hardy McNeil, *America, Britain, and Russia* (London, 1953); William Appleman Williams, *The Tragedy of American Diplomacy*, rev. ed. (New York, 1962).

For surveys of various aspects of U.S. diplomacy in regard to Germany during the war and postwar periods the reader ought to consult: John H. Backer, *Priming the German Economy: American Occupation Policies, 1945–1948* (Durham, 1971); John L. Chase, "The Development of the United States Policy Towards Germany during World War Two," Ph.D. thesis (Princeton, 1952); John Gimpel, *The American Occupation of Germany,*

Politics and the Military (Stanford, 1968); Manuel Gottlieb, *The German Peace Settlement and the Berlin Crisis* (New York, 1960); Paul Y. Hammond, "Directives for the Occupation of Germany: The Washington Controversy," in *American Civil-Military Relations*, ed. Harold Stein (Birmingham, Ala., 1963), pp. 311–460; E. F. Penrose, *Economic Planning for the Peace* (Princeton, 1953); John L. Snell, *Wartime Origins of the East-West Dilemma over Germany* (New Orleans, 1959).

Studies in more specific areas include: Nicholas Balabkins, *Germany under Direct Controls* (New Brunswick, 1964); Michael Balfour and John Mair, *Four Power Control in Germany and Austria, 1945–1946* (London, 1956); Ray S. Cline, *The War Department: Washington Command Post* (Washington, 1951); Robert Coakley and Richard M. Leighton, *The War Department: Global Logistics and Strategy, 1943–1945* (Washington, 1968); Harry L. Coles and Albert K. Weinberg, *Civil Affairs: Soldiers Become Governors* (New York, 1964); F. S. V. Donnison, *Civil Affairs and Military Government: North-West Europe, 1944–1946* (London, 1961); David Ginsburg, *The Future of German Reparations* (Washington, 1947); Edward H. Litchfield, ed. *Governing Post-War Germany* (Ithaca, 1953); Forrest C. Pogue, *The European Theater of Operations* (Washington, 1954); William Ratchford and W. D. Ross, *Berlin Reparations Assignment* (Chapel Hill, 1947); Robert Slusser, ed. *Soviet Economic Policy in Postwar Germany* (New York, 1953).

Useful articles include: William M. Franklin, "Zonal Boundaries and Access to Berlin," *World Politics*, 16 (1963–1964), 1–36; Manuel Gottlieb's "The German Economic Potential," *Social Research*, 17 (1950), 65–89, and "The Reparations Problem Again," *Canadian Journal of Economic and Political Science*, 16 (1950), 22–41; George C. Herring, Jr., "Lend-Lease to Russia and the Origins of the Cold War, 1944–1945," *Journal of American History*, 56 (1969), 93–114; Leonard Krieger, "The Inter-Regnum in Germany, March–August, 1945," *Poltical Science*

Quarterly, 64 (1949), 507–532; Thomas G. Paterson, "The Abortive American Loan to Russia and the Origins of the Cold War, 1943–1946," *Journal of American History,* 56 (1969), 70–92.

The Morgenthau plan has generated a literature of its own. I have found the most relevant material in the following: Morgenthau's own work, *Germany Is Our Problem* (New York, 1945), and "Our Policy toward Germany," *New York Post,* November 24–27, 1947; John Morton Blum's two narratives in *From The Morgenthau Diaries: Years of War, 1941–1945* (Boston, 1967), pp. 327–416; 451–464, and *Roosevelt and Morgenthau* (Boston, 1970), pp. 559–649; John L. Chase, "The Development of the Morgenthau Plan through the Quebec Conference," *Journal of Politics,* 16 (1954), 324–359; Walter Dorn, "The Debate over American Occupation Policy in Germany in 1944–1945," *Political Science Quarterly,* 72 (1957), 481–501; Frederick H. Gareau, "Morgenthau's Plan for Industrial Disarmament in Germany," *Western Political Quarterly,* 14 (1961), 517–534; Sven Palme, "Politics and Economic Theory in Allied Planning for Peace, 1944–1945," *Scandinavian Economic History Review,* 7 (1959), 67–78.

Also of interest is the "journalistic" literature on the American occupation of Germany, written in the years immediately following the war. I found the following most helpful: Julian Bach, *America's Germany* (New York, 1946); Lewis Brown, *A Report on Germany* (New York, 1947); Basil Davidson, *Germany: What Now?* (London, 1950); Russell Hill, *The Struggle for Germany* (New York, 1947); Joachim Joesten, *Germany—What Now?* (Chicago, 1948); Marshall Knappen, *And Call It Peace* (Chicago, 1947); Drew Middleton, *The Struggle for Germany* (Indianapolis, 1949); Norbert Muhlen, *The Return of Germany* (Chicago, 1953); Saul K. Padover, *Experiment in Germany* (New York, 1946); Hoyt Price and Carl E. Schorske, *The Problem of Germany* (New York, 1947); Wilhelm Ropke, *The Solu-*

tion of the German Problem (New York, 1947); Gustave Stolper, *German Realities* (New York, 1948); James P. Warburg's *Deadlock over Germany* (Toronto, 1948), *Germany—Bridge or Battleground* (New York, 1946), *Germany, Key to Peace* (Cambridge, Mass., 1953), and *Germany, Nation or No-Man's Land* (New York, 1946); and Arnold Wolfers, *United States Policy Toward Germany* (New Haven, 1947). The reader might also want to consult Wolfgang Friedmann, *The Allied Military Government of Germany* (London, 1947), and Harold Zink's *American Military Government in Germany* (New York, 1947) and *The United States in Germany, 1944–1955* (Princeton, 1957).

When intelligently read, the memoirs of strategically placed officials continue to be a crucial source for students. Hull's *Memoirs*, 2 vols. (New York, 1948) are excellent for the ideological viewpoint expressed. More substantively important are James F. Byrnes, *All in One Lifetime* (New York, 1958), and *Speaking Frankly* (New York, 1947); Lucius Clay, *Decision in Germany* (Garden City, 1950); Robert Sherwood, *Roosevelt and Hopkins: An Intimate History*, rev. ed. (New York, 1950); Walter Bedell Smith, *My Three Years in Moscow* (Philadelphia, 1950); Edward R. Stettinius, *Roosevelt and the Russians*, ed. Walter Johnson (Garden City, 1949); Henry L. Stimson and McGeorge Bundy, *On Active Service in War and Peace* (New York, 1947); Harry Truman, *Memoirs*, 2 vols. (Garden City, 1955, 1956); Nathan I. White, *Harry Dexter White* (Waban, Mass., 1956).

The State Department publication, *Foreign Relations of the United States*, is now almost complete through 1946; it is an indispensable set of documents. The *Morgenthau Diary* (*Germany*), 2 vols. (Washington, 1967), published for the Senate Subcommittee to Investigate the Administration of the Internal Security Act and Other Internal Security Laws of the Committee on the Judiciary is also most valuable. The Office of the Military Government (US) issued much material of interest. Of most significance are: the *Monthly Reports* of the Military Governor, U.S. Zone, September 1945–September, 1946; *Functional Reports* for the same period; *Economic Data on Potsdam Germany: Special Report of the Military Governor* (September 1947), and *Three Years of Reparations: Special Report of the Military Governor* (November 1948). Another primary source of interest is the State Department collection of documents edited by Harley Notter, *Postwar Foreign Policy Preparation* (Washington, 1949).

The State Department files are the most important manuscript collection; they are open through 1945 to qualified researchers, and the scholar must be grateful to Dr. Arthur G. Kogan and his staff for their helpfulness and many kindnesses. I was not able to get access to military and War Department files. My notes indicate more fully the manuscript sources I have used, but some of these bear special mention. Of the available open manuscript collections of major figures, only Henry Stimson's at Yale, Edward Stettinius' at the University of Virginia, and Henry Morgenthau's at Hyde Park fully repay research time and effort; the material in the Stettinius collection, however, duplicates that in the State Department files, and even Morgenthau's famous Diaries contain little material in this area that is not published in the *Morgenthau Diary (Germany)*. There are papers of lesser figures that are extremely significant: the Isador Lubin and Charles Fahy papers at Hyde Park; the James Pollock papers at the University of Michigan; the Richard Scandrett papers at Cornell; and the Manuel Gottlieb collection in the Littauer Library at Harvard.

Index

Davies, Joseph E., 96, 153, 184
Davis, Norman H., 15, 22-23
Deane, John, 96, 98, 112
deindustrialization of Germany, *see*
 Morgenthau plan
demilitarization treaty, 215-216
Directive of March 10, 1945, significance for reparations, 86-92
Directive of March 23, 1945, 90-91,
 115
dismemberment of Germany
 discussed at Moscow Conference,
 28-30
 discussed at Potsdam Conference,
 164-166
 discussed at Tehran Conference,
 30-32
 discussed at Yalta Conference,
 74-76, 164
 effect of U.S. reparations plan on,
 145-147, 155-166, 181-184, 224,
 231-233
 Roosevelt on, 23, 24-25, 26-27,
 30-32, 74-76, 164
 State Department plans for, 22-24,
 25-27, 164-166
 Summer Welles on, 23-24, 244
 see also reparations
Dodd, William, 16
Douglas, Lewis, 185
Draper, William, 187
Dunn, James, 86
Durbrow, Elbridge, 99, 103

Eastern Europe, 6
 and Soviet-American relations before end of war, 103-113, 121,
 122, 177-180, 215, 228
 in postwar period, 171, 182, 215-
 216, 223-224, 231, 233
 see also Hungary, Poland, Rumania, Soviet Union
Echols, Oliver, 194
economic disarmament of Germany,
 see State Department
Eden, Anthony
 at Moscow Conference, 28-30
 at Potsdam, 145, 165
 at Yalta, 75-76, 78-80, 82-83
 on Soviet Union, 70, 104, 130

 spokesman for British views on
 Germany, 24-25
 see also Great Britain
Eisenhower, Dwight D., 48
European Advisory Commission
 (EAC), 32, 33-34, 35-36, 39,
 46, 72, 164, 245

Feis, Herbert, 82, 172, 174-176, 224
first-charge principle
 and level of industry plan, 198-
 204, 208-210, 220-222
 discussed at Potsdam, 145, 148-
 149, 151, 158-160, 173-174,
 208-210
 explained, 134-139, 259
 see also level of industry plan
Foreign Economic Administration
 (FEA), 110
 view on American occupation
 policy, 86-87, 115, 193-194
Foreign Ministers Conference, October 1943, *see* Moscow Conference
Foreign Ministers Conference, May
 1946, 216
Forrestal, James, 221, 227, 230, 249
Fowler, Henry, 193
France
 and Control Council for Germany,
 194-198, 214, 217
 participation in reparations discussion, 129-131
 see also Control Council *and* occupation
Friedmann, Wolfgang, 189

Gimbel, John, 186n, 214-215
Gousev, F. T., 70, 71
Great Britain, 126, 130, 240
 occupation policy of, 191-192,
 194-195, 202-203, 212, 221
 plans for postwar Germany, 28-
 30, 31-32, 33, 53-54, 75-83,
 164
 views on American plans for Germany, 158-160
 see also Winston Churchill, Anthony Eden
Grew, Joseph, 116, 128-129

(Roosevelt, Franklin, *cont'd*)
on dememberment of Germany,
23, 24-25, 26-27, 30-32, 74-76,
164
on economic relation of Germany
and Britain, 53, 57-58, 63, 64,
72-73, 77-78, 89-91, 227
on in kind reparations, 81-82,
138-139
personal diplomacy of, 14, 30-31,
32-34, 35, 129
Ruhr, 53, 58, 153, 154, 165, 191,
193, 195, 207, 216, 224-225
discussed at Potsdam, 164
see also occupation *and* zones of
occupation
Rumania, reparations policies in,
177-180
Russia, *see* Soviet Union

Sayre, Francis, 16
Scandrett, Richard, on reparations
negotiations, 132-133, 258-259,
262
Schlesinger, Arthur M., Jr., on
Soviet policy, 95-96, 97, 107
Snell, John L., on reparations
policy, 85-86
Sokolovsky, Vassily, 221
Soviet Union
and cautious views on Germany,
28-29, 69-72, 74-76, 164, 180,
218-219
and compromises at Potsdam, 150-
155, 168-169
and conflict with United States,
10, 73, 103-113, 120-140, 167-
182, 195-204, 206-224, 227,
229-233
and German dismemberment, 29,
164-166, 174-175
and harsh views on Germany, 28-
30, 40, 69-72
at Yalta, 74-85
interpreting behavior of, 93-96
occupation plans of, 24-25, 28-32,
42, 69-70, 75-81, 112, 133-
134, 145, 147, 150-159, 165,
168, 169, 206, 209, 261

occupation policies of, 194-204,
206-224
views on reparations, 2, 42-43,
69-72, 76-85, 99-101, 111-113,
133, 143-144, 145-163, 168-
169, 177-180, 194-204, 206-
224
see also Lend-Lease, loan, V.
Molotov, Joseph Stalin, State
Department
Stalin, Joseph, 70, 104, 105, 215
and dismemberment, 24-25, 31-
32, 75-76, 164
at Potsdam, 154-155, 158-159,
165, 169
at Tehran, 31-32
caution of, 69-70, 74-76
Standley, William, 96, 98
State Department
and economic disarmament of
Germany, 22, 25, 40, 84-85,
170, 173-174, 205, 234
and Franklin Roosevelt, 8, 23-27,
32-34, 46, 50-54, 56-64, 100-
101
and planning for dismemberment
of Germany, 22-24, 25-27, 28-
29, 164-166
and political plans for Germany,
25-26, 28, 38, 174-175
and postwar planning, 19-20, 61,
84-85
and postwar planning for Germany, 21-26, 28-30, 34-35, 39-
46, 53-64, 65, 84-85, 114-120
and Treasury Department, 48-49,
53-56, 62-63, 72, 84, 86-91,
114-117
and War Department, 34-39, 47-
48, 53-56, 72, 84, 86-91, 117-
120, 156-157, 189
on the occupation, 34-35, 189,
190-194
reparations policies of, 39-46, 48-
49, 58-61, 62-63, 85-91, 118,
169-180
unrealism of, 2, 7, 38-39, 45-46,
65, 68-69, 93, 113, 125, 180-
184, 190, 203-204, 220-221,
225, 232-233, 234

American Policy and the
Division of Germany

Designed by R. E. Rosenbaum.
Composed by Vail-Ballou Press, Inc.,
in 11 point linotype Caledonia, 3 points leaded,
with display lines in monotype Bulmer.
Printed letterpress from type by Vail-Ballou Press
on Warren's 1854 text, 60 pound basis,
with the Cornell University Press watermark.
Bound by Vail-Ballou Press
in Columbia book cloth
and stamped in All Purpose foil.

Library of Congress Cataloging in Publication Data
(For library cataloging purposes only)

Kuklick, Bruce, date.
  American policy and the division of Germany.

  Bibliography: p.
  1. World War, 1939–1945—Germany.   2. World War,
1939–1945—Peace.   3. World War, 1939–1945—Reparations.
I. Title.
D821.G4K85   940.53'14   78-38121
ISBN 0-8014-0710-9